Guardians of the Sundoor

"Of course, ultimately, the most interesting thing[s] about the 'gate' . . . are the *conditions* subject to which it can be passed through. In other words, what is the *use* of this iconography anyway? If thieves cannot make off with the treasure to which they have no right, what qualifies the Hero and gives him the right? His state of being — when he realizes Who he really is."

❧ • ❧

"The tree or pillar . . . is a symbol of the Divinity and refers to the *Logos* from which male and female derive, being accidents rather than the essence of (Inner) Man. The pattern of the *Logos* after which Man in this man or woman was made is bodiless and neither male nor female but a unity of both at once."

❧ • ❧

"In all that change is a dying — 'No creature can attain a higher grade of Nature without ceasing to exist' [St. Thomas Aquinas.] The Ether is the soul's immortal covering — its subtle or glorious body."

❧ • ❧

". . . when this Perfection has been realized, it will not be found to have been effected by our toil . . . our toiling was not essential to the *being* of this Perfection, our own Perfection, but only dispositive to our *realization* of it. As Eckhart expresses it, 'When I enter there no one will ask me whence I came or whither I went'. *The weary pilgrim is now become what he always was had he only known it.*"

—*Ananda K. Coomaraswamy*

Guardians of the Sundoor:

Late Iconographic Essays and Drawings of Ananda K. Coomaraswamy

Edited with a Preface
by Robert A. Strom

THE FONS VITAE QUINTA ESSENTIA SERIES

FONS VITAE

Fons Vitae
49 Mockingbird Valley Drive
Louisville, Kentucky 40207-1366 • U.S.A.
fonsvitaeky@aol.com • www.fonsvitae.com

These essays have been presented as A.K. Coomaraswamy left them over a half century ago. The general reader need not become involved in the multitude of details under discussion; nor is it essential to deal with the many references cited in Sanskrit, Greek, Latin, Arabic, German, *et al.* The text as a *whole* literally plunges a person into the astounding mentality of the ancient world and the genius of the early authorities whose systems of metaphysics, iconography, analogy and symbolism provide us with both new levels of meaning and reassurance for our lives today.

"... all the dragons, walls and inactive doors of the myths are nothing but the symbols of our own inadequacies and failures." —*A.K.C.*

— *The Publisher*

Cover illustration with the kind permission of The J. Paul Getty Museum, Malibu, California. *Clazomenian Sarcophagus, 480–470 B.C., attributed to the Albertinum Group.*

Typesetting and book design by R.G. Renzi • rgrenzi@worldnet.att.net

Printed in Canada.

ISBN 1-88-7752-59-5
Library of Congress 2003116977

Table of Contents

"Not that the One is two, but that these two are One."

— *Hermes Trismegistos*

Foreword — On Ananda K. Coomaraswamy

Rama Coomaraswamy

Ananda Coomaraswamy, both as a person and as a scholar, is hardly remembered in our day. To some degree, this is how he would have it — for he constantly held that, if he were to be remembered, it would only be for his works and not as an individual. He repeatedly refused to indulge in autobiographical details and felt that such was *aswarga*, and as such against the very principles in which he believed and to which he devoted his life. In this, he was like the true artist and craftsman, whose products have always carried the stigma of anonymity. While giving a talk at the University of Hawaii, a Ph.D. candidate informed me that his request to do his thesis on Ananda Coomaraswamy was rejected because "Coomaraswamy said nothing new." This would have delighted him, though it in no way contradicts the fact that he was able to give expression to what had already been said in clearer and better ways — *better* in being more suitable to our times.

It is, however, of value to provide some historical background. Born in Colombo, Ceylon (now Sri Lanka) in 1877 to an English mother and a Sri Lankan father, he returned to England at the age of three when his father passed away from Bright's disease (now called glomerulonephritis). He schooled at Wycliffe College (*college* being a term used for private schools in England), where he first manifested his interest in both geology and language. After graduation he proceeded to London University, where he took his degree in both Geology and Botany. At the age of twenty-three he returned to Sri Lanka, where he conducted a geological survey which is still of value and in use today.

During the course of his geological studies, he became interested in the arts and crafts of Sri Lanka, which were rapidly being destroyed by the inroads of ugly and cheaply-produced products from the west, as well as by the corruption of the tastes and values of consumers as a result of both modern education and their desire to imitate the English. It was but a short step from this to his developing interest in the nature and meaning of art itself.

He then traveled extensively throughout India, both studying and collecting examples of Indian art, offering his collection to the government if they would build a museum to care for it. This offer was refused, and hence it was that the collection returned with him to England. During this period he published many articles on Indian and Buddhist Art, as well as on Buddha and the Gospel of Buddhism, myths of the Hindus and Buddhists, etc. Back in England, he continued his studies and published, among other items, his classical two-volume work on Rajput paintings and Mediaeval Singhalese art, and *The Dance of Shiva*.

During the first World War (1914-1918), he refused to fight in the British Army on the grounds that India was not a free nation. As a result he was "exiled" to the United States, where he was given the appointment at the Boston Museum of Fine Arts as Curator of Indian and Mohammedan Art, and where he lived for the rest of his life. It was here that his many works on art were published, such as *The Origin of the Buddha Image* and the *History of Indian and Indonesian Art*. However, with the course of time his interests in the meaning of art — and hence in metaphysics — became increasingly consuming. From about 1933 on, while he continued to publish articles dealing with art, he was able to bring to his knowledge of metaphysics both his Eastern experiences and his extraordinary linguistic abilities, producing a corpus of works which can only be described as extraordinary. While his bibliography lists over a thousand items, one might mention in passing as it were, *A New Approach to the Vedas*, *The Darker Side of Dawn*, *Angel and Titan*, *The Christian and Oriental Philosophy of Art* and many significant articles, some of which were gathered together by Roger Lipsey and published in a two-volume collection by Princeton University Press, Bollingen Series LXXXIX, under the title of *Collected Papers*.

In 1947 Ananda Coomaraswamy retired from the Boston Museum of Fine Arts with the intention of returning to India, where he hoped to finish up some of his writings, translate some of the *Vedas*, and take *Sanyasa*. God, however, had other plans, and he passed away peacefully and alertly shortly thereafter.

It was only his ashes, carried by his wife, which returned to both India and Ceylon.

Needless to say, many of the unfinished writings were left in disarray. His wife did yeoman work in bringing much of the material together, but the material on the Sagittarius was so complex that she made no attempt to deal with it. In the course of several moves the text, notes and photographs were further disrupted. Several scholars to whom the collected material was shown felt that they could not deal with it in an adequate manner. For a time, I felt that his final works would probably never see the light of day.

Fortunately, Robert Strom — who is probably the only person alive who has the capacity to deal with this material — undertook the task. The result, a work of several years, is truly remarkable. Not only has he presented the finished product much as Coomaraswamy himself would want it done, but he has done it with the same spirit of anonymity and virtue that the original author embraced. It has been both a search for truth and an exposition of truth which leaves one a little breathless. It is no exaggeration to say that without the work of Robert Strom, this material would probably never have become available to us.

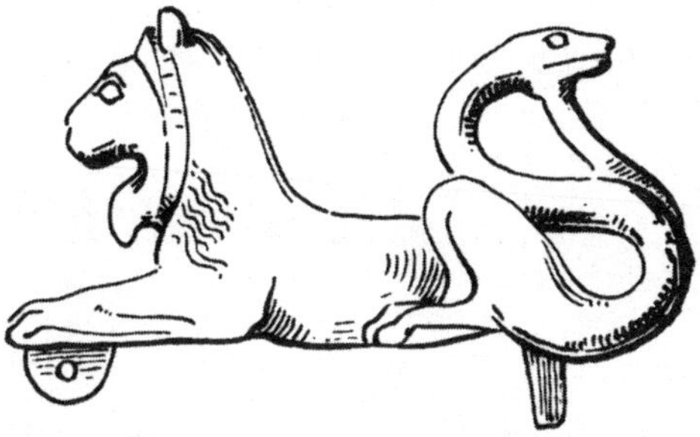

INTRODUCTION

Rama Coomaraswamy

Ananda K. Coomaraswamy's *Guardians of the Sundoor* is one of the last remaining unpublished group of essays of this prolific author; it is also in many ways the culmination of his life's work. Although the material is presented in a scholarly manner, it is also the story of a spiritual journey: his, and possibly ours. As he wrote in an earlier essay, "When the deceased reaches the Sundoor, the question is asked, 'Who art thou?'" Depending upon the answer, one is either allowed to enter in or "be dragged away by the factors of time." The present work aims at providing us with the correct response and at teaching us how to negotiate the difficult passage between this world and the next.

A.K.C. was by vocation a scholar, who dedicated the last decades of his life to "searching the Scriptures" — something made possible by his extraordinary linguistic ability. He read and spoke some thirty languages, which enabled him to seek out the original sources. Because he wrote primarily for fellow scholars, it has been suggested that an introduction — providing the potential reader with a brief outline of some of the issues under consideration, while avoiding the multiplicity of unfamiliar linguistic references — would be of use. Without this simplification — hopefully, one that does not violate the depth of content — many who would greatly benefit from the text itself would perhaps be frightened off. It is because the content is of such spiritual importance — that our very souls depend upon both our understanding and following the paths set out by the author — it is of equal importance that a few "sign posts" be provided to enable us to follow in his footsteps.

The ideas and concepts discussed go back to prehistoric times, but show a consistency of meaning that those imbued with evolutionary ideation would find difficult to accept.[1] Metaphysical ideas, however, are best expressed by analogy and hence by symbolism. Indeed, as A.K.C. has elsewhere explained, "symbolism is a language and a precise form of thought; a hieratic and metaphysical language and not a language determined by somatic or psychological categories . . . symbolism can be defined as the representation of reality on a certain level of reference by a corresponding reality on another . . . traditional symbols are the technical terms of a spiritual language that transcends all confusion of tongues and are not peculiar to any

1 This is not surprising. Augustine, as a Christian, said that the very thing that is now called the Christian religion was not wanting among the ancients from the beginning of the human race, until Christ came in the flesh — "after which the true religion, which had already existed, began to be called 'Christian'." (Stephen Cross, *Avaloka,* VI, 1992, p. 56.) And Origin says, "There has never been a time when the saints did not have the gift of spiritual salvation pointed towards Christ. The Word became man at the final hour; He became Jesus Christ. But before this visible coming in the flesh, he was already, without being man, mediator for humanity." (*Commentary on Gospel of John*, 20.12).

one time and place. Indeed, they are the technical language of the *philosophia perennis*." As Professor S.H. Nasr has said, "The symbol is the revelation of a higher order of reality in a lower order through which man can be led back to the higher sphere. It is not accidental that Christ spoke in parables."

What could be more common than a doorway? To quote Gray Henry: "It is more than coincidental that many doorways throughout the world exhibit a corresponding set of symbolic motifs that point to the One manifesting itself as duality — a duality and a world that must return to that One." One must pass through the duality of the door jambs to the unity which is only to be found in the centre. As Christ said, "I am the door," and "No one comes to the Father but through Me." The passage through the door is always a passage that at least symbolically involves a change of state, and what is required metaphysically is a casting off of the "old man" much as a snake casts off his skin. In our prosaic lives we easily forget that the door both allows us "in" and keeps us "out." We forget that the husband carrying his wife over the threshold symbolizes a psychopomp carrying the soul to another world — hopefully a paradise where the couple will be "happy ever afterwards." Should the husband stumble, it is a sign of bad luck or impending misfortune. On the other side of the door is the "One" or "centre" which is represented by the Tree of Life, the *Axis Mundi*, the Fountain of Immortality, a throne, a mountain, royalty, a sun disc, and so on. Also, the centre can refer to the garden of Paradise where the tree and fountain are located.

The entrance is, however, not open to everyone — as mentioned above, the door functions both as entrance but also as an excluding barrier. And so it is that the Door or the Tree is guarded by "cherubim" who each hold "a flaming sword, turning every way, to keep the way of the tree of life" (*Genesis* III.24). The affronted cherubim are themselves the "contraries" (of past and future, ruling and creative powers, etc.), of which the wall is built — and, therefore, the appropriate ornaments on the wall of the Temple as in *Ezekial* XLI.18. Each and every pair of affronted cherubim represents the clashing jambs of the living door through which the strait way leads — "strait," because the line that divides past from future, evil from good and moist from dry is — literally — what is so often called "a razor edge." Thus it is that sacred structures — churches and temples — almost invariably place flanking guardians at their entrances. As Gray Henry has pointed out, "One finds paired lions at the door of each Burmese Buddhist shrine, sphinxes at the entrances of Egyptian temples (not to be confused with the famous Egyptian Sphinx), and affronted male and female griffins over the gates to Christian churches. The configuration still continues to be used for secular doorways, which often exhibit palmettes (representing the Tree of Life) and urns or vase motifs (indicating the Font of Living Waters). The threshold of the *yurt* in Central Asia is decorated with the image of the Tree of Life flanked by two mountain sheep, which are represented by their horns." Such is appropriate and understandable when one conceives of the home as a mini-shrine or church — for a genuine "home" is a sacred enclosure. (This is why in many cultures one leaves one's shoes at the doorstep.) One even sees an appropriate secular reminder of this in libraries (presumably the depository of wisdom), whose entrances are flanked by lions. Through time, these guardians have been of various types, including "Scorpion-men, sleepless and baleful serpents or dragons, centaurs (notably 'Sagittarius'), Gandharvas, cherubim and in many cases armed *Automate*" (*Symplegades*).

Every sacred enclosure is representative of Paradise. The central point of a Christian church, as traditionally conceived, is either the Cross — the upright stem of which is the Tree of Life — or the Dome open to heaven, under which is the Tabernacle containing the Body of Christ — Who is Himself the Door. The very cruciform structure of the church repeats this principle, as does the maze found in many mediaeval cathedrals. Again, every genuine Catholic altar has as its prototype the altar in the Holy of Holies guarded by the cherubim. Between the cherubim is the *Shakina*, or the Divine Presence now replaced by the Tabernacle. Similarly the well of Zam Zam situated in the sacred precincts of the Kabba in Mecca represents the Divine Centre, where is to be found the *Fons Vitae*, a pattern repeated in the fountains of mosques around the world. The water functions to wash the "old man," and hence to purify the worshipper. And of course our bodies are also sacred enclosures, for the Kingdom of Heaven is within the human heart.

The well-guarded doorposts also represent the duality — the past and future, regret and anticipation, etc. — which must be overcome if one is to enter into the Present or the presence of God — a place where, to use the words of Eckhart, "neither virtue nor vice ever entered in." Such statements may confuse, but not if one listens to Nicholas of Cusa, who tells us: "The walls of Paradise in which Thou, Lord, dwellest, are built of contradictories, nor is there any way to enter but for one who has overcome the highest Spirit of Reason who guards its gate." This would seem to be a common doctrine recognized throughout the history of the world. If we are to reach the other shore — which is in Dante's words, a place "where every where and every when are focused," (*Paradiso* xxix.22) we must pass through this Door of duality, though "here, under the Sun, we are overcome by the pairs" (xxii.67). As the *Maitri Upaniṣad* teaches: "Every being in the emanated world moves deluded by the mirage of the contrary pairs, of which the origin is our liking and disliking . . . but only those who are freed from this delusion of the pairs . . . freed from the pairs that are implied in the expression 'weal and woe' reach the place of invariability." As Boethius said, "Truth is a mean between contrary heresies" (*Contra Eutychen* vii). Another word for this duality is *Maya*, which both points to unity and at the same time obscures it. As Coomaraswamy explains, the "Vedantic *maya-veda* doctrine must not be understood as meaning that the world is a 'delusion', but that it is a phenomenal world and as such a theophany and epiphany by which we are deluded if we are concerned with nothing but the wonders themselves, and do not ask 'Of what' all these things are a phenomenon."

Coomaraswamy explains the process each of us must undergo. The passage through the Door is always a "Middle Way" and is frequently symbolized by the "clashing rocks" of mythology through which the "hero" must pass. As A.K.C. said in his essay on the Symplegades, "the severing *Logos* (itself symbolized by a flashing sword) is at once the narrow path which must be followed by every Hero, the door that he must find, and the logical Truth and Highest Spirit of Reason that he must overcome if he would enter into the eternal life of the land 'East of the Sun and West of the Moon'. This is also the '*Logos* of God', the trenchant Word that like a two-edged sword 'sunders' soul from spirit (*Hebrews* IV.12); 'sunders', because whoever enters must have left himself, his 'Achilles heel', behind him; our sensitive soul being the 'mortal brother' and the 'tail' or 'appendage' of which the Master surgeon's knife — the Islamic *Dhu'l-fiqar* — relieves us, if we are prepared to submit to his operation."

Again, this desired locus is described as a place where "shine no stars, nor sun is there displayed, there gleams no moon; (and yet) no darkness there is seen." It is here that Dionysius' "Divine Darkness is entered and where one is 'blinded by excess light,'" where the Darkness and the Light stand not distant from one another, but together in one another. Darkness and Light, Day and Night, are contraries that must be overcome and passed through — which can only be done at dawn and dusk, when these archetypal contraries that were divided "in the beginning" are surpassed. Christ said He was the door through which we must pass, but having done so, united to Him, we are also united to the Father — for as He said, "I and the Father are one." Rūmī wrote, "Our Soul is, as it were, the day and our body the night: We, in the middle, are the dawn between our day and night."

The well at the world's end is not to be found by walking, for it is within us. It is the Spirit within us that, having shaken off our bodily attachments (and above all our attachment to our little self or ego), can make the journey. The priest in approaching the altar prays for the joy of his youth, which as Eckhart says is the casting off the "old man." He also prays that God will lead him to the light, the truth and the Mountain in which He dwells. Reverting to the symbolism of the "clashing rocks," it is clear that one must pass them in a "flash." This "moment" of transition corresponds to the "single moment of full awakening" (The Buddha is not by accident called the "Wake"), for all spiritual operations are necessarily "sudden."

Clearly the Hero's quest is never meant to be a one-way street — The Holy Grail must be brought back to the world of manifestation. The Hero becomes a "soma-thief," where Soma is the waters of life, the Golden Fleece or the golden apples of Jason. It is also called the "vessel of plenty." "No dweller on earth partakes of the true elixir, but only of substitutes 'made to be Soma' by rites of transubstantiation, participation being a prefiguration or anticipation of the blessed life of the deceased." This transubstantiation is achieved in a ritual sacrifice that allows the sacrificer to identify himself with the Hero who is always a Christ figure, and who as it were crosses over and brings back the Soma. It is the Catholic priest, who identifies himself with Christ, who crosses over or through the clashing rocks — between the Cherubim — and brings back Bread and Wine, (both crushed like the soma branches), the Body and Blood, for others to participate in.

Space only allows us to but touch upon some of the basic ideas in this work. Tied in with these are a host of treasures explaining the symbolic meanings of a variety of associated ideas, drawn from all the genuine traditions of the world — such as the meaning of "Sacrifice," "Ether," "Space," "Solar Symbols," etc. The Sphinx, then, which Philo identifies with the Cherubim made of the creative Fire, is also identified with the *Logos* and with Wisdom. The Sphinx is also represented by the Eagle or the Indian Garuda. This explains the symbolism of the "rape of the *Nagi*" — or of Ganymede, which is the inverse of the "Rape of the Soma." Here, as A.K.C. explains, "the Sphinx represents the Psychopomp who bears away the soul of the deceased, as she bore away the Thebans 'to the inaccessible light of the Ether'." Here we have a further elucidation of the traditional symbolism — for as A.K.C. explains, quoting Euripedes: "The spirit dies away into Ether" which is nothing but its return to God Who gave it. This is at once the background for Philo's pronouncement that when, at our death, the four lesser elements are returned to their origins, "the intellectual and celestial species of the soul departs to find a father in Ether." In the words of A.K.C.: "We have seen in the mythological formulations, verbal and visual, that winged pneumatic powers, whether we call them sirens, sphinxes, eagles or angels, convey the soul to the heavenly realms of ethereal light. The soul itself not being winged, only clings to its bearer." On the other hand, Plato in the *Phaedrus* speaks of the soul itself as growing her wings; Philo, similarly, says of souls that are purified from mundane attachments that "escaping as though from a prison or the grave, they are equipped for the Ether by light wings, and range the heights for ever" (*Somn.* I.139).

In the same way, Dante speaks of those who are — or are not — "so winged that they may fly up there" (*Paradiso* x.74). In India, likewise, both formulations occur; on the one hand, it is the eagle that conveys the sacrificer, who holds on to him (*TŚ.* III.2.1.1), by means of the *Gayatri*, whose wings are of light and that one reaches the world of the Suns. On the other hand, it is asked *what is their lot who reach the top of the Tree (of Life)?* The answer is "the winged, those who are wise, fly away, but the wingless, the ignorant, fall down (*PB.* XIV.1.12.13). Uplifted on wings of sound, "the Sacrificer both perches fearless in the world of heavenly light, and also moves" i.e. at will, "for wherever a winged one would go, all that — it reaches."

A.K.C. points out: "We are ourselves the Sphinx. Plato himself implies as much by his 'etc.' when he discusses the problems of man's relation to Chimaera, Scylia, Cereberus and other composite animals. Plato equates the two parts of the composite creature with the two parts of the soul, the better and the worse, immortal and mortal; the composite represents the whole man, the human head the Inner man, the lion or dog, the mettle." He might even have gone further and pointed out that the serpent tails of these creatures correspond to the appetites — equating the two animal forms, those of the lion and the snake, with the two parts of the mortal soul, as Philo assuredly would have done. In any case, Plato says, that man is one who can be described as *just* (or in Christian terms, is *justified*), in whom the Inner Man prevails and is not pulled about by the beasts, but makes an ally of the lion or dog and so cares for the other beasts as to make them friendly to one another and to himself. On this basis, one might say that the composite animal that he really was carries him off at last, either to punishment in case the beasts have prevailed, or to the beatific life if the Man in the man has prevailed: The question is really just that of the *Prasna Upaniṣad*: "In which, when I depart, shall I be departing?"

In concluding these introductory comments I must, first of all, express my admiration for the work of the Editor, Robert Strom — who when faced with a confused mass of notes and illustrations, was able to collate and bring together this difficult material. Equally remarkable has been the work of Rebecca Renzi who, working from the notes of Mr. Strom, has typeset a text involving several languages with great accuracy. One must also be grateful to Gray Henry, for whom this has been a work of love as well as spiritual growth. Her contributions are by no means limited to the role of publisher, for she has been responsible for the collating of illustrations — many of which she has herself found and replaced when they were missing from the original text. Finally and most important, thanks are due to Peter Schroeder, whose patronage made the entire work possible.

Chimaera. Attic, 6th century B.C.

Preface

Robert A. Strom

I

THE WIDELY AND PROFOUNDLY LEARNED ANANDA KENTISH COOMARASWAMY (1877-1947), art historian and metaphysician, is not as well known as he deserves to be. In the East he is best known for his earliest works, in which the critique of the colonial economic system and the advocacy of traditional arts and crafts tend to predominate. Those who are most willing to commend his work too often exhibit a discreet silence, or have been unable to fully access and evaluate his latest and most important writings. In the West, where he lived most of his life, academia has been very slow to welcome the grand Coomaraswamian scientific synthesis.

Coomaraswamy would have asserted that his work was only a beginning at restoring a fully integrated world view of the ancients. Moreover, he would have said that it leaves out the entire regimen of practice — without which any theorizing, however comprehensive, is little more than the raising of dust. On the other hand, the serious problem posed by the absence of spiritual masters in the modern world is easily overrated where the theory is not understood. The restoration of the primordial vision of man in the cosmos as offered in these essays — which are published for the first time — is another such beginning and can lead to the manifestation of a seasonally spoken, creative and life-giving Word.

As for the practicum, Coomaraswamy knew the need for this very well as an ideal or not, and seriously intended to retire to a Himalayan hermitage where the truth he so assiduously pursued could be fully realized. Before that was to occur, probably in 1949, the essays presented here — along with a number of others he had been working on for years — would very likely have been brought to finish and found their way into print somewhere in the world. We believe they favorably augment his already published *oeuvre* and are important additions to the study of iconographic traditions in East and West, a field to which he had given many of his best years and for which these essays were doubtless intended to be both a literal and a figurative capstone.

II

Coomaraswamy probably began working on the first essay in this volume, "The Early Iconography of Sagittarius," in the spring of 1943. However, it was the appearance in 1937 of Willy Hartner's "Pseudo-Planetary Nodes of the Moon's Orbit," a study dedicated to Ananda Kentish Coomaraswamy on his sixtieth birthday, which must have set his mind on course. The earliest reference to the work in his surviving correspondence dates from 4.8.43 in a letter to J.C. Cuttat:

> . . . Your mention of Scorpio (who was originally a celestial janitor) is curious, because I am just now working

> at the iconography of Sagittarius (another janitor) in which that of the Scorpion-man is also involved. These types were originally the guardians of the door (*Janua coeli)* of the abode of Anu (= Varuna) and of Tammuz (= Soma) that grew in Anu's "garden." The Tree was robbed by the Firebird (Aquila) in order that "we" might have life, and ultimately eternal life. Scorpio is one of the equivalents of the cherubim who "keep the way of the Tree of Life" in *Genesis*, where the "flaming sword that turns every way" is an example of the widely diffused type of the "active door." The guardians are evil from our present point of view, who are shut out, but no more absolutely than St. Peter who keeps out those who have no right to enter. It is in the same sense that pearls are to be withheld from swine. Hence, I think you are right in saying that *tamas* can be associated with *ananden* as its locus (*loka*); indeed, the analogy serves to explain *why* it is that human intercourse (which reflects the "act of fecundation latent in eternity") ought to take place only in the dark (*cf.* *ŚB.*VI.1.5.19), and to explain the covering up of the Queen and the Stallion in the *Asvamedha* . . .

Some months later, on 7.1.43, in a letter to Ad'e Bethune, he would continue these themes:

> . . . I wish I could send you all the new material I have collected on the *strait gate* but it would amount to a pamphlet and must wait 'til I have made it ready for publication (in an article on Sagittarius) — who can be equated in the last analysis with the angel of the flaming sword which burned every way) . . .
>
> Of course ultimately the most interesting thing about the 'gate', practically, [are] the conditions subject to which it can be passed through. Nicolas of Cusa is particularly good on this . . .

Coomaraswamy appears to have been somewhat sidetracked from this project throughout the remainder of 1943, reporting to Margaret Marcus on 12.27.43 that he "hoped to get back soon and perhaps finish 'Early Iconography' [. . .]." It appears that the earliest full rescension of the work probably dates from 1943. Sometime in early 1944 he left this version in midsentence and started over, basing the new version on the first thirteen pages and the concluding three pages of the earlier work. We present this early version of the "Sagittarius" as the second entry in this volume with a new title: "Guardians of the Sundoor and the Sagittarian Type." The later version has become our first entry. We know that there had been many intervening tasks in that year, among which was the composition of a new article for his friend George Sarton's *festschrift*. The new essay would be titled

"Symplegades" and can be dated from late October and November of 1943, though it would not be published until 1946. From bibliographic references in both early and late "Sagittarius" manuscripts, it is clear that the "Symplegades" was under way towards the *terminus ad quem* of the earliest and probably completed before the composition of the latest "Sagittarius" manuscripts.

In the early summer of 1944, there was a discussion of many "Sagittarian" themes in the correspondence to G. Carey. This material, beginning with the card dated 6.13.44, was never precisely incorporated in A.K.C.'s formal work:

> . . . One might also say that as red agrees with the "ardor" of the seraphim, so blue with the cooler "knowledge" of the cherubim. But this would be a moral rather than metaphysical explanation.

The topics were continued in a letter to Carey dated 6.14.44:

> From the Indian point of view (dark) blue and black are equivalent. The three, blue, black and white, correspond to the *tamasic*, *rajasic* and *sattvic* qualities. Indian images can be classified in these terms as ferocious, royal and mild or spiritual in aspect. Now while knowledge and love are the characteristic *qualities* of cherubim and seraphim, their primary *functions* are defensive and apotropaic and looked at purely from an Indian point of view, one would think of the colors blue and red as corresponding to this *militant* function. God Himself would be white — or what is essentially golden. Gold being the regular symbol of light, life and immortality.
>
> From within the Christian-Hebrew tradition one would recall that Seraphs are "*fiery* serpents" and connect the red with this as well as with their characteristic *ardor*.
>
> I am just now writing the part of the "Early Iconography of Sagittarius" which deals with Cherub and seraphs. They are both militant and fierce types that "keep the way of the Tree of Life" — and nearest to God (with the Thrones) in knowledge and love because they are his "bodyguards," a sort of "King's own" regiment, an elite of the angels.
>
> I am not quite able to explain the blue from the Christian-Hebrew sources. Possibly the blue is for the Virgin; considered in her aspect as Sophia . . . From my outlook blue or black is appropriate for the Virgin in view of her identity with the earth (Goddess), the Mother — of which I was reminded the other day when seeing the film, *The Song of Bernadette.* (Which is very fine and you

must see.) This is the accepted explanation of the "*Vierges Noires*" (of Durand-Lefebure, *Études sur l'origine des Vierges Noires*, Paris 1937 and Rowland's article on the Nativity in the Grotto, *Bulletin of the Fogg Art Museum*, III, 1939 (cf. p. 63).

In conjunction with the above, we excerpt here a small portion of a letter to Ms. Bethune from 7.26.43:

> . . . I was for the moment surprised by Maria as *Janua coeli* (since Christ's words are "I am the door"), but at once remembered that both Sun and Moon are the doors and no doubt it is in her lunar aspect that Mary is the door.

The color symbolism would also be the subject of the letter to Carey, dated 7.29.44:

> . . . Answers on the color symbolism are not quite so easy. On the whole I agree with your remarks: However, I suggest that *essentia* is only *apparently* modified by matter; in the same way that space is only apparently modified by its enclosure in, say, a glass jar. We see this when the jar is broken: In the same way with *Essentia* when the material conditions determining *Esse* are dissolved. So I would say "God created the universe by revealing whatever of Himself is susceptible of manifestation." Over and above this remains all that is not susceptible of manifestation. I do not like the expression "passing *Esse* through *Posse*." As you say:
>
> Pure Being — White
> both invisible
> Pure Potency — Black
>
> Between these two lies the colored (red) world of action. These are the 3 "gunas" of Indian cosmology: Cf. *Paradiso* 29.31-6. These are the "3 worlds" of tradition — all under the Sun and other than the otherworld. Blue, black and green are more or less the same traditionally: The implication of emptiness is right, but this is also potentiality, since emptiness demands ful*fil*ment.
>
> The four castes and four quarters are white, red, yellow, black. The "high lights" (as you imply) are representative of higher values. Purple rightly associated with black: Purple connected with royalty [also mourning], as black is with death.
>
> Prism: So "life stains the white radiance of eternity." I hardly think the light returns to God by the rotation of

> the wheel, but rather when it is *stopped*, i.e., when the circumference is reduced to the centre: Then the centrifugal ray by which the circumference was, so to say, pushed out, returns on itself to its source. As Heracleitus says: "The way up and the way down are the same." The wheel continues to turn until the circumference is contracted to the motionless centre ([the] "rolling up" of time and space).
>
> I wonder if you are not using *Esse* (existence) where you mean *Essentia* (being), . . . *Essentia* apparently modified by matter = *Esse.*

Only a month later, as we see in this quotation from a letter to Marco Pallis dated 8.20.44, Coomaraswamy was still at work on the "Sagittarius":

> . . . I am rather appalled by your suggestion of *my* writing a book of the nature of a critique of Occidentalism for Indian readers. . . . In the long run the long piece on the "Early Iconography of Sagittarius" on which I have been engaged for over a year, with many interruptions, seems to me more important than any direct addition to the "literature of indictment" . . .

From a letter to Bernard Kelly dated 12.30.44, we know that the work on the "Sagittarius" had continued up to that time, but now we also find mentioned the earliest reference in the extant correspondence to the "Ether" essay, the fourth of those presented in this volume.

> I am just now working on two rather difficult papers, one on *aiqhr*, akasa as *quinta essentia* and name of God, the other on the early iconography of Sagittarius who is ultimately a Cherub or Seraph, guardian of the sources of life.

Only a month later, in a letter to R. Parker, dated 1.27.45, we find a similar picture:

> I am still deep in *Sagittarius* and have started a piece on Gr. *aiqhr* and Skr. *akasa*, both = *quintessentia* — fascinating material! But I get so much interruption . . .

It was much the same a few days later in a letter to G. Sarton, dated 2.6.45:

> I have a number of things in the press that will interest you. I am still working on the "Early Iconography of Sagittarius," but am almost bogged down in the mass of material (cherubs, centaurs, *Janua coeli*, Rape of soma, etc.); and on the concept of Ether in the Greek and Sanskrit sources.

As it turned out, he *was* stymied and both manuscripts of "Early Iconography of Sagittarius" end at that point where the material corresponds to and is continued in the "Ether" essay. This is possibly reflected in a letter to Gretchen Warren dated 4.2.45, which incidentally contains the earliest reference in the correspondence to the "Sphinx" essay, the third of those presented in this volume:

> Both "Sagittarius" and "Ether" became so extensive that I paused to write up the material on the Sphinx (*not* the Egyptian "Sphinx") separately and hope at least to finish that this month.

Less than a week later, on 4.7.45, he would send this pertinent card to E. Goodenough of Yale, the prominent Philo scholar, with whom many of these subjects had been explored:

> . . . Re the Hermetic 2 *dorujoroi* that a comparison with *Rep.* and with *Phaedo* 107f. shows that *both* are called *hgemwn* and *daimwg* and one is the guardian angel of the past life and one the guardian angel of the new life. Representing thus the soul's *past and future* they correspond to the Cherubim, the opposites, between which (as Symplegades) stands the Now through which our Way — the very *strait* leads.

We see in a letter to Ethel Mary Coomaraswamy Mairet, dated 6.1.45, the state of these manuscripts at that time:

> At the present time I have long been working on the early forms of Sagittarius; I have had to separate from that a discussion of "ether"' in Greek and Sanskrit doctrine; and from that again to separate out a long paper on the Sphinx (not the so-called Egyptian variety, of course), which may get finished this summer. All this has to do with cherubim, and with the distinction of Destiny from Necessity — i.e. *Dharma* from *Karma*.
>
> I, too, hope to live a number of years more; at the same time I do prepare for death, as far as possible, in the Platonic manner. In a few years more we plan to go home to India (northern) permanently, when I will in a certain way retire, rather than dying in harness; that is, I want to contact and realize more immediately the actuality of the things of which my present knowledge is more "intellectual" than direct.

The contemporaneous letter to Walter Shewring, dated 6.5.45, will be extensively quoted:

> As to *moira* ("share," *qismet* and *bhagam*) and *eimarmenh* these represent our participation in the divine

nature, and our "freewill" is as to whether or not we shall consent to and cooperate with the *will* which these imply, whether we seek or not to reach our *destin*ation. Nothing could be more un-happy than to be *amoira*. *Moira* as will and destiny then corresponds to *dharma*, of which each one's allotment is his *sva-dharma*, vocation, the natural means of his entelechy. On the other hand, *anagkh* represents the ineluctable operation of mediate causes, and corresponds to *kharma*, which may help or hinder our destiny, but with respect to which we can only submit with a good grace, endeavoring to fulfill our destiny as best we can. This endeavor itself becomes a mediate cause in turn and thus creates a better *anagkh* — *kharma* for tomorrow. Thus our lives are actually determined in part by our intentions and in part by our environment. . . . [Note] the valuable treatment of *moira*, etc. in Philo and Hermetica, etc. As Philo maintains God alone is truly free, but we are given a share (*moira*) in this freedom: And all such shares are in amounts proportionate to our receptive capacity — all is *offered*.

I am still at work on Sagittarius, Ether, and Sphinxes, and shall try to complete articles on these three closely related themes, in the reverse order, i.e., Sphinxes first. The concept is ridiculous. *Sjiggw* has practically never this sense, but = *dew* (in *desmos* and *dei*) and is almost always used with respect to the Golden Chain that unifies all things. On the other hand the verb of which Sphinx is most often the subject is *arpaxw*, to carry off: And you know how and of whom this verb is used in NT. In other words, the Sphinx, like the Eagle, appears in tombs chiefly in the capacity of psychopomp — who, as Euripedes says "carries off the Cadmena kin to the untrodden light of Ether" — or as Philo says, "to find a father in Ether" (a reminiscence of the early equation *Zeus estin aiqhr*). That is a very brief outline of what the Sphinx article is to be. After I had got this far I was delighted to find that Clement of Alexandria explains the Sphinx in precisely the same way. (Of course, I am talking about the Gk. and Western Asiatic Sphinx only, not the so-called Egyptian Sphinx of which the origins are different, although there is, as biologists would call it, a "convergence.")

I recently came across this admirable aphorism: "Our choice is (as it always was) between metanoia and paranoia."

The summer of 1945 may have been occupied with other tasks so that by September 25, in a letter to Helen Chapin, Coomaraswamy would confess that "[his] work on Sphinxes, etc. seems rather slowed up." One of these new projects was the composition of the essay "*Rgveda*" 10.90.01 "*aty atiṣṭhad daśan̄, gulám*," later published in the spring of 1946 by the *JAOS*. This excellent work has never been republished and is in need of careful editing. It contains many echoes of the essays we publish in this volume, with "Note 36" especially relevant to the "Ether." We believe that most of the first three sections of the "Sphinx" presented below were probably composed by the late summer 1945. A new effort to order and refine the material presented itself with an invitation to lecture at the University of Michigan, Ann Arbor, early in 1946. A.K.C. would write to his host, James Marshall Plumber, on 11.26.45 as follows:

> . . . I think my talk for you must be on "The Riddle of the (Greek) Sphinx" because I have worked on that last and have good material for slides, which I must get made in time.

This lecture was given at the university's Student Religion Association, Lane Hall, on January 2, 1946. It survives in two manuscripts with indicated illustrations in the margins. Both manuscripts are closely related, and appear to have been composed "back-to-back" over a short period of time. As in the manuscript published below, the main concern is with the Greek iconographic and literary traditions. The "riddle" itself is given short shrift; Coomaraswamy saw the answer in the nature of the Sphinx herself. We have used part of the latter of these two versions in a "Conclusion" to the essay. After returning to Boston, the "Sphinx" manuscripts may not have been worked over again, as we can infer now from letters dated 5.13.46 to Mrs. Roger Foster and Willy Hartner from 8.1.46. By that date, Coomaraswamy's last book [published in his lifetime], *Time and Eternity*, was in preparation and would occupy his attention for a few months. Towards the end of 1946, the project of a book titled *Reincarnation* would develop in which Coomaraswamy would return to the study of "ether' "for the early but finally only tentative chapters. A portion of this material, our Section I of the "ether" essay in this book, titled "'Ether' in Plato," was completed and sent to the *Journal of the Hellenic Society* early in 1947 but was apparently not accepted. Later that spring, Coomaraswamy's heart condition worsened and he was able to do very little in finishing the essays printed in this volume. On the morning of September 9, 1947, Ananda Coomaraswamy passed away at his home outside Boston. His ashes were returned to Ceylon and the Ganges eighteen years later, in September 1965.

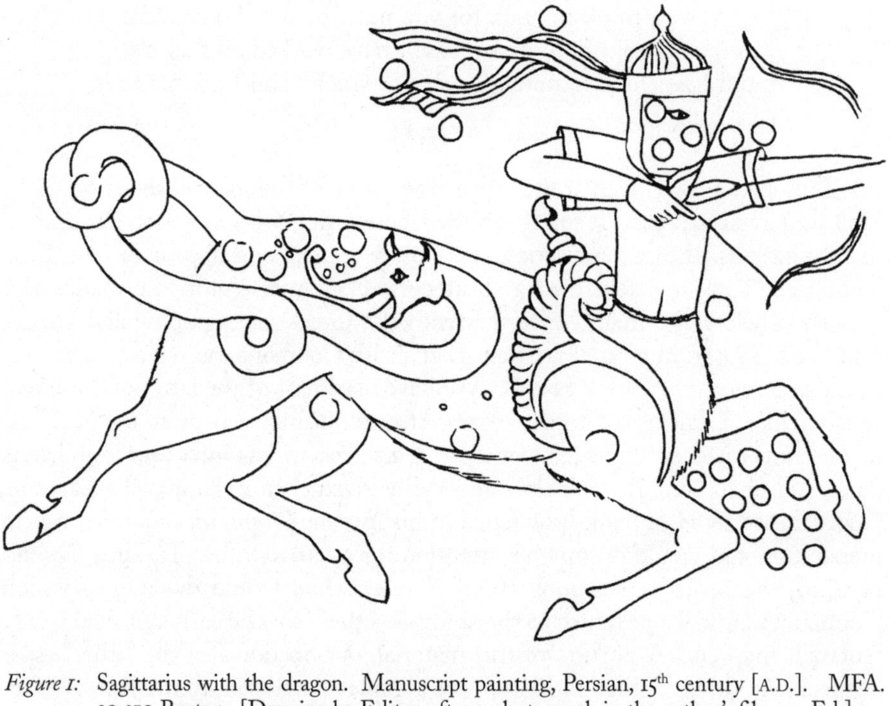

Figure 1: Sagittarius with the dragon. Manuscript painting, Persian, 15th century [A.D.]. MFA. 30.210 Boston. [Drawing by Editor, after a photograph in the author's file. — Ed.]

Chapter I

The Early Iconography of Sagittarius — *Kṛśānu*[1]

"L'Asie Occidentale applique les lois d'une iconographie rigoureuse," G. Conteneau, *Manuel d'Archéologie orientale*, p. 377.

WHATEVER ASTRONOMER'S PURPOSE THEY MAY SERVE, THE ACTUAL FORMS of the signs of the Zodiac are of mythological rather than astronomical origin.[2] It is proposed to discuss the older background of the sign Sagittarius (τοξότης), of which the surviving type is that of the centaur-archer whose place lies between Scorpio and Capricornus and below Aquila and Serpentarius — collectively a significant ensemble.

The fundamental questions to be asked will be, *At what is the archer shooting?*, and *What is he defending?* Intimately connected with these questions is the problem of the Islamic iconography in which the centaur-archer's tail is not that of a horse, but that of a snake or dragon (Fig. 1). This problem has already been ably discussed by Dr. Willy Hartner, who remarks that "This combination . . . evidently originates not in a doctrinal astrological conception, but in a purely mythical, or rather *metaphysical* one"; while as regards the dragon tail he says that "the question remains entirely unsolved as to why this dragon was combined with the constellation of Sagittarius . . . some of the features belonging to the scorpion also seem to have passed over to Sagittarius; and, still, we must not forget that the scorpion itself had always been closely related to the snake, symbol of the inferior, antisolar world, the region of the dragon." He is, in fact, entirely on the right track in going on to say that "the solution of the problem has to be sought in the ancient oriental mythology — indeed, there certainly exists a connection with the 'scorpion man' watching, in the Gilgamesh epic, at the entrance of the inferior world."[3] Except that we should have preferred to say "other" rather than "inferior" world,[4] this is a

[1 The present title, expanded by the addition of "*Kṛśānu*," follows that given in Ananda Kentish Coomaraswamy's "Symplegades," see R. Lipsey, Ed., *Coomaraswamy: Traditional Art and Symbolism*, Princeton, 1977, Note 29, p. 534. — Ed.]

2 Hardly any of the Greek, Chinese or modern signs of the Zodiac are recognizably manifested by the actual arrangements of the stars; they cannot have been derived from, but have been imposed upon the visible starry sky.

3 Willy Hartner, "Pseudoplanetary Nodes of the Moon's Orbit," *Ars Islamica*, V. pp. 138, 149.

4 The "inferior" and "superior" worlds, Zeus and Hades are very often in the Greek sources only different aspects of one and the same "otherworld" of the dead; and the like is true in Celtic mythology, and even Christian eschatology. For Greece, cf. Heracleitus fr. 127, "One and the same are Hades and Dionysos"; Plato, *Laws* 727 D, "Hades . . . realm of the Gods yonder"; *Republic* 363 C, D; *Phaedo* 68 B, "Hades, where and only is true wisdom to be found"; *Timaeus* 44 C; *Apology* 29 B, 41 A, 80 D; Euripedes, Nauck, fr. 912 "Ruler of all . . . by whatsoever appelation thou wouldst be called, or Zeus or Hades thou": J. Harrison, *Prolegomena* . . . p. 17; "Zeus-Hades": G. H. Macurdy, *Troy and Paeonia*, 1925, ch. VIII "Helios-Hades"; also Justin, *Cohort*, c. 15, "One Zeus, one Hades, one Helios, one Dionysos, Yea, in all three things One God, why speak I his name asunder?"

W.A. Nitze, in *PMLA*. XXIV, 1909, rightly speaks of the "Hades-Paradise" myth of the Babylonians. Arallū, "the land of no return" (an expression often used of the Indian *Brahmaloka*

(Continued on following page.)

conclusion that only needs to be reinforced and extended by a more detailed examination of the "ancient oriental mythology" both Western Asiatic and Indian; this it is proposed to undertake without pretending to add anything to Dr. Hartner's very able treatment of the purely astronomical aspect of the Nodes of which the knots in the serpent's tail are an indication.

As Jerphanion remarks, "*Ce que l'archéologue cherche dans la monument, c'est l'expression d'une pensée*";[1] and though it involves what may seem to be, at first sight, a lengthy digression, it will be indispensable to provide a background for the history of the iconography of Sagittarius by outlining the myth of the Quest for Life, or Rape of Soma from which we learn where and what it is that the archer defends, and against whom, and why it is that the Archer is so often armed not only with arrows but with a sting.

In India, Soma is at once a "person" and the tree, plant, food or Water of Life of the gods, especially Indra, on whose behalf it is defended by dragons and an "active door." In Greece, the source of life is Dionysos, Semele's son who "though a god, is poured out as a libation to the gods, so that through Him men may win good things,"[2] or is represented by the Golden Apples, or Golden Fleece that is guarded by a dragon and stolen by a hero. In Hebrew, this is the Tree of Life, or Suftung's "Mead," the blood of a sacrifice, that Odin wins.[3] In Grail and Celtic folklore, the source of life is a Vessel of Plenty or other talisman won by the Hero of a Quest who crosses a bridge or ford and overcomes the defender of an "active door." In Christianity, Soma is represented by the "living water" of *John* IV.10-14 and the "bread" of VI.50-51 — "The sweetness which is hidden from all has truly come into this heavenly vessel."[4]

(Continued from preceding page.)

and of the Irish Otherworld) is the "Land of Darkness" to which "went the souls of *all* men" and where the good reposed in peace and the wicked in bondage (Langdon, *Semitic Mythology*, pp. 161, 162.) There Ningiśzida or Nergal rules. This Land of Darkness in which so many traditions locate the Fountain of Life becomes the Divine Darkness of Christian mystics and the subject of the *Contemplatio in Caligine*. In Celtic mythology Joyous Garde and Dolorous Garde are one as places, but differ according to *our* point of view; on this dual aspect of the Otherworld, cf. Josef Baudis in *Folklore* XXVII, 1916, pp. 39, 40, "one of a beautiful blessed country and the other of a dangerous region." There could be no better proof of the real identity of the empyrean Otherworld with the world of the dead "from which there is no return" (except for the living hero who achieves the Quest for Life) than is afforded by the convivium of the deceased with the Gandaharvas and Yama (God of Death) in *Ṛgveda* IX.113 and *Atharva Veda* IV.34.4. As Eckhart [also says]: "The Kingdom of God is for none but the thoroughly dead."

So in the Boehme's dialogue of Heaven and Hell it is emphasized that the *fire* is one, but experienced as love or wrath according to the nature of the experient. The distinction of Heaven and Hell as places is purely esoteric, and however inevitable on this level can have no place on the metaphysical level of reference to which our symbols refer and in which the distinction is not of places but of states of being.

1 G. de Jerphanion, *La voix des monuments*, 1930, p. 16. In the present state of our science it might have rather been said that "*doit chercher*" than "*cherche*"!

2 Euripedes, *Bacchae* 284.

3 G. Vigfusson and R. York Powell, *Corpus Poeticum Boreale*, I, pp. 20-3 and 463-6. For these authors "son" or "*soma*" is the root in *Suftung* (*Suptungr = Sum-t-ung*); the remark that "the Holy Mead was fetched from Hades beyond the outskirts of the inhabited earth."

4 Meister Eckhart, *Pfeiffer*, p. 215.

King Soma's place is in the Otherworld, "the third heaven from here," or "highest heaven," an arcanum of which the equivalent in Sumerian mythology is Ea-Anu's "secret chamber."[1] No dweller on earth partakes of the true elixir, but only of substitutes "made to be Soma" by rites of transubstantiation.[2] Soma, guarded by and assimilated to his gaoler, Vṛtra-Varuṇa, is "in the rock,"[3] that is, behind or within the rockwall or mountain that must be pierced or opened by whoever would reach him, or in other words, within the "castle" or behind the "murity" of the Sky that divides this world from the hyperuranian Empyrean than can be entered only by way of the guarded Sundoor. That is "the wall of the Paradise in which thou, God, dwellest, built of the coincidence of contraries, and none may enter who has not overcome the Highest Spirit of Reason who guards the entrance,"[4] *viz.* the "harsh divinity" whose name is "Truth" and who keeps the door against all who are unqualified to "pass through the

Figure 2: "Rape of Soma." Relief from Bādāmī, Cave IV, 6th century A.D. [Drawing by Ananda Kentish Coomaraswamy. — Ed.]

1 *RV.* IX.86, 15, 27; *TS.* III.5.7.1; *ŚB.* III.6.2.8, etc.: S. Langdon, *The Legend of Etana*, Paris, 1932, p. 3.

2 *RV.* X.85.3.4; *AB.* VII.31; *ŚB.* III.4.3.13; XII.7.3.11.

3 *In* which he is enclosed or imprisoned, *RV.* X.68.8 and from which he is wrung, *RV.* I.93.6, like "honey from the rock," *Deut.* XXXII.13.31. Soma was set or hidden in this rock by Varuṇa (*RV.* V.85.2 *varuṇo . . . adadhāt somam adrau*), to whom he belongs and to whom he is assimilated before his purification (*RV.* IX.77.5; *TS.* I.2.10.2 *varuṇo 'si dhṛtavrato, vārūṇam asi*, VI.1.11 *varuṇo iva*; *TB.* I.7.8.3 *somorājā varuṇaḥ*; *ŚB.* III.3.4.25, 29, 30 *vāruṇya*), or sacrificial disenchantment, as he is to Mitra after it. It is similarly that Agni is Varuṇa at birth, and becomes Mitra when kindled (*RV.* V.3.1; *AB.* III.4). These two, Agni and Soma, are the "dry and moist" principles of life. To say that they are in or in the power of Varuṇa is to say that they are in or in the power of Vṛtra, as they are explicitly in *TS.* II.4.12. So it is "for Agni and Soma" that Indra smites Vṛtra, *TS.* VI.1.11.6.

In the Soma-*haraṇa* (Rape of Soma) reliefs at Bādāmī (Fig. 2), Varuṇa and his *makara* are seated beside Soma as guardians. Varuṇa's enclosure of Soma is paralleled in the Younger Edda by the shutting up of the Holy Mead in the Lockhill (Knitberg), to which there is no access but through its solid rockwall.

4 Nicolas of Cusa, *De vis. Dei.* Ch. 9.

midst of the Sun"[1] — "I am the door: By Me if any man shall enter in, he shall be saved."[2] Of this *Janua Coeli* the leaves or jambs are those very contraries of which the wall is built, and through which none can pass but the Hero who can dart between the "Clashing Rocks" of every dialectical alternative — *inter genas saevantium dentium . . . draconum!*[3]

The associations of Soma are in particular with Varuṇa, Yama (the God of Death), Tvaṣṭṛ (the Titan Smith) and the Gandharvas (of whom more later). Priests are said to "lap the rich milk of the Aśvins, by their inspired-contemplations, there in the Gandharva's stronghold" (*RV.* I.22.4); the sacrificer "drinks Soma in a symposium with the gods" *sadhamādam devaiṃ somam pibati*, *TS.* II.5.55); and these participations are a prefiguration or anticipation of the blessed life of the deceased who "sits by Yama, goes to the gods and drinks with the Soma-loving Gandharvas" (*AV.* IV.34.3), with Yama and the gods (*RV.* X.135.1). In Yama Vaisvavata's realm of immortality, where Soma flows, every desire is fulfilled in yonder realm of Heaven's gate (*RV.* IX.113.8 f.).[4] King Soma is ever guarded by the Gandharva (*RV.* IX.83.4), who stands up pointing his bright weapons at the Eagle as he approaches Yama's seat to carry off the elixir (*RV.* X.123.6, 7). A typical version of the myth of the Rape of Soma begins: "Soma was in the Sky, and the gods were here (below).[5] They desired, "Would that Soma might come to us; then might

---

1 *Jaiminīya Upaniśad Brahmaṇa* I.5.1.

2 *John* X.9.

3 *Apuleius* VI.15. Cf. the formula *mā mā santāptam*, "Do not burn me up" (*VS.* V.33 etc.) addressed by the sacrificer to the door-posts (*dikṣā* and *tapas*, *ŚB.* III.6.2.9) of the *sadas* as he enters this ritual equivalent of the Otherworld; and further, in my "Symplegades," to appear in the *Festschrift for Professor George Sarton.*

4 "Heaven's gate": The *avarodhanam divah* (*Sāyana, bhūtānām pranveśanam*) is the Sundoor (*Janua Coeli*) of *Muṇḍ. Up.* I.2.11 and *MU.* VI.30, etc., and the World-door of which *CU.* VIII.6.5 speaks as "a way-in for the gnostic, and a barrier for the agnostic" (*lokadvāram, viduṣām prapadanam, nirodho' viduṣām*) [; cf.] Parmenides in *Adv. Dog.* It is with reference to this defense that the "celestial penetralia" (*diva ārodhanāni*, *RV.* IV.7.8), with which the Firebird (Falcon or Eagle) is so well acquainted (*ib. vidutaraḥ*; IV.8.4 *vidvān*) are so called.

The convivium of *RV.* IX.113.8 and *TS.* II.5.5.4 (*sadhamādam*), (cf. XI.4; II.3 and VI.5.5.2) corresponds to the Greek conception of a συμπόσιον τῶυ ὁσίων in the Otherworld, cf. Plato, *Republic* 363 C, D and *Phaedrus* 247 B; and in G. Weicker, *Der Seelenogel*, 1902, Fig. 9, vase painting of five drinkers reclining round the Tree of Life.

5 Soma's descent is for the sake of "all gods," ancestors and men, i.e. all sacrificers (*ŚB.* III.9.3.6, *TS.* VI.4.3.1). "All gods" may be said with particular reference to the sensitive powers of the soul (*prānah*) "in which one sacrifices metaphysically" (*TS.* VI.14.5) in what is called the "Interior Burnt-Offering."

The intellectual superiority of the Gandharvas to the gods whose natural preoccupation is with pleasure is often emphasized; they know and repeat the Vedas and are expert in the Sacrifice, at the same time that they are the original possessors and guardians of Soma (*RV.* X.177.1., 2; *AV.* II.1.1, 2; *BU.* III.3.1; *ŚB.* III.2.4, 5; XI.2, 3, 7; *TS.* VI.1.6.6; etc.) When Purūravas, to whom the immortal Asparas Gandharvī has condescended, is admitted to their palace (as in Celtic mythology, Heroes are admitted, or succeed in entering Otherworld castles) the highest boon that he can ask for is to become one of themselves; it is only by sacrificing that he is at last able to do so. Purūravas (who is represented in ritual by the upper fire-stick (*pramanthana*) may be compared to Prometheus, but is given and does not steal the sacred fire. There is, nevertheless, additional evidence for the equation Pramanthana = Prometheus in the fact that the production of fire by attrition is called an *upavarohaṇa*, literally "making descend."

The Gandaharvas of our text correspond to the Igigi of the Etana myth, and the gods to the Annunaki; the former, or "Gods of heaven and earth, hated mankind," while the latter or "Gods of the lower world, planned good things for him" (S. Langdon, *Legend of Etana . . .*, pp. 1-10).

we sacrifice with him (as our offering) . . . " The Gāyatrī (metre, becoming the Falcon, or Eagle) stole (*āharat*) Soma from the Sky. He was concealed behind two golden leaves that were razor-edged and closed together at every winking of an eye . . .[1] Moreover, yonder Soma-guardians (*soma-rakṣāḥ*)[2] watched over him" (*Ś.B.* III.6.2).

Iconographically, Soma can be represented either by a plant or a tree, or by the full and overflowing chalice (*kalaśa* = κυλιξ) from which a plant is growing; or can be thought of as an inexhaustible spring. The Fountain of Life or Plant of Life can be represented as springing from the open jaws of a *makara* (Figs. 3, 4). Soma as an extracted fluid, originally mixed with blood,[3] is at once the ichor of a dragon and the sap of a tree; in other words, the life-blood of a Dragon-tree.[4]

Soma's original nature is ophidian. He is the "brother of the snakes" (*RV.* I.191.6), and his procession is an emergence from the old snake-skin (*RV.* IX.86.44), or resurrection of the body of death (*VS.* XIX.72). His sacrificial passion is thus "not really his death, but the death of his 'evil'" (*Ś.B.* III.9.4.17, 18) and a release or disenchantment by which he is brought into his kingdom as a guest and

Figure 3 (top), Figure 4 (bottom): Lotus and *makara*. Bas-reliefs from Amaravati, 3rd century A.D. From A.K. Coomaraswamy, *Yakṣas*, II, 1931, pl. 38.1.2.

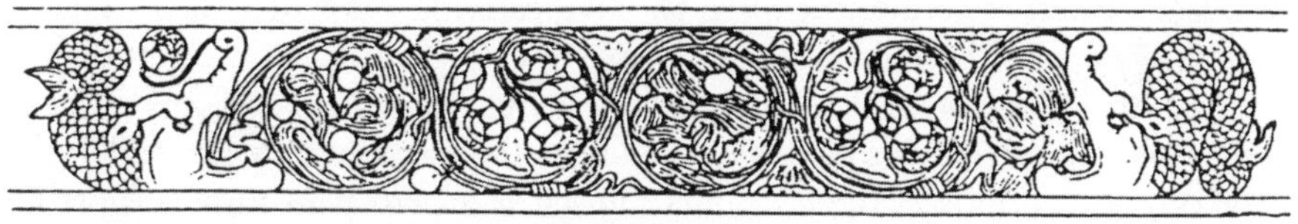

1 Again, the Symplegades, see page 4, Note 3, above. Represented in ritual by the jambs of the door of the *sadas*, which the sacrificer must be qualified by initiation and ardor to enter; they are addressed as divine, and invoked not to injure him, cf. page 4, Note 2, above.

2 *Raksa* (root *rakṣ*, protect, guard; αρέω, *arceo*) corresponds to Greek αλκα (the "fire-breathing, three-bodied" Chimaera, guardian of Euripedes, *Ion* 202-4), cf. Clement, *Stromata* V.7.2 ἀλκῆς (*sphina*). *Rakṣa*, *rakṣas*, *rākṣasa* acquire their pejorative sense of "demon" only from the fact that in their capacity as Soma-guardians the *rakṣa* is inimical to the Sacrifice; this is especially clear in *ŚB.* III.9.3.15, and 18-22 in connection with the recovery of the "ichor (*rasa*) of the sacrifice," i.e. Soma, from the water.

3 The mixture of blood and Soma in Vṛtra's veins (*ŚB.* XII.7.3.4) is similarly indicated for the Gorgon, in Euripedes, *Ion* 1003-15, where the old nurse has *two* drops of Gorgon's blood, one of deadly venom, the other "for the healing of disease and the fostering of life." Hence the Vedic "separate drinking" (*vipānam*, *VS.* XIX.72, Comm. *viviktaṁ lohitāt somapānam*); cf. M. Fowler, "The Role of Sura in the Myth of Namuci," *JAOS.* 62.36-40, and C.R. Lanmann, "The Milk-drinking Haṁsas of Sanskrit Poetry," *JAOS.* 19 (2), 150-8. Vṛtra, Namuci, etc. are designations of one and the same ophidian principle, the first possessor of the sources of life.

4 "Dragon-tree" and "dragon's blood" are traditional designations of various balsam-yielding trees, and of wine. These conceptions underlie the symbolic connotations of amber, resins, gums, vegetable oils and incense as preservatives from corruption. Greek ἀμβροσία, Arabic *'anbar* and Sanskrit *amṛta* are of cognate meaning and probably cognate etymology.

Figure 5: Soma guarded by Varuṇa and *makara*. Relief from Bādāmī, Cave IV, 6th century A.D. [Drawing by Ananda Kentish Coomaraswamy. — Ed.]

made a friend.[1] In other words, as we are repeatedly told, Soma was Vṛtra (Ahi, Namuci, Pāpman, Mṛtyu) [in] that he is sacrificed, but [it is] as Mitra (Friend) that he comes forth (*ŚB.* III.9.4.2 etc.). As Lord of the World he is urged to move forward to his stations, becoming a Falcon and evading the Gandharva Viśvāvasu (*TS.* I.2.9), thus assuming a form identical with that of the Firebird, Falcon or Eagle, who carries him off — "Thee for the Falcon, the Soma-bearer!" (*TS.* I.2.10.1) (Fig. 5). That carrying-off is the "Rape of Soma (*soma-haraṇa*), and the Falcon is the "Soma-thief" (*soma-hārin*) who overcomes or eludes the "Soma-guardian" (*soma-rakṣa*). But from the sacrificer's point of view Soma is not so much stolen as rescued from the magicians, thieves and misers by whom he is imprisoned; and Soma himself is a hero who turns against his "brothers"[2] and is praised as a Dragon-slayer (*RV.* IX.88.4, etc.) As von Schroeder expresses it: "*Der gefangens, streng behutete Soma-Haoma sucht sich zu befreien, sucht zu entfliehen.*"[3]

Similarly in the Sumerian mythology the "Plant of Birth" and bread and water of immortal life grew in the third or highest heaven, the abode of Anu, thought of as a hidden garden or secret chamber. As the Kiśkanu tree it flourishes "in an undefiled dwelling like a forest grove: Its shade spreadeth abroad, and none may enter in"; in its depths are Shamash and Tammuz, while as an elixir or living water it is represented by the "overflowing vase" in the hands of Anu or

---

1 *ŚB.* III.3.2.6, III.3.10; *TS.* VI.1.11, etc.

2 In Vedic mythology, the Gods (*Devas*) and Titans (*Asuras*) are both the children of Prajāpati; but the Gods are the younger brothers of the Titans, and this "brotherhood" is synonymous with "enmity," e.g. of men with "snakes" (*ŚB.* IV.4.53) or with Namuci, Pāpman in particular (*ŚB.* XII.7.3.4). See further my *Spiritual Authority and Temporal Power in the Indian Theory of Government*, 1942, Note 22. [New edition, IGNCA and Oxford University Press, 1993, Note 37.]

3 L. Von Schroeder, *Herakles und Indra*, Vienna, 1914, p. 45.

Ea,[1] who corresponds to the Indian Varuṇa. King Soma, the sacrifice, is, in fact, no other than the Sumerian Dumuzi (Tammuz) who, by his epithet *uśumgal* is not merely a vegetation spirit, plant or tree, but a "great serpent";[2] and at the same time the Greek Dionysos, the true vine whose blood is wine and who may be called a man, a bull, a lion, or a many-headed serpent.[3]

The myth of the Rape of Soma is briefly formulated in *RV.* IV.27.3.4; "When the Falcon (*śyena* = Avestan *saeno*) screamed and left the Sky, he bore away the Plenisher (Soma), and when Kṛṣānu, the footless (ophidian) archer loosed the string and let fly at him . . . then, as he sped in middle course, a winged feather of the Bird fell down."[4] Kṛṣānu is literally *arcitenens*, "Sagittarius"; and that in *RV.* X.64.8 he is associated with the constellation Tiṣya, the arrow, suggests an astrological association.[5] The epithet "footless" is an unmistakable indication of

---

1 S. Langdon, *Semitic Mythology*, pp. 94-96; H. Frankfort, *Seal Cylinders*; p. 124; R.C. Thompson, *Gods and Evil Spirits of Babylonia*, I.200 ff. (Tab.K.11.183-95); E.D. Van Buren, *The Flowing Vase and the God with Streams*, 1933.

The *Fons Vitae* is a fountain both of Life and Knowledge or Truth. (Cf. Philo, *Fug.* 97.197-9.1.) The great result achieved by Indra's defeat of Vṛtra-Namuci (to whom are applicable the words of *Ezekial* XXXIX.3, "the great dragon, which hath said, 'My river is mine own'") is the release of the waters" or opening of the sluices (*khāni*) of the "seven rivers" (*RV.* II.15.3; IV.28.1; *TS.* II.3.14.5; etc.); i.e. seven streams of consciousness that pass through the doors of the senses to reach their objects (*AV.* X.2.6; *KU.* IV.1). "Our senses and perceptions, such as they are, are (but) a single drop in those rivers" (Rūmī, *Mathnawī* I.2719). The meaning of this release of living waters from their still but inexhaustible source is nowhere better indicated than in the tale of "Cormac's Adventures in the Land of Promise" where Manannan explains that "the fountain which thou sawest, with the five streams out of it, is the Fountain of Knowledge, and the streams are the five senses through which knowledge is obtained. No one will have (true) knowledge who drinks not a draught (both) out of the Fountain itself and out of the streams" (T.P. Cross and C.H. Slover, *Ancient Irish Tales*, 1936, p. 507.)

The streams are of Soma (*RV.* I.32.12). The place of "the inexhaustible fount of Mead," milked by the Naruts (the aforesaid powers of perception) is "where the servants of the God rejoice" (*madanti*), identified by Sāyana with Brahmaloka (*RV.* I.64.6; I.154.51), as it must be also with Varuṇa's dwelling "where the rivers rise" (*RV.* VIII.41.2). In all these contexts the Hero of the Quest is Indra, and it is by his achievement that the Waste Land is renewed.

2 S. Langdon, *Tammuz and Ishtar*, 1914, pp. 114 f.

3 Euripedes, *Bacchae* 284 and 1017-20; J. Harrison, *Prolegomena to Greek Religion*, 2nd ed., 1908, pp. 410-53.

4 The motive of the "fallen feather" is an inseparable part of our myth, and essential to any understanding of the iconography of feather crowns and cloaks and the use of feathers in rites of healing, a subject that demands much fuller treatment elsewhere. In many of the *ŚB.* versions the fallen feather (or leaf) becomes the *Palasa*, tree of life and knowledge on earth. In the *Mbh.* version Indra casts his bolt at Garuḍa as he flies off with Soma, and though Garuḍa cannot be injured even by this cosmic weapon, of his own freewill he lets a feather fall, saying: "You shall never find its end." In the Persian *Manṭiqu 't-Ṭair* it is the Sīmurgh (Saeno Muruk, Verethragna), equivalent of the Indian *śyena* and *Garuḍa*, that drops a feather, and we are told that it falls on Chinese soil, and that "the saying, Seek knowledge even in China, points to this" (E.G. Browne, *Literary History of Persia*, II, p. 512). In the well-known version in Grimm's *Kinder und Hausmärchen*, there is a king in whose garden grows a tree that bears golden apples, which are stolen as soon as they ripen; armed with a bow and arrow, the gardener's youngest son keeps watch; when the robber appears, he lets fly, but only a single golden feather falls to the ground.

For some characteristic later representations of the archer and the robber bird, in their mythological pertinence, see Karl von Spiess, "*Der Schusse nach dem Vogel*" in *Jhrb. f. hist. Volkskunde*, II, 1926, p. 102 and V, VI, 1937, pp. 212 f.; and for another good illustration, my *Mediaeval Sinhalese Art*, pl. XVI.

5 In astrology Ninurta was identified under various names with the complex of stars under Sirius, called "the arrow," the Bow-star composed of ε, δ, τ of Canis Major, and κ, λ of Puppis and Orion, wherein the Babylonians probably saw a gigantic hunter drawing an arrow on his bow (S. Langdon, *Semitic Mythology*, p. 135). Ninurta is an ophidian or draconian deity of fertility, the opponent of Zū (Imgig,

(Continued on following page.)

ophidian nature,[1] of which there is another indication in *VS.* V.34 where the words "Look ye not upon me with the eyes of a Friend," i.e. not with a serpent's or "dragon's" naturally "evil" eye, are addressed to the sacrificial fires which represent, in ritual, Kṛṣānu and the other Soma-guardians. Grassman (*Rig-Veda* II, 1877, p. 499) plausibly equates Kṛṣānu with the Ahīśuva of *RV.* X.14 (an adversary elsewhere associated with Vṛtra, Arbuda and other of Indra's ophidian or draconian enemies), where he "leers at" or "watches for"[2] the Falcon Soma-thief.[3] Kṛṣānu appears again in *TS.* I.2.7 (cf. *VS.* IV.26, 27) where, in another phase of the myth Soma is "bought" from his guardians Svāna ("Hiss"), Bhrāja ("Glare," φλοξ, *flamma*, Blitz), Kṛṣānu and four others; and analogically (*ib.* I.3.3. and *ŚB.* III.6.2.18) these are the names of the Fire-altars by which the Soma is guarded on earth,[4] the main (*āhavanīya,* sacrificial) after being addressed as "King Kṛṣānu" In *TS.* VI.1.10 the episode of the purchase of Soma is more fully developed; in the mimetic file the Vendor is represented by Śūdra,[5] who is cheated of his price,[6] cursed with darkness, and struck with a black knot of

---

(Continued from preceding page.)

Aquila) and associated with or to be identified with Ningiśzida (Sīru, Hydra, one of the warders of Anu's gates), Ningirsu, Ab-u and Dumuzi (Frankfort, "Gods and Myths on Sargonid Seals," *Iraq* I, 1934, pp. 10, 11, 16, 27; E.D. Van Buren, "The God Ningiśzida," *Iraq* I; and further discussion below).

In Chinese astrology Sagittarius has three parts or aspects of which that one associated with the unicorn (*hsieh*, 4423, or *chai hsieh*, 245-4423, or read as *chi* = reptile) is the genius of military matters. The *chai hsieh* distinguishes right from wrong and gores the wicked; it eats fire and is furious. In the Boston painting 11.4001 Sagittarius appears with the other zodiacal signs surrounding the "Buddha of the Blazing Crest" (Prajvāloṣṇīṣa) who must be regarded as the Sun (cf. *RV.* X.149).

1 "Footless," Sanskrit *apad*, like Philo's τὸ ἄπουγ, *De migr.* 65. In *ŚB.* I.6.3.9 Indra's adversary is Vṛtra "in that he rolled" and Ahi (serpent) "in that he was footless." Cf. my "Darker Side of Dawn," Washington, 1935; "Angel and Titan," *JAOS.*, 55, 1936; "Ātmayajña," *HJAS.*, VI, 1942, pp. 390-1; and "Sir Gawain and the Green Knight; Indra and Namuci," *Speculum*, XIX, 1944.

2 *Ava didhet = dipyati*, implying a scorching glance, cf. *BG.* XIII.50: *Nētrāg-nināswīsavad didhakạuḥ.*

3 On Kṛṣānu (and also Savitṛ, Rudra, Tvaṣṭṛ, Varuṇa, Vṛtra, Gandharva as Soma-guardians, and in this sense from the human point of view maleficent) see further A. Bergaigne, *La religion védique*, 1883, III, pp. 30-67; and on the significance of the epithet Asura, *ib.* pp. 67-88, with the conclusion that this term "*doit désigner des êtres concu comme les maîtres des sources de la vie et comme habitant un séjour mysterieux.*" As Bergaigne clearly saw, the subject of our Quest is not of "life in the popular and empirical sense, but of the sources of life, in other words the *Fons Vitae* itself." I take this opportunity to say that in my opinion Bergaigne remains to this day the greatest of all European students of the mythology of the *Ṛgveda*.

4 The Gandharvas propose to the Gods: "Even as in yonder world we were Soma's keepers (*goptarah*), so also will we be his keepers here" (*ŚB.* III.6.2.18). For analogous reasons the doors of the Indian temples are even now guarded by Janitors (*dvārapāla*) in the shape of *Rakṣases* or *Nāgas*.

5 Representing the Asuras of *Kāth. Saṁ.* XXXVII.14. One infers from *RV.* where the word *Śūdra* occurs only in X.90.12, not that there were originally only three castes but that the Asuras, Dāsyus, Paṇis etc. are the "Śūdras." This is explicit in *TB.* I.2.6.7 and *PB.* VI.1.6-11 where Brāhmans, Kṣatriyas and Vaiśyas are Aryans with corresponding gods, and the Śūdras to whom none of the gods corresponds are consequently excluded from the Sacrifice. This division of men into two classes, corresponding to a distinction of Gods and Titans, and each having its own functions (*dharma*, *TS.* I.8.3), is met with in many cultures: Cf. A.M. Hocart, *Les castes*.

6 Just as in Odin's Mead, won from Gunfled is "fraud-bought" (*vel-keptz*), in the Indian versions Soma is bought at the price of Vac (dear to the Gandharvas because they are "fond of women") who is really the messenger of the gods and given by them only that she may return to them with the stolen Soma (*TS.* I.2.4.2. etc.); a form of the widely disseminated motive of "*La fausse fiancée*" (see G. Dumeznil, *Le festin d'immortalité*, 1924, pp. 21, 25, 224, 228).

wool,[1] in the twisting of which the buyer says: "Thus do I entwine the necks of the biting serpents,"[2] and "O Svāna, Bhrāja" — for "they indeed, in yonder world guarded the Soma."

The seven Soma-guardians of *TS.* I.2.7, together with Viśvāvasu and others, are described in *TA.* I.9.3 as "a company of Gandharvas" by whom the gods are poisoned. In *Kāth. Saṁ.* XXXVII.14 Soma is with the Asuras, notably Śuṣṇa (the Scorcher), and Indra, himself becoming the Falcon, snatches him from Śuṣṇa's jaws.[3] *JB.* I.287 describes the jealous Soma-guardians, Agnis and Gandharvas, as Āsīviṣāḥ, venomous serpents or basilisks.[4] In the

1 "With lead, with mind, and woolen thread the thoughtful poets (sacrificing priests) weave a thread" (*VS.* XIX.80). On the apotropaic qualities of lead or alternatively "river foam" cf. *AV.* I.16.24; *VS.* XXI.36; *TB.* I.7.8.2; and Bloomfield in *JAOS.* 15 p. 158. The knot may have been tied in the form of the *nodus herculaneus* discussed below and of which the caduceus is another type.

2 Viśvavāsu, the "All-wealthy," the celestial Gandharva, Savitṛ, the Sun, opposed by Indra who opens the rocky doors, though "full well he knew the serpents' power" (*RV.* X.139, cf. *TS.* VI.1.11.5).

3 Śuṣṇa's *māyāh*, *RV.* VI.20.4 (= Vṛtra's in *RV.* X.111.6) mentioned in a Rape of Soma context are no doubt of the same word as *yā me māyāh* of the *Suparṇādhyāya* 25.1 where these are the devices or "engines" protecting Soma for Indra; just as the *cakra* (wheel) of 25.3 corresponds to the *amṛtasya yat rakṣakam cakra-yantram* of *Kathā Sarit Sāgara* VI.3.47. Of much the same sort must have been the "net and trap" that seems to have been made by Enki, the "carpenter god" to protect the entrance to the underworld of the dead, whither Gilgamesh goes in search of Enkidu (Langdon, *Semitic Mythology*, pp. 263, 265), and the "net and trap" of Shamash (Sun-god, Marduk) which in the myth of Etana are respectively Earth and Sky and a defence against Zū (Langdon, *Legend of Etana*, 1932, pp. 22, 23). We cannot, of course, agree with Langdon that the Gilgamesh epic is historical, but much rather equate Gilgamesh with Etana, and consider both as "kings of Erech" only by euphemerisation. For the great antiquity and Sumerian origin of the Gilgamesh epic see S.N. Kramer in *Bull. Am. Sch. Or. Res.*, No. 94, 1944.

That the Otherworld is defended by automatic devices, armed automata and self-operating gates is one of the most characteristic features of our myth not only in its Eastern, but also in its Western, and notably Celtic forms; cf. J.D. Bruce, "Human Automata in Classical Tradition and Mediaeval Romance," *Modern Philology*, X, 1913, pp. 511-26; M.B. Ogle, "The Perilous Bridge and Human Automata," *Modern Lang. Notes* XXXV, 1920, pp. 129-36; and my "Symplegades" to appear later; and for the Bridge, D.L. Coomaraswamy, "The Perilous Bridge of Welfare," *HJAS.* VIII, 1944.

4 On Āśīviṣa ("poison-fanged") see *HJAS.* IV, p. 131; and page 9, Note 2, above. Āśīviṣa corresponds to Avestan Azhivishapa and the ophidian Azhi Dahāka, [of] the Zohāk epic, who is represented in human form with a pair of serpents growing from his shoulders, and in whom we shall later on recognize the old Sumerian deity Ningiśzida. Azhi Dahāka is described as a three-headed and six-eyed Druj (Sanskrit *druh*), "treacherous," Vedic epithet of Ahi, Suṣṇa, etc., and in *AV.* II.10.1 of Varuṇa and in XVI.6.10 of Namuci) conquered by Thraetona ([of the] Farīdun epic) *Yasht* V.34, just as the three-headed Visva-rupā, brother or doublet of Vṛtra, is overcome by Trita (*RV.* II.11.19, X.8.8). This Trita (Ārtya, cf. *RV.* X.45.5), friend of Indra, is a form of Agni (or Soma) and may be compared with Zeus Tritos, Pantocrator, Soter, Oikophulax (Aeschylus, *Cho.* 245, *Suppl.* 25 and *Eum.* 759); cf Macdonell, *Vedic Mythology*, pp. 67 ff.; K. Rönnow, *Trita Āptya*, Uppsala, 1927; and M. Fowler, "Polarity in the Rig-Veda," *Rev. of Religion* VII, 1943, pp. 115-23.

Again, the Avestan Ātar, Fire, overcomes Azhi Dahāka in a contest for the possession of the "Glory that cannot be forcibly seized" (*hvareno*, *Yasht* XIX.46 f.); and there can be no doubt that this Glory (in [the] New Testament "the kingdom, the power and the glory") is the same "unconquerable Glory" (*anapajayyaṃ yaśas*) that was won by the Vedic Gods from the Asur-Rakṣas, or from Makha-Śoma (*ŚB.* III.4.2.8; *TA.* V.1.1-5; *PB.* VII.5.6), cf. *D.* II.259 "the Vāruṇa deities with Varuṇa and Soma with Glory" (*yaśas*).

Again, Keresāspa ([of the] Garshāsp epic, Sanskrit *kṛśāsva*) overcomes Azhi Dahāka together with the horse-eating serpent Srvara and the green-heeled Gandarewa (archtype of Khwāja Khidr, the Master of the Water of Life) in the aerial sea Vouru-Kasha (*Yasht* V.38; XIX.38-41; etc.); and since Gokard, the "Tree of the Falcon" (*seno*), i.e. the White Haoma (Soma) tree grows there

(Continued on following page.)

Suparṇādhyāya,[1] 23.1-6 and 29.6, the first-names and probably chief of the Soma-guardians is the "footless Bhauvana, the ready archer,"[2] while among the other ophidian and Gandharva defenders of the "deathless food" are Arbuda, Nahuṣa, Pipru, Namuci and Rāhu;[3] of whom Namuci is Vṛtra and the Buddhist Gandhabba Māra, Death; Rāhu is the dragon of the eclipses discussed by Hartner, and Arbuda must be the Arbuda Kādraveya[4] of *AB.* VI.1 and *KB.* XXIX.1 (cf. *PB.* IV.9.5; IX.8.2) where he is an Āsīviṣāḥ (cf. page 11, Note 4), i.e. poison-fanged, evil-eyed[5] (cf.

(Continued from preceding page.)

(*Bundahish* XIV.11 etc.), and the Falcon is one of the forms of Verethragna ([of the] *Bahrām epic*; Sanskrit *vṛtrhan*), "slayer of Vṛtra," characteristic epithet of Indra and sometimes of his allies), it can hardly be doubted that all these battles were fought for the possession of Sources of Life that were originally jealously guarded be Serpents and/or Gandharvas. As M. Dumézil has shown, the Avestan Gandharewa and his congeners are at home in the waters, and "*en rapports (hostiles d'ailleurs) avec le monde des morts*" (*Le problème des centaures*, 1929, p. 85).

On these matters see further E. Benveniste and L. Renou, *Vṛtra et Vereoragna*, Paris, 1934; L. von Schroeder, "Heracles und Indra," *Denkschriften d. k. Akad. Wiss.* Wein, 58 Bd., 3 Abth., 1934, pp. 43-8.

1 "Book of the Eagle" (or "Falcon"). See K.F. Johanson, *Solfägeln i Indien*, Uppala, 1910; and J. Carpentier, *Die Suparnasage*, Uppala, 1920.

2 Again the ophidian archer, probably Kṛṣ̄ānu. There is a rather intimate and semantic connection of serpents with archery, connected with the facts that there are actually species of snakes that spit poison, aiming at their victims' eyes, and that arrows are often poisoned Sanskrit *iṣu*, from [the] root *iṣ*, to project or shoot, appears also in *viṣa*, poison e.g. in *viṣa-dhara*, poison bearer, serpent. *Iṣu* and *viṣu* are cognates of ιός, which is (1) "arrow," and (2) "poison," especially of serpents (Eur., *Ion* 1015). Ἰοβολέω is (1) to shoot arrows and (2) to emit poison. Ἰοβόλος, "shooting arrows," and τὰ ἰοβόλοι "venomous beasts" suggest that in *Ion* 997, Οώρακ' ἐχίδγς, περιβόλοις ὡπλσμένον, and *Phoen.* cf. *Illiad* V.739 περὶ . . . εστεφάνωται is not exactly Way's "fenced with ring on ring of snakes" but rather "fenced with a ring of Echidna's (poison-) darters," i.e. snakes. The iconography never shows us ring on ring of snakes, but only a fringe of open-mouthed snakes on the shield of Heracles described by Hesiod, who said that they clashed their teeth when Heracles fought. All these contexts are significant for the apotropaic significance of a number of "decorative" motifs to be discussed later, cf. my "Iconography of Dürer's 'Knots' . . . ," *Art Quarterly*, Spring 1944, p. 127, Note 43.

The equation of arrows with snakes occurs in Indian contexts and also in Aeschylus, *Eum.* 181-2, Apollo speaking: "Get ye gone . . . lest ye may be even smitten by a winged glittering snake shot forth from the golden bowstring." The whole connection moves in a circle; arrows are like snakes because their heads are poisonous, and snakes like archers because they strike as if with poisoned arrows; cf. our "toxin," from τόξον, bow, and τόξα, arrows.

3 These are all well-known opponents of Indra in *RV.*, but now appear as Soma-guardians on Indra's behalf. We have seen already that once the Soma has been carried off, its former defenders exercise their original functions, but now as vassals of the conqueror and on his behalf. The "thief," moreover, either restores it to Kṛśānu by offering on the fire-altar called after him and addressed as "King Kṛśānu," or by drinking it makes an offering of it to the fire in his belly which is really Vṛtra's. The myth is not, in fact, concerned with an unique or one-way event, but with an unending cycle, that of the "circulation of the Shower of Wealth."

4 Matronymic from Kadrū, the Earth Goddess, and mother of all serpents, terrestrial, and celestial, by Kaśyapa their father; Kaśyapa being also the father of Garuda (Tārksya) by Vinatā. Thus Eagle and Serpent, although opposed to one another, are sons of the same father by different mothers. With Kadrū may be compared the Babylonian Mother Ummu (Vedic *ambā*?) Khubur, "the mother of venomous serpents, as though divine, so that fright and horror might overcome him who looks upon them," and of eleven other monsters including the Scorpion-man (*girti-bili* = Sagittarius) and the Horned Dragon (*mušḫuššu*), Viper, Ravening Dog, Fish-man (*kulilu* = Aquarius).

5 Arbuda himself plays the part of Grāva-stut in the Sacrifice of Soma, but because of his baleful glance must be blindfolded, and it is after him that the Grāva-stut priest in the human ritual mimesis, in which the original Sacrifice is "extended" or "continued," is likewise blindfolded as a protection against the evil-eye.

page 9, Note 3) and a maker of "incantations" (*mantra-kṛt*), the last with reference to *RV.* X.94, a hymn in praise of the Soma-pressing stones. The situation is further clarified by the battle hymns *AV.* XI.9 and 10, where serpents Arbudhi and Nyaroudi (sons of Arbuda, and like their father, ophidian) are enjoined, by their agreement made with Indra when they had been overcome in the beginning, to "conquer on this side, not on that," i.e. to battle now on behalf of the Devas and against the Asuras. They are accordingly called upon to employ their arrows and other weapons; and, what is of particular interest in connection with the "serpent knots" to be discussed below,[1] to "bind themselves together" (*saṁnahyadhvam*) and to "fasten upon the armies of our unfriends with knottings-up and knottings-together" (*ādāna-saṁdānābhyam*),[2] and to "surround them with their coils" (*bhogebhiḥ pari vārayaḥ*);[3] the enemies of the devas will be destroyed when their venomous vassals "strike and bite" (*hate . . . radite*). It is perfectly clear that the serpents, once opposed to the gods, having been overcome by them, are now their sworn allies, who poison and "constrict" their enemies.

Perhaps the fullest and most interesting version of the Rape of Soma is that of *Mahābhārata* (in the Pūna edition, I.29). Soma is in the sky and guarded as in the closely related *Suparṇādhyāya* by a whole company of warlike gods, including Indra and a regiment of Gandharvas. The only Soma-guardian explicitly so-called is Bhaumana, "the incomparable archer," whom we naturally identify with the "footless archer" Kṛśānu of *RV.*, "the footless Bhauvana,[4] the ready archer" of the *Suparṇādhyāya*, the "footless archer" of *ŚB.* I.7.1.1, and with the Asura Maya, the Titan Craftsman of the *Kathā Sarit Sāgara*;[5] and in the last analysis

---

[1] Cf. also my "Sarpabandha" in *JAOS.* 62, pp. 341-2.

[2] Saṁdāna is etymologically σύνδεσμος.

[3] We can only note in passing that *bhoga* can be either "coil" (of a serpent) or "enjoyment" and that in the same way for Philo the "serpent," as a psychological principle, is *delectatio*, ἡδονη, pleasure.

[4] Bhaumana and Bhauvana are adjectival, and both are epithets of Viśvakarman, the "All-maker" and "All-sacrificer" of *ŚB.* XIII.7.1.14, 15 and *KB.* VIII.21, and elsewhere also of Indra or Agni. *RV.* VIII.48.2 (*AV.* II.2.2) speaks of the celestial sun-skinned Gandharva as "the remover of the theft of the gods" (*avayātā haraso daivyasa*), i.e. as solar Soma-defender, while *AV.* II.2.2 calls him also "Lord of the World" (*bhuvanasya pati*), which is *RV.* IX.86.36. In sum, Bhaumana-Bhauvana can be regarded as the "Divine Architect."

[5] In *KSS.* VI.3, Somaprabhā, daughter of Maya, exhibits a variety of automata, and explains that these "crafty engines" (*māyā-yantra*) were "made by my father of old." Five kinds are based on the five elements, "like that great engine, the world," "but the Wheel-engine (*cakra-yantra*) that guards the Water of Life (*amṛtasya yat rakṣakam*), that only he comprehends." This wheel is, of course, a form of the well-known "Active Door," which can appear as a wheel also in many Celtic contexts, notably *Wigalois* (cf. in A.C.L. Brown, *Iwain*, 1903, pp. 80, 81).

It should be observed that the word "automaton," for the Greeks and Indians applicable to persons, properly means "one who acts of his own will and power," an independent and intelligent agent, *kāmacārin*. An almost exact equivalent is τὸξαυτοὺ κινεὶν, and this "self motion," implying "authentic power," (ἐνκράτεια, *svaraj*) is the essential character of living things and notably of "soul" (Plato, *Laws* 895 D, 896 A), and "it is regards the best in us that we are really God's toys" (*ib.* 644, 803, 804). Something of this survived in the seventeenth century, when Robert Boyle could still speak of "these living automata, human bodies" (cf. *MU.* II.6). "Automaton" in the modern sense has an almost opposite meaning, that of "one who follows a routine without active intelligence" (Webster 3); while the traditional automaton has nothing in common with the "mechanism" of the materialists, whose belief in a mechanical universe represents a revival of the fallacy of the perpetual motion machine.

(Continued on following page.)

with Tvaṣṭṛ (*māyā vet* in *RV.* X.53.9) and other mythical smiths, Hephaistos *et al.* The footless Bhauvana defends the Active Door;[1] and this is described as a revolving, razor-edged, sun-bright wheel, an engine (*yantra*) "fitly devised by the gods for the cutting to pieces of Soma-thieves." Garuḍa, the Eagle, strikes him down, and darting between the spokes of the Wheel finds the Soma within still defended by "two great serpents glowing like blazing fires, with tongues of lightning, most awful; whose fiery mouths spat venom, and whose eyes never closed, but were ever on the watch; to be seen by either would be to be reduced to ashes. But all of a sudden he filled their eyes with

Figure 6: Combat of the bird and serpent. This exemplar from the *Beatus* tradition retains the ancient form. [From Ananda Kentish Coomaraswamy's file, probably eleventh century French. — Ed.]

(Continued from preceding page.)

Hence, if the Golden Gates are called "automata," said to "roar," and represented in art as "winged," all these verbal and visual symbols mean the same, *viz.* that the Divine Doors (*devī dvārau*) are living beings, empowered and ensouled and such that only the Divine Architect *could* have made them; while the automata that have been made by hands are, like all human works of art, imitations of the divine *artificiata* (*AB.* VI.27) and only "as if" self-moving.

1 The Active Door (= Symplegades) recurs in all the traditions both of the Old and New Worlds. In *Iliad* V.749-50 and VIII.393-4 it is said that "Sky's self-moving portals roared (αὐτόμαται δέ πύλαι μύκον οὐρανοὺ), cf. *TS.* V.1.11.2 *kavayaḥ . . . dvāro devīḥ*), which the orae keep, to whom are entrusted Great Sky and Olympus, whether to throw open the great cloud (νέφος, Sanskrit *nabha*; nimbus) or shut it to"; and one can hardly doubt that these automata had been made by Hephaistos for Zeus. The interest of this passage is increased for us by the fact that the Horae are "Seasons" (or sometimes "Fates"), since in *JUB.* III.14.1, cf. *JB.* I.18, it is precisely the Seasons that drag away from the Sundoor whoever has reached it but cannot make the right *responsum* to the watchman's *signum* ("Who goes there?"). The "roaring" of the doors is indicated visually on many Babylonian seals by the representation of open-mouthed lions on the jambs, while their self-moving power is indicated by the attachment of wings to the doors themselves. In the *Suparṇādhyāya* 25.1 the Active Door that keeps the way of Soma, and that Indra calls his "magic" (*māyā*), is "*von eigen Willen leuchtend*" (Charpentier's rendering). Similarly in Egypt: For the justified Pharoah, who ascends to heaven, flying like a bird, "the gates of heaven open, the bolts slide of themselves, the door-keepers make no opposition" (A. Moret, *The Nile and Egyptian Civilization*, 1927, p. 180).

dust,[1] and unseen, attacked them from every side and cut them to pieces; the strong son of Vinatā rushed up to the Soma between them, then swiftly flew off with the Water of Life." On the other hand, in the *Suparṇādhyāya* (XXXIV.2, 3) the leaves of the Active Door itself are sleepless, razor-edged lightnings, that strike from every side; in Apuleius the Eagle darts between the jaws of raging dragons (*Met.* VI.15, 18); in *Genesis* III.24 the "way of the Tree of Life" is guarded by Cherubim "and a flaming sword which turned every way;[2] in the *Book of Enoch* (LXXI, 7) there are "Seraphim, Cherubim, and 'Ophannin' (wheels); and these are they who sleep not, and guard the throne of His glory." These are important variations; what we are concerned with is rather the nature and function of the guardians, than their precise numbers or positions; though it may be noted that the *Mbh.* account is in agreement with Gudea's vase (Fig. 7 [page 14]), where there are both external janitors and paired serpents within. The "flaming sword" of Genesis has been regarded by many as a "lightning,"[3] or identified with the fiery solar *Logos*,[4] Nicholas of Cusa's "highest spirit of Reason," whom all must overcome who would enter into the Paradise of God, of which the walls are built of the contraries,[5] i.e. the Sundoor, *Janua Coeli*, "all covered over by rays" and of which it is asked "Who is able to pass through it?"[6] By the same token, it is as the Active Door that "one sees Him (Brahma), as it were, a sparkling wheel of fire, of the color of the Sun";[7] and that way in which the *Logos*, Christ himself, identifies himself, when He says that "I am the door: By me if any man enter in, he shall be saved . . . no man cometh unto the Father but by me."[8]

---

1 Cf. *MI.* 159, where a monk, by the power of his contemplative practice, "puts a darkness on the footless (ophidian) Māra, and so blinds him" thereby passing him safely. An illustration of the subject appears in a ninth century Spanish *Beatus* manuscript in the Rylands Library (R.W. "Miraculous Birds," *J. Warburg Inst.* I.253-4 and pl. 33); the text explains that there is an oriental bird that when fighting with a snake covers himself with dust in order to deceive his opponent, and makes this a type of Christ putting on the flesh. In the picture, however, in R.W.'s words, "one sees over the bird a blue mass signifying the dirt which the bird has thrown off in order to pierce the brain of the snake," and this interpretation accords more nearly with the Indian formula. R.W., admitting the possibility of Mozarabic or even Indian influence, suggests a derivation of the motive from the habits of the Ichneumon; and in any case, *gua* "snake-fighters," Bird and Ichneumon, are equivalent and interchangeable symbols, cf. *HJAS.* VI, pp. 393-8. Another illustration of the same subject, from an unspecified French XIth century source, is published by A. Leroi-Gourhan in *Revue des Arts Asiatiques* XII, 1938, p. 166, Fig. 285, [and our Fig. 6 in this Chapter. — Ed.]

2 One of the forms of the Active Door in Celtic folklore (cf. A.C.L. Brown, *Iwain*, Boston, 1903, pp. 54, 55, 66, 67, 77, 80, 81) is that of a whirling wheel set with sharp swords.

3 T.G. Foote, "The Cherubim and the Ark." *JAOS.*, 25, 1904, p. 283, cf. *Zech.* IX.14 where the arrow of the Lord is a lightning; and *Ezekial* I.13, "out of the fire went forth lightning." Cf. *BU.* II. 3.6: (Brahma) *yathāgny-arciḥ . . . yathā sakṛd-vidyut*, and V I.2.15 *vaidyutam*; *Kena Up.* 29 *yad etad vidyut*; *JUB.* I.26.8 *vidyuti puruṣas . . . tad brahma tad amṛtam. Vi-dyut*, "lightning" corresponding to *vi-bhava* (ἐξ-ουσία) and *vi-rāj* (dominion), and illuminating all things simultaneously. "Lightning" is one of the primary symbols of Brahma.

4 Philo, *Cher.* 26-28. Philo identifies the "fiery sword" (1) with the whirling Sun and (2) with the burning *Logos*.

5 *De vis. dei* Ch. IX, *ad. fin.*

6 *JUB.* I.5.6 ff; Philo, *Opif.* 71, *Spec.* 37.

7 *Maitri Up.* VI.22.

8 *John* X.9 and XIV.6. On the Door and the Door-God see more fully my "*Svayamātṛṇṇā*: *Janua Coeli*" in *Zalmoxis* II, 1942; also see "Selected Papers." In architectural symbolism the Sundoor is represented by the oculus or luffer of the dome and in that of the body of the bregmatic fontanel, see my "Symbolism of the Dome," *IHQ.* XIV, 1938. Whatever underlies this open door is open too and can receive the Light-stream from above, which is the significance of all "hypaethral" structures.

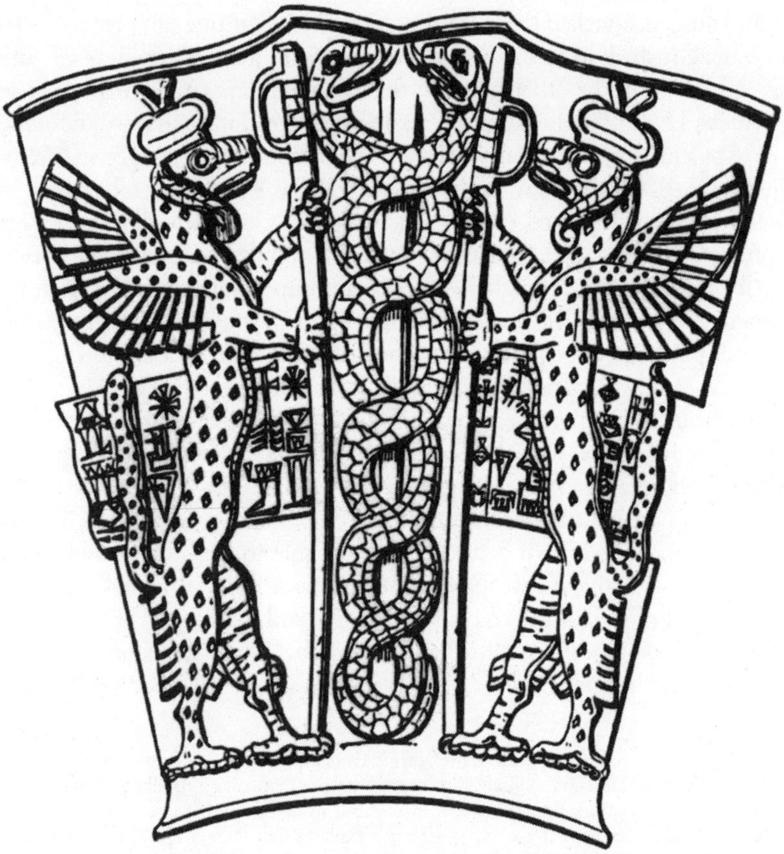

Figure 7: Vase of Gudea — libation vase from Girsu (modern Tello), dedicated to Ningiśzida. Neo-Sumerian period, ca. 2120 B.C. Dark-green speckled steatite, 9¼ inches in height. Paris, Louvre.

The God Himself, whose throne the Cherubim protect, is the *Fons Vitae, Sapientiae et Veritatis*[1] or, alternatively, the Tree of Life[2] and Wisdom. In the iconography, for the most part — Gudea's vase is exceptional — we do not see the door itself or any fountain, but only the affronted Cherubim — Philo calls them δορυφόι, "guardsmen"[3] — and between them (ἐνμέσῳ, *madhye*) the Tree of

1 Philo, *Fug.* 97 and 197-9.

2 Philo, *Mut.* 140, "the Tree of his Eternal Nature," and *LA.* III.52-79); Irenaeus, "the Tree which is itself also called Gnosis" (*Adv. Haer*, I.27), cf. *ŚA.* XI.2 Brahman, "as it were, a great green tree, standing with its roots moistened," cf. *Maitri Up.* VI. 4; *Śvet. Up.* III.9, VI.1; Agni as Vansapati, *RV. passim.*

3 The affronted Cherubim are themselves the "contraries" (of past and future, ruling and creative powers, etc.) of which the wall is built, and therefore the appropriate ornaments of the wall of the Temple, as in *Ezekial* XLI.18. Each and every pair of affronted Cherubim represents the clashing jambs of the living door through which the strait way leads — "strait," because the line that divides past from future, evil from good and moist from dry is literally, what it is so often called, a razor edge (*TS.* II.555.6 "the Sacrifice is razor-edged," *KU.* III.14 "the sharpened edge of a razor, hard to

(Continued on following page.)

Life, generally represented by a pillar with Ionic volutes.[1] The formula, illustrated by our Fig. 8, is ever repeated, and is more fully treated below. In the later Christian angelology the Seraphim are regarded as "excelling in ardor," the Cherubim in "fullness of knowledge,"[2] but it is never forgotten that their primary function is one of guardianship, for, as St. Bernard says, the Seraphim covering the feet and face of the Lord "were so placed, I think, in order that, just as the entrance to Paradise is forbidden to sinful men by Cherubim, so a bound may be set to thy curiosity by Seraphim."[3] The Seraphim of [the] Old Testament are "fiery flying serpents"; the root meaning of *sāraph* is to "burn," and the word can be used in qualification of or apposition to, or by itself as a synonym of *nāhash*, serpent," as

Figure 8: Mycenean (Late Hellenic) *kylix*. [Ananda Kentish Coomaraswamy's rendering from the *Bulletin of the Museum*, Rhode Island School of Design, Providence, Rhode Island, XXVII, 1939, p. 12. — Ed.]

(Continued from preceding page.)

be traversed"), or bridge of light, no wider than a hair (cf. D.L. Coomaraswamy, "The Perilous Bridge . . .," *HJAS*. VIII, 1944). Philo's *Logos Tomeus* and *Sunagogos* (*Fug.* 100) in the midst, is Cusa's "highest spirit of Reason," the solar Truth of *JUB*. I.5, whom the perpetrator must overcome, if he is to enter into the world that is really "but not logically." Now — the "now without duration" — is the appointed time; *brahma-bhūti*, literally "theois," is therefore also "twilight," that is the timeless interval that intermediates night and day.

1 *Genesis* 28.16-18 "Surely the Lord is in this place . . . And Jacob . . . took the stone . . . and set it up for a pillar"; *JUB*. 1.10.9 "They called the Sun a sky-supporting pillar." Clement of Alexandria, *Misc.* I.24 "The ancients erected pillars, and reverenced them as statues of the Deity." A.J. Evans, *Mycenean Tree and Pillar Cult*, London, 1901; A.J. Wensinck, *Tree and Bird as Cosmological Symbols in Western Asia*, Amsterdam, 1921; Uno Holmberg, *Finno-ugaric and Siberian Mythology*, Siberian Ch. III, "The Pillar of the World."

2 Dionysius, *Coel. Hier.* VII; St. Thomas Aquinas, *Sum. Theol.* I.108.5. "Ardor" and "knowledge" parallel the "glowing" (*tapas*) and "initiation" (*dīkṣā*) — both are "fires" — that "the weal-asking prophets, the finders of the Light (*ṛṣayaḥ svar-vidaḥ*), besieged (*upaniṣeduḥ*) in the beginning" (*AV.* XIX.41.1) and that identified with "the ever-clashing Gandharva guardians of Soma," represented in the ritual by sacrificial fires (*ŚB*. III.6.2.9). Like the Seraphim and Cherubim, to whom they correspond, the Indian Gandharvas are so distinguished by their equally erotic and intellectual powers and by their guardian function.

3 *De grad. humiltatis* X.35.

in *Numbers* XXI.8, 9 "Make thee a fiery serpent (*sāraph*) . . . Moses made a serpent (*nāhash*) of brass."[1] For Dante, seraphim, cherubim and thrones are all "loves."[2] The description of these fiery powers as "loves" is of interest because our modern Cupids (*Amori*, *Erotes*) with their bows and arrows are by no means accidentally but properly Sagittarii, forms of Sagittarius himself, who is not merely ardent but also venomous. Already in Apuleius, we find Amor described by the Milesian oracle, foretelling Psyche's marriage, as an "evil, fierce and savage Viper, who flies on wings in the high firmament and doth subdue all things with his flame, and sap the strength of each with his iron dart," while Psyche's sisters warn her that her husband is "a great and venomous serpent who will swallow her up"; until at last, so bewildered she is, that *in eodem corpore odit bestium, diligit maritum.*[3] We cannot overlook that in all traditions Love and Death are contrasted aspects of one and the same power; He is one and the same who slays and makes alive.[4] That he devours as well as generates his children can be said as well of Krishna[5] as of Death;[6] while the Gandharva, whose aspects are manifold, is at the same time "inexorable Death" (*Mṛtyu*) and the "fair love" (*Kāma*) whose consorts are "burning longings;[7] a situation that survives in Buddhism, where the Gandhabba Māra is also Kāmadeva. In the Greek tradition, the special connection of Eros with Psyche, parallel to that of the Gandharva to the Apsarases, is rather late; the winged human figure, originally armed with a dart or javelin, had originally been a more generalised fertility spirit and daimon of generation, a *Kēr* "of double nature, good and bad . . . fructifying or death bringing."[8] The *Kēres* in turn are closely related to such other winged beings as harpies, sirens and gorgons; the latter was originally male, as the beard denotes, and almost certainly a solar type, while as regards Medusa it is noteworthy [that] she can be represented as a Centauress.[9] *Kēres* or harpies can also be represented in the form of the Sphinx, lion-bodied like the Syrian Cherubim, watchdogs of the Tree of Life. An old gloss on Euripedes, *Phoen.* 1760 attributes a snake's tail to the Sphinx[.] A two-headed type from Carchemish, having the heads of a man and a lion, is also known (Fig. [72 in Chapter III, "Concerning Sphinxes, page 68." — Ed.]).[10]

The Greek Sphinx must not be confused with the Egyptian, to which the name is applied only by analogy. The type is of Oriental origin; originating in Babylonia and by way of the Hittites the type was transmitted to Asia Minor, Phoenicia, Syria and Crete. The Greek type is almost always feminine, but there are examples

---

1 Cf. also *Deuteronomy* VIII.15, *Isiah* XIV.29 and XXX.6. For Philo, the Serpent set up by Moses represents "self-mastery," and is the natural opposite of the serpent of Pleasure, and of brass so as to resemble gold (*LA.* II.79 ff.).

2 *Paradiso* XXVIII, 94-105.

3 Apuleius, *Met.* IV.33, cf. V.18.

4 *I Sam.* 2.6; *I Kings* 5.7.

5 *BG.* XIII.6.

6 *PB.* XXI.3.1.

7 *TS.* III.4.7.2.

8 J. Harrison, *Prolegomena*, pp. 175, 631.

9 Boetian vase in the Louvre, *Bull. de Corr. Hell.*, XXII, 1898, pl. V; J. Harrison, *Prolegomena*, Fig. 21. Cf. Roland Hampe, *Frühe griechischer Sagenbilder*, 56 f. and pls. 36, 38.

10 Hittite examples [in] E. Kasmuth, *Het. Kunst*, pls. 14, 15 [and] Moortgart, *Bildwerk und Volkstum Vorderasiens zur Hethiterzeit*, Fig. 35.

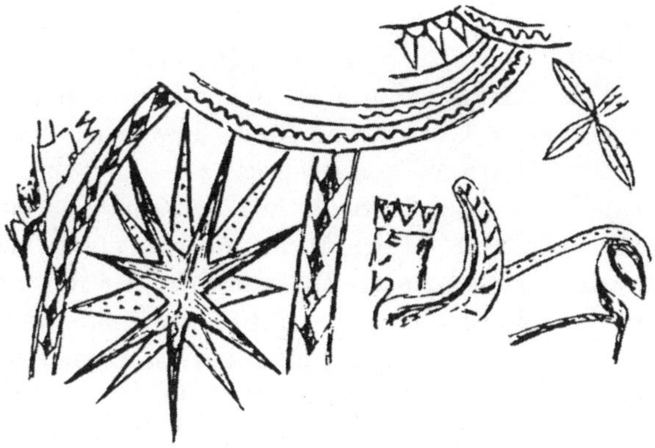

Figure 9: Bearded sphinx from a fragmented vessel. From Van der Osten, *Alisher Huyük*, III, 1937, Fig. 73, a 824. Second half first millennium, B.C.

of bearded sphinxes from *Alisher Huyük* and Cyprus (Figs. 9, 10).[1] It may be asked, by way of introduction to Philo's penetrating interpretation of the Cherubim, what was the fundamental significance of the Greek Sphinx?[2] In the first place, the word itself derives from σφίγγω, and is understood to mean the "Throttler" or "Strangler," with reference to the slaughter of the Thebans and others; but I should prefer to say "Constrainer," rather in a favorable than in a pejorative sense, though there is nothing against a *double entendre*. For if we collate Empedocles fr. 185 (σφίγγει), Plato, *Timaeus* 58 A, B (σφίγγει) and Philo *Fug.* 112 (σφίγγει) and *Heres* 188 (σφίγγεται) it will be found that a "constraint" is exercised by Titan Ether, i.e., Father Zeus, by the circumambiance of Heaven, or by the fiery *Logos* — the Wisdom (σοφία) of God[.][3] [4]

Figure 10: Bearded sphinx from the Hubbard amphora. Cyprus Museum, ca. 900 B.C. *Ann. Brit. Sch. Athens*, XXXVII [1940], pl. 7. Cf. G. Weicker, *Der Seelenvogel*, 1902, Fig. 48. [Ananda Kentish Coomaraswamy's drawing. — Ed.]

---

1 Van der Osten, *Alisher Huyük* III, 1937, Fig. 73 and pl. 21 "winged sphinxes, each wearing a cidaris." *Ann. Brit. Sch. Athens*, XXXVII, 1940, pl. 7 (Hubbard Amphora, Cyprus Museum).

2 See, in general, Roscher, *Lexikon*, *s.v.* Sphinx, discounting the Egyptian derivations.

3 This last is a common identification in Philo, e.g. *LA.* I.65 and cf. E.R. Goodenough, *By Light, Light*, pp. 22-23. From this point of view it may be assumed that Philo (who must have been familiar with the Syrian representations of cherubim as sphinxes), had he been interpreting the pagan iconography, would have called *the* Sphinx a symbol of Σοφία.

[4 The manuscript ends here with a comma. Ananda Kentish Coomaraswamy turned at this point to the composition of his "Ether." Our continuation, which follows, is based on three typed pages related to the manuscript of "Ether," either partially excised or scattered in the Princeton archive. We believe that Coomaraswamy probably intended to somehow transfer this material back to the "Sagittarius," where it perfectly serves to conclude this work. — Ed.]

What results from these collations is that the fiery etherial *Logos* that unites and *constrains* all things is in fact *the* Sphinx (σρίγξ); and this conclusion is in perfect agreement with Philo's interpretation of the Cherubim as made of the creative Fire, and as representing the Creative and Ruling Powers of "the median *Logos*," "the third uniting both" (τρίτον δὲ συναγωγόν μέσον . . . λόγον);[1] and equally with the Western Asiatic iconography in which the Cherubim are affronted sphinxes, with a palm tree between them.[2] It has been argued very plausibly that this Tree of Life as it occurs on painted pottery and elsewhere is a representation of the Mother Goddess, *Nutrix Omnium*.[3] Certainly, from Philo's point of view, this would not have hindered it from representing also the *Logos*, since he identifies the *Logos* with Sophia,[4] and as he says "the Tree of life, that is, of Wisdom (τὸ τῆς ξωῆς ξύλον, τουτέστι σοφίας).[5] Now the Greek Sphinx, whose qualities are fundamentally those of enigmatic wisdom, love and death, is typically represented seated on the top of an Ionic pillar exactly like the pillars that are guarded by the paired sphinxes (cherubim) of Palestinian art; it is certainly in her oracular capacity and as σοφήπαρθένος that such a sphinx must have been dedicated at Delphi[6] and in her riddling and enigmatic capacity that the type is represented with Oedipus.[7] If the same form was set up on graves, the symbol is surely not simply one of Death but — like that of the Eagle, raptor of Ganymede, or like that of the Indian Garuḍa[8] — the representation of the Psychopomp, who bears away the soul of the deceased, as she bore away the Thebans "to the inaccessible light of the Ether" (αἰθέρος εἰς 'άβατον φαῖς).[9] *Mors janua vitae!* For when we give up the ghost, as Euripedes says elsewhere, "the spirit dies away into the Ether" (ἀπέσβε πνεῦμ᾽ ἀφεὶς ἐς αἰθέρα),[10] which is nothing but its return to God Who

1 *Cher.* 27, cf. *QE.* II.66-67; *Dec.* 6, 7; Goodenough, p. 31, *sc.* "in bonds of love," as with cities; *Protag.* 322 C; and cf. *Timaeus* 32 C, Eur. *Phoen.* 537-8.

2 As on the walls of Solomon's temple, *Ez.* XLI.18, 19[.] On the representation of cherubim as sphinxes see W.F. Albright, in *The Biblical Archeologist*, I, 1938, p. 2, and E. Conn-Weiner, *Die judische Kunst*, 1929, pp. 40, 41, "*Cherubim . . . Sphingen . . . Damonen-gestalten*" and Abb. 20 ("*Stilisierter Baum zwishen Cherubim*," or in the text "*zwei einander zugewandte Sphingen zu seiten eines Baumstammes saulenartiger Form*").

Plato would surely have seen in these Cherub-Sphinxes those "terrible guards of Zeus" that Prometheus could not evade (*Protagoras* 321 D). [Cf.] Aesch. *Prometheus* 803-4.

3 H.G. May, "The Sacred Tree on Palestine Painted Pottery," *JAOS.* 59, 1939, pp. 251-259.

4 E.R. Goodenough, *By Light, Light*, pp. 22-23 ("Philo flatly identifies the *Logos* with Sophia"), cf. *Fug.* 51, 52 where "the daughter of God, even Sophia, is not only masculine but father, sowing and begetting." In Scholastic philosophy, Christ can still be called the "art" of God, since it was by him as *Logos* that "all things are made."

5 *LA.* III. 52; cf. *Genesis* III.6. Irenaeus, *Adv. Haer.* I.27 "the Tree which is itself also called Gnosis." Brahma as *eko svattha . . . eko' sya sambodhayitṛ*, *MU.* VI.4.

6 Darenberg *et* Saglio, *Dict. des Ant. Grec. et Rom.*, Fig. 6544, [which is a] representation of Eur., *Phoen.*

7 Darenberg *et* Saglio, *loc. cit.*, Fig. 6547.

8 See my "Rape of a Nagi," *Boston M.F.A. Bulletin*, nos. 209, 210, 1937.

9 Euripedes, *Phoen.* 809. Cf. Philo, *Heres* 282, 283 "to find a father in Ether."

10 Euripedes, Fr. 971 (in Plutarch, *Mor.* 416 D where, in the Loeb Library edition, Babbit makes the mistake of rendering αἰθήρ by "air"). The wording is of particular interest because σβένυνμι (with or without a prefixed particle) is regularly used of wind, fire, and passion and so of Man, whose life is kindled and quenched like a candle, Heracleitus Fr. LXXII; and employed with reference to the fire of life, corresponds exactly to Sanskrit *udvā* and *nirvā*; the return of the spirit to its etherial source is its *nirvāna*, a quenching of the fires of its existence in the quintessential "Ether, that holy Fire and unquenchable ασβέστοσ) flame," the celestial Fire of which the Sun is a portion (*Conf.* 156-157, with almost literal equivalents in *MU.* VI.35 and VII.11).

gave it,"[1] since Ζεύς ε̉σ̃πναἰθηρ.[2] This is at once the background for Philo's pronouncement that when, at our deaths the elements are returned to their origins, "the intellectual and celestial species of the soul departs to find a father in Ether," the fifth and purest of essences and that of which itself was a spark or offshoot (απόσπασμα)[3] or apportionment (μοῖρα);[4] and the equivalent of the Indian entering of the Spirit into Ether *ākāśam ātmā apyeti*.[5] The Sphinx may be called the Hound[6] of Heaven-or-Hades, the Otherworld, but we are nowhere told that she "throttles" her victims, only that, like the Indian Garuḍa, she devours them or carries them off, assimilates and ravishes them; and the "constraint" implied by the name of "Sphinx" is simply that of the "bonds" (δεσμοί) *sc.* of love (φιλίας, *Timaeus* 32 C), that are laid upon all things by the *Logos*, to keep them in being and that they may not be lost.[7] The Sphinx, in other words, is the single form of Wisdom, Love and Death, and corresponds to Philo's "intelligible light," whence proceed the contraries visible to sense, represented by the affronted Cherubim;[8] these three, of which only the two are actually represented as sphinxes in Palestinian art, composing Philo's "Trinity."[9]

1 *Eccl.* III.20, 21, XII.7; perhaps the most significant eschatological pronouncements to be found in the whole of [the] Old Testament.

2 Aeschylus, *Fr.* 65 A; cf. Empedocles' *Titan Zeus and Titan Aither*, and Cicero, *De. nat. deor.* II.66, Jove = Ether.

3 *Heres* 282-3. Σπάν related to Sanskrit *sphur*, "sparkle," cf. *MU.* VI.24 (Brahma like a sparkling wheel, of which the sparks are living beings).

4 *LA.* III.161.

5 *BU.* III.2.13, cf. *CU.* 1.9.1 *ākāśah parāyaṇam*[.]

6 Aeschylus, *Fr.* 129 (236) κύνα [and] *Prom.* 803-4.

7 "Taking wise forethought that the things bound (δεθέντα) and pendant, as it were, from a chain (σειρά), and should not be loosed," *Migr.* 167, 181; *BG.* VII.7 "All this is strung on Me, like rows of gems on a thread"; *Tripurā Rahasya, Jñāna Khaṇḍa* V.122-123, "Without Him [the proceeding Breath, *prāṇa-pracāraḥ*, the guardian of the 'city'] the citizens would all be scattered and lost, like pearls without the string of the necklace. For He it is that associates me with them all, and unifies the city; He, whose companion I am, is the transcendent Holder-of-the-Thread (*sūtra-dhārah*, ωευρο-σπάστης, puppeteer, also stage-manager, architect) in that city." Cf. Philo, *Fug.* 46 "Know thyself and the parts of thyself... who it is that invisibly pulls the strings and moves the puppets."

8 Philo's thought[:] The *Logos* is actually thought of as the "turning fiery sword" of *Genesis* [III.24]; and in the art it is actually represented either by the pillar with its Ionic capital or by the occupant of a throne.

9 E.R. Goodenough, *By Light, Light*, 33 f., 364-365.

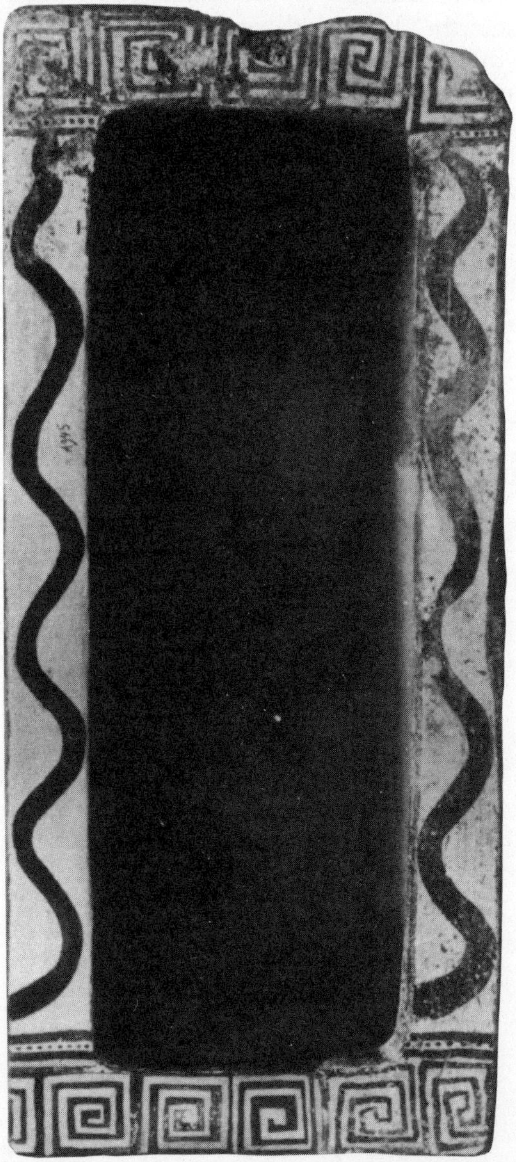

Sarcophagus lid from Clazomenia (Western Turkey, situated between Izmir and Ephesus). Sixth century B.C. Greek.

Chapter II

[THE GUARDIANS OF THE SUNDOOR AND THE SAGITTARIAN TYPE[1]]

IN A LATER, BUDDHIST RECENSION OF OUR MYTH[2] [OF THE GUARDIANS], THE essential features are retained; the medicinal waters are possessed and guarded by a serpent or dragon, and won by a hero who flies through the air and overcomes the Defender. Mahā Sumana, a youthfully precocious saint, has become the pupil of the Buddhist elder Anuruddha. The latter, having fallen sick, asks his accomplished pupil to bring him a jar of the healing waters of Lake Anottata.[3] The lake is guarded by the *Nāgarāja* Paṇṇaka,[4] who covers it with his hoods, and is "of fierce fiery-energy (*tejas*) and mighty strength." Mahā Sumana flies through the air, and on reaching the lake explains his errand. The Serpent-king refuses to let him take the water, and Sumana says that he means to have it with or without consent. To that the serpent replies, "My congratulations: By all means carry off (*harassa*, 'steal') my water, if there be in thee the manhood of a hero!" Sumana then tramples on the serpent's hoods, and as they are displaced, fountains of water rise between them; he fills his jar and returns through the air to his Master's hermitage, where the cure is effected. In the meantime, Paṇṇaka has been vainly pursuing Sumana, and follows him to the hermitage; there Anuruddha remonstrates with him until he realizes the error of his ways and asking for pardon becomes Sumana's friend and promises to supply him with the living water whenever it is needed. That is, of course, the normal sequel of a successful quest; the Defender of the sources of life remains their guardian, but now for and no longer against the victorious Hero, who was in effect "so winged that he could fly up there."

In another Buddhist myth,[5] five hundred "merchants" are journeying through a waste land and at the point of death for want of food and water; they find a Banyon tree invested with a dragon (*nāgapariggahītaṁ nigodha-rukkham*) that proves to be for them a veritable tree of life, for its branches yield them water, food and treasure; in this case, the dragon is a willing benefactor, but in another version of the story, told in the same context, the greedy merchants cut down the tree with the hope of obtaining greater treasure, and a host of dragons fall upon them and cast them into bonds from which they cannot escape. In these two versions, the two possible denouements of our myth are represented.

[1 This essay, the first full version of the "Early Iconography" above, is here given a new title. Coomaraswamy only based his latest manuscript on the first eighteen pages and not the last two of this work; our editing preserves just that part not used elsewhere. — Ed.]

2 *Dhammapada Atthakathā* IV.129-137. For snakes and dragons as guardians of fountains and deities of rain see J.P. Vogel, *Indian Serpent-Lore*, *passim*.

3 *An-ottata* = *ana-avatapta*, "not shone upon," *i.e.* in the Land of Darkness, not under the Sun; in accordance with all later traditions.

4 Ambiguously, the "Feathered" ("Winged") or the "Leafy"; a "Dragon-Tree," *Parna* often *palāśa*; and in *Śatapatha Brāhmaṇa* VI.5.1.1 is identified with *Soma* and the Moon.

5 *Jātaka* No. 493 (*J.* IV.350 ff.). The story is illustrated in a well known relief from Barhut (2nd century B.C.), and at Bodhgayā; see my *Yakṣas*, Pt. II, 1931, pl. 25, Figs. 1 and 3.

It may have been noticed that in the *Dh. A.* version, the Hero is pursued as he flies away with the booty, as is also the case in many of the older Indian versions, especially those in which the motif of the fallen feather appears. The same pursuit takes place in the Eddic version. The Hero, in other words, is never safe, even if he has successfully carried off the Plant of Life, until he reaches his destination. There are Greek and Assyrian versions in which the Hero is finally unsuccessful just because the Plant is stolen from him on his way back; and it is noteworthy that in both cases the Plant is recovered by a snake connected with a pool or spring. In the Gilgamesh epic, the Hero takes a bath, and "whilst there a serpent discovered the whereabouts of the plant through its smell and swallowed it. When Gilgamesh saw what had happened he cursed aloud, and sat down and wept . . . over the waste of his toil."[1] In the "Ogygian Myth" related by Nikandros, "Zeus sent a load of youth to mankind, who put it all on the back of an ass. Man, being thirsty, went to a spring for a drink, but found a snake there. The snake asked for his load as the price of the water, and the ass consented; hence a snake can cast his skin and grow young again, but man grows inevitably old."[2]

The Indian Āsīviṣa, referred to above, corresponds to Avestan *azhi-vishapa* and the ophidian Azhi-Dahāka, [of] the Zohāk epic, who is represented in human form with a pair of serpents growing from his shoulders, and in whom we shall recognize the old Sumerian serpent-god, Ningiśzida, defender and "Lord of the Tree of Truth."[3] Azhi-Dahāka is described (*Yasht* V.34) as a three-headed *Druj* (Sanskrit *druḥ*; fiend, deceiver)[4] conquered by Thraetona ([of the] Farīdun epic); just as the three-headed Viśvarūpa, brother of Vṛtra, is overcome by the Vedic Trita, the friend of Indra (*RV.* II.11.19, X.8.8).[5] Ātar (Vedic *Atri*, fire) also overcomes Azhi-Dahāka in a contest for the possession

---

1 British Museum, *Babylonian Legends of the Deluge and the Epic of Gilgamesh*, 1920, p. 55.

2 H.J. Rose, *Handbook of Greek Mythology*, 1933, p. 340B, summarising Nikandros, *Theriaka* 343 ff. Nikandros wrote in the 2nd century B.C. Langdon, *Semitic Mythology*, pp. 227-8, cites the legend of the serpent's theft of the plant from Aelian, and also finds a reference to the story in a Sumerian incantation in which the words occur, "the serpent in the water, the serpent at the quay of life, seized the watercress: O woe, the dog-tongue, the watercress it seized"; and he remarks that "the myth explains the annual rejuvenation of the serpent, and adds to the legends of Adapa and Tagtug still another legend of how man lost eternal life" — of which, throughout the traditions that we are studying, the sloughing of the inveterated skin is symbolic.

3 On the term *Āśīvisa* (which survives in Buddhism as an epithet of the Ahi-nāga of the Jaṭilas' Fire-temple), see *HJAS.* IV.131. Arbuda plays the part of Grāva-stut in the Soma-sacrifice, but because of his baleful glance must be blindfolded, and it is after him that the Grāva-stut priest in the ritual is blindfolded, as a protection against the evil eye. Cf. the American Indian monster "Starry-eyes-that-kill" whom the Hero Nayenezzani blinds (Wheelright, *Navajo Creation Myth*, 1942, p. 54); and more generally. A.H. Krappe, *Balor with the Evil Eye*, 1927; A.C.L. Brown, "Arthur's Loss of Queen and Kingdom," *Speculum*, XV, 1940; and *Origin of the Grail Legend*, 1943, p. 233 (Balar, "a god of the dead whose look kills"). Cf. Polyphemus and Siva's "third-eye."

4 In *Ṛgveda* a designation of Śusna and Rakṣases generally; in *Atharva Veda* II.10.8 and XV.6.10, an epithet of Varuṇa and of Namuci from whose bonds the sacrificer would be liberated.

5 On the Vedic Trita see McDonell, *Vedic Mythology*, 67f.; K. Rönnow, *Trita Āptya*, Uppsala, 1927; M. Fowler, "Polarity in the Rig-Veda," *Rev. of Religion* VII, 1943, pp. 115-23. As the "Son" Trita can be equated with Agni or *Soma*, or both (Agnīṣomau); and with Zeus Tritos (Pantocrater, Soter, Oikophulax), cf. Aeschylus *Cho.* 245, *Suppl.* 25, and *Eum.* 759.

of the "Glory that cannot be seized" (*Yasht* XIX.46 f.).[1] In the same contexts, Keresāspa ([of the] Garshāsp epic; Sanskrit *Kṛśāśva*, "having a lean horse") overcomes Azhi-Dahāka, the horse-eating serpent Svara, and the green-heeled Gandarewa[2] (Sanskrit Gandharva) in aerial sea Vouru-Kasha (*Yasht* V.38; XIX. 38-41). And inasmuch as the tree Gokard, the "Tree of the Falcon" (*seno*, Sanskrit *śyena*), *viz.* the White Haoma (Sanskrit *soma*) grew in this sea,[3] and the Falcon is one of the forms of Verethragna ([of the] epic *Bahrām*, Sanskrit *vṛtra-han*) "Smiter of Vṛtra" (an epithet of Indra and some of his allies), it can hardly be doubted that all of these battles were fought for the possession of a "Life" that was originally jealously guarded by ophidian or draconian "Gandharvas" or "cherubim."[4] Guarded, that is to say, against all but the spiritual Hero who can evade the Clashing Rocks and overcome "the highest Spirit of Reason who wards the gate of the Paradise in which thou, God, dwellest";[5] "to keep the Way of the Tree of Life" against the fallen whose thinking is in terms of "good and evil," the types of the very contraries of which, as Cusa also says, the wall of the Paradise is built, and from which man must be delivered if he would reenter there where, as Meister Eckhart says, "neither vice nor virtue ever entered in."

The forms, or as Indians would express it, *avatāras*, of Verethragna, "the most victorious of those to whom sacrificial worship is due" are those of the Wind (*vata*), Bull, Horse, Boar, Youth, Bird Varaghna, Ram, Buck and Man with the Golden Sword made by Ahura Mazda.[6] *Yasht* XIV.7.19 refers to the Bird (a form of Verethragna, as the falcon is of the Indian Vṛtra [. . .]) as "the swiftest of birds, the lightest of all flying creatures," significantly adding that "he alone of all living things outflies the arrow, however well directed." In almost the same words Dante says that "before the eyes of the full-fledged in vain the net is spread or the arrow shot" (*Purgatorio* XXXI.62-3). All that is as much to say that the "flight" is intellectual; what "flies" so fast is "that swiftest of things in us, swifter than the flight of birds, the understanding" (Philo, *Sacr.* 65). "Mind (*manas* = νοῦς) is the swiftest of flying things" (*Ṛgveda* VI.9.5 etc.). Agni is "mind-swift" (*Jaiminīya*

---

1 Presumably the "glory" (*yaśas*) for which the gods compete in *PB.* VIII.5.6, cf. *ŚB.* XIV.1.1; and the "unconquerable victory and glory" won by the gods in their conflict with the Asura-Rakṣas, *ŚB.* III.4.2.8. For the connection of "glory" with Soma, cf. *D.* II.249, "the Vāruṇya deities with Vāruṇya and Soma with Glory (*yaśas*)."

2 Archtype of Khwājā Khizr, the green-heeled Master of the *Fons Vitae* who is often equated with Elias, see *Ars Islamica* I, 1924, p. 181. As demonstrated by M. Dumézil, the Avestan Gandarewa and his congeners are at home in the waters, and moreover "*en rapports (hostiles d'ailleurs) avec le monde des morts*" (*Le problème des centaures*, 1929, p. 85).

3 *Bundahish* XIV.11, XVIII.9, XXIV.11.29; *Zād-Sparam* VIII.4.5; *Rashn Yasht* X.

4 Cf. G. Dumézil, *Le problème des centaures*, Paris, 1929 (ch. II on the Gandarewa, etc.); P. Beneviste and L. Renou, *Vṛtra and Vṛagna*, Paris, 1934; L. von Schroeder, "Herakles und Indra," *Denkschriften d.k. Akad. Wiss*, Wien, 58 Bd., 3 Abth., 1934, pp. 43-8.

5 Cusa, *De vis. Dei* IX, *ad fin.* Cusa's "wall," like the Islamic "murity," (*jidāriyya*, see Nicholson, *Studies in Islamic Mysticism*, 1921, p. 95), and the "thick cloud" (νέπος = Sanskrit *nabha*, cf. *nimbus*) of *Iliad* V.751, is that of the Sky dividing what is under the Sun from what is beyond. The significance of the "contraries" or "pairs of opposites" is discussed in my article on the Symplegades (Sanskrit *mithasturā*), [available in Volume I of *Selected Papers of Ananda Coomaraswamy*, edited by Roger Lipsey, Princeton University Press, 1977].

6 *Yasht* XIV *SBE.* XXIII.231 f.); J. Charpentier, *Kleine Beiträge zur indo-iranishen Mythologie*, Uppsala, 1911, p. 27 ff.

Brāhmaṇa I.50 etc.), and a "divine vehicle," that is to say the mind, for "it is the mind that most of all conveys him that hath mind to the gods" (*Śatapatha Brāhmaṇa* I.4.3.6); it is always in a mental (*manomaya*) body, never in the flesh, that in Hinduism and Buddhism one ascends to the Brahma world, from which there is no return. It is important to bear in mind that our Bird is primarily a Firebird rather than a Sunbird; and that the universality of its form is essentially that of the Phoenix described by Lacantius, combining in itself every kind of flying creature — *contrahit in caetum sese genus omne volantum.*

In connection with the animal forms of the Hero, Langdon (*Semitic Mythology*, p. 281) cannot understand how the ancient combat of Marduk (Sagittarius) with Zū (Aquila) can have been represented as one of Marduk with "such harmless animals as mountain deer." But not only are deer by no means harmless from a gardener's point of view; an even weaker animal, the hare, is also a recognized type of the thief, and this is the theme of the old and so widely diffused theme of the pursuit of the hare by a hound or hounds (Fig. 11), protectors of the garden.[1] The point is that it is not so much by mere brute force, but far more by his speed, lightness, courage, or wit that the master-thief succeeds. The Defender is the proprietor of a "garden"; and consequently, the Hero may be represented by any of the creatures, large or small, or strong or weak, that are the kinds that naturally devour the fruits or leaves that are grown in gardens. As it is typically a fruit-bearing tree that is guarded, so it is typically against a bird that it is protected, the Defender in this case appearing in the form of the natural enemies of the bird, i.e. as an archer or as a

Figure 11: [Hare with hounds. Ananda Kentish Coomaraswamy's drawing of a capital from the transcript of the Zurich Munster, 12th century A.D. in K. Von Spiess' "Die Hasenjagd," *Jahrb. f. Hist. Volkskunds* V, VI, 1937, pl. 3, Fig. 13. — Ed.]

[1] Cf. E. Potter, "*L'histoire d'une bête*," *Revue de l'art ancien et moderne*, t. XXVII, 1910, pp. 419-436, and *Bull. de Corr. Hellenique*, 1893, p. 227; L. von Schroeder, *Arishe Religion*, II, 1923, p. 664; and especially K. Von Spiess, "*Die Hasenjagd*," *Jahrb. f. Hist. Volkskunde* V, VI, 1937, p. 243 ff. D'Arcy Thompson, (*Science and the Classics*, p. 91), citing the *Phaenomena* of Aratus, says that the poem tells "how under Orion's feet the Hare is seen, and how she is hunted every day; and evermore the great Dog Sirius follows on her track. 'And so it is, for every morning as the Hare rises, close behind her comes the Dog; and still the Dog presses close upon her as she goes down at evening in the west.'"

Figure 12: Centaur archer from a 13th century casket. French or German, Bargello, Florence in Von Spiess' "Der Schuss nach dem Vogel," *Jahrb. f. Hist. Volkskunds* V, VI, 1937, pl. 7, Fig. 22.

snake.[1] Whether in purely human form, or as a centaur, the archer survives into Mediaeval European art (Fig. 12) and is finally secularised; a notable example can be cited also from Ceylon.[2] Whether as archer (with poisoned arrows) or as a snake, etc., the Defender is characteristically venomous; the Robber Bird, on the other hand is a master of anti-venins.[3] On the other hand, if the source of life is thought of rather as a plant (*Lebenskraut*, Herb of Life, etc.) than as a tree, then the thief will naturally be represented by such animals as the horse, deer, elephant or hare that do in fact feed on leaves or grasses, and the Defender, if not in human form and armed with a bow or other weapon, will be a lion or a dog or any of the dangerous creatures whose food is flesh. If there are many respects in which the Thief and Defender may resemble one another (both, for example, are typically winged) this is because, like Christ and Anti-Christ, and "the two Agnis that hate one another" (cf. *TS.* V.2.4.1 "hatred" of Agni, for the "Agni" that was not), they are strictly antitypal; one might, for example, cite the case of the Buddha's conflict with the *Ahi-nāga* (described as *āsiviso ghoraviso*, etc.), in which he assumes the counterform of a "human *Naga*" and "fights fire with fire" (*Mahāvagga* I.24-25), though in the fight about the Tree with Māra (*Death*, a *Nāgarāja* and is identified with Kāmadeva = Eros[4]), whose arrows fail to reach him, the Buddha remains the victor solely by his impassibility (*Jātaka* I.73). The bow itself, however characteristic of Sagittarius = Kṛṣānu (Buddhist *Māra*, etc.), is not infallibly an attribute of the Defender; there is, for example, an exceptional group of seals (Fig. 13 [page 26]) represent[ing] an archer aiming at a horned serpent (= Ningiśzida), and there can be no doubt that the former is the Hero and the latter the Defender. The one infallible sign by which the Defender can always be recognized is his venomous ophidian character, of which the scorpion or serpent's tail is the most conspicuous indication; this is, indeed, the bared tail that survives, together with the serpent's horns, in Mediaeval representations of the Devil, whose iconography in these respects is perfectly correct, since it is the Devil that opposes Christ who, in his despite, *aperuit nobis januam coeli*.

---

1 Cf. *Euphorio* III, where the keeper of the garden is a snake.

2 My *Mediaeval Sinhalese Art*, 1908 [reprinted by Pantheon Books, New York, New York, 1979], pl. 16, a Paradise garden with central Sun and flowering trees, archer defenders and bird and rabbit thieves. For the motive generally see the admirable discussion by Karl von Spiess, "*Der Schuss nach dem Vogel*" in *Jahrb. f. Hist. Volkskunde* V, VI, 1937, pp. 204-235.

3 So notably the Peacock, *Ṛgveda* I.191.14.

4 Cf. Apuleius, *Met.* IV.33 describing Cupid as of no mortal birth, *sed saevum atque vipereumque malum, quod pinnis volitans super aethera*; and (*ib.* V.17, 18) a venomous serpent "with many-knotted coils" (*multinodis volumininibus*) by whom she [, Psyche,] will be devoured. Love and Death are one divinity (cf. references in *JAOS.* 60.47)[;] accordingly the dragon (*makara*) vehicle and ensign are common to Varuṇa and Kāmadeva (cf. *MFA. Bulletin* No. 202, 1936, "An Indian Crocodile"). "The terrible cherubim are also "Loves," and Cupid is rightly represented as a cherub.

Figure 13: Archer, sacred tree and horned serpent from Moortgart, *Vorderasiatische Rollsiegel*, 1940, No. 691, cf. Weber No. 349 and also Moortgart Figs. 689-695.

The myth confronts us with the problem of the so-called "jealousy" (φθόνος) of the High Gods of Life. Langdon (*Semitic Mythology*, p. 185) speaks of the "gods of fertility, probably Ningizśida and Tammuz, of whom the serpent was symbolic" as "jealous of that man who would attain immortality like themselves." Similarly in the *Ṛgveda*, the Asura possessors and guardians of Soma or other treasures are often referred to as "misers" or "traders," and we find, too, that the sacrificing (terrestrial) deities, when they reach the other world, actually invert the sacrificial post, and so block and bar the way against the after-comers who would follow them (*Taittirīya Saṁhitā* III.4.6; *Aitareya Brāhmaṇa* II.1, 2, etc.). Darmetester observes that "in the Vedic mythology, the Gandharva is the keeper of the Soma, and is described now as a god, now as a fiend, accordingly as he is a heavenly Soma-priest or as a jealous possessor who grudges it to man" (*SBE.* XXXIII.63, Note 1). It would, nevertheless, be a great mistake to think of this "jealousy" as actually "miserly" in any human sense, however it may be contrasted with Indra's "bounty." To do so would be to accuse the Cherubim of *Genesis* 3.24, the "harsh deity" of the *Jaiminiya Upaniṣad Brāhmaṇa* I.5.1, Rūmī's "friend" (*Mathnawī* I.3056-65), Cusa's "highest spirit of reason," and likewise St. Peter and every other Janitor of the Golden Gates of simple avarice — not to mention him who shuts the door on the foolish virgins and keeps them from the wedding feast (*Matthew* XXV). The mythical level of reference is metaphysical; and we shall not understand its formulae unless we recognize that the derogatory terms employed by the contesting powers are as purely symbolic as the weapons of the visual iconography. Or does anyone suppose that in these aerial battles fought at the Sundoor, "bows and arrows" of human manufacture were employed, or that the Cherub's sword in *Genesis* had been made on Earth before the first forge had been built? This would be no more intelligent than it would be to ask, "What was God doing before He made the world?" The door is guarded, not to keep out those who *can* overcome the "highest spirit of reason" or to exclude any of those who *are* "so winged that they can fly up there" and are so eagle-eyed that they can fix their gaze upon the Sun (*Paradiso* X.74 and *passim or* the perfected τελέαι, etc.) who can and will follow through the ἄκπαν ἀψῖδα to participate in the supercelestial convivium (Plato, *Phaedrus* 247 B, cf. Philo, *Opif.* 71), but only those who are unable or unfit to enter. Unable and unfit are not two different, but one and the same qualification; it is precisely "by their ability-and-fitness (*arhaṇa*) that the gods attain their immortality" (*Ṛgveda* X.63.4). All the dragons, walls, and inactive doors of the myths are nothing but the symbols of our own inadequacies and failures. Whoever has the key receives a royal welcome.

The myth itself announces the opposition of contrasted powers and the possibility, therefore, of taking sides with one or the other, or with neither. The story will be colored in accordance with our point of view; far more often than not, of course, our sympathies are with the (human or semi-divine) Hero, whom we applaud, while the (superhuman) Defender becomes a fiend, and in the last analysis the Devil himself. Appolonius Rhodius (*Argonautica* IV.1432 f.) tells the story fairly: The Argonauts regarded Hercules, in that (like Indra) he had freed the waters, as a hero and saviour, but from the point of view of the Hesperides, the slaughter of the guardian serpent and the theft of the Golden Apples were acts of wanton violence, and Hercules himself a ruthless brute. The Celtic myths are almost always told from the Hero's point of view, with which we identify ourselves. In the *Ṛgveda* the slaughter or dismemberment of Vṛtra and the Rape of Soma are glorious feasts, for which the heroic Indra and the Eagle can never enough be praised; nevertheless it is explicit that the Rape of Soma is a "theft," and the dismemberment or decapitation of Vṛtra is an "original sin" from which the ritual Sacrifice, in which "the head of the Sacrifice (Vṛtra, Soma, Makha, Viṣṇu, Prajāpati, etc.) is put on again" and the dismembered deity thus made "whole and complete," is a deliverance.[1] If we are to understand the myth and the *raison d'être* of its variant and yet inconsistent iconography, it must be realized that the opposition of the powers of light and darkness to one another is strictly relative and valid only under the Sun. It is, in fact, our attachment to one or the other of these contradictories that shuts the "active door" in our face, for this is the door that leads beyond the good and evil[2] that occasioned our Fall. We must take this point of view, who is not subjected to or distracted by these contrary predicaments, and for whom "in all these conflicts, both sides are right" (*Ṛgveda* II.27.15). If we mean to stay on the metaphysical level of reference to the marvels themselves, we must interpret them in the terms of immutable justice, not in those of equity.

A designation of one or the other of the opposing Champions as "good" or "evil" can only lead to unnecessary confusions. For example, Frankfort (*Seal Cylinders*, pp. 133 ff.), taking Ninurta's side, refers to Zū, led captive before the enthroned Ea, as "an evil being." The capture and judgment of the Bird-man is, indeed, a common subject on Akkadian seals[3] and the crime for which the "evil bird" is tried is, of course, that of the "illegal possession" of stolen property.

---

1 See my "Ātmayajña" in *HJAS.* VI, 1942, pp. 358-98 [reprinted in Volume II of *Selected Papers of Ananda Coomaraswamy,* edited by Roger Lipsey, Princeton University Press, 1977], and "Sir Gawain and the Green Knight: Indra and Namuci" in *Speculum* [XIX, Jan.] 1944, [pp. 104-125].

2 These are "the lion and the lamb" that lie down together. We need hardly say that the doctrine of a "beyond good and evil" has been taught for millennia, and was not invented by Nietsche; or that it does not contravene the validity of their distinction here and now!

3 I must strongly dissent from Frankfort's remark (p. 135) to the effect that "the primitive mind" thinks of everything "concretely," *e.g.* of "life" and "death" as *objects* in the text:

> ". . . the gods, in their first creation of mortals, Death allotted to man, but life they retained in their [keeping.]
> (R.C. Thompson, *Epic of Gilgamesh*, p. 46[.])

(Continued on following page.)

Elsewhere, however, (Frankfort, "Cretan Griffin . . . " pp. 128 ff.)[1] the "Griffin" (the Defender) is "a terrifying power, against which the Griffin-demon [the Bird-man, Hero and Thief] affords protection"; the griffin-demon "appears throughout as beneficial to man." It is he, indeed, who brings down from above, at the risk, or even the price, of his life, the gifts of life and knowledge that are necessary to man's very existence. But if so, why call him a "demon"? In the last analysis the Defender is the "Father" and the Hero is the "Son," whose cosmic crucifixion parallels the punishments of Zū and of Prometheus and the decapitation of Dadhyañc.

We are now in a better position to investigate the archer's iconography. It must, however, be premised that the designation "dragon" has too often (e.g. by Langdon, Legrain and Frankfort) been misapplied to the Hero; it should be reserved for the Defender, whose alone is the "evil eye," as the word δράκων itself implies.[2]

The surviving type of Sagittarius is, as we remarked above, that of a centaur armed with bow and arrow, like Dante's centaurs "armed with arrows, as they were wont on Earth to go hunting" *Inferno* VII.56).[3] But, as Hartner points out, in the Islamic iconography the centaur-archer has a knotted serpent's tail,

---

(Continued from preceding page.)

We need hardly say that the *symbols* with which we think are necessarily, both for us and for the "primitive," concrete, visible things standing for invisibles (cf. *Romans* I.20). The assumption is quite unwarranted (and contrary to all we know of the abstract and algebraic quality of "primitive" mythology and art) to assert that in using concrete terms the "primitives" are referring only to concrete things! This is the error into which we fall when we call the early Ionian philosophers "naturalists," forgetting that the "nature" of which the Greek philosophers speak was not our own *natura naturata*, but *natura naturans, creatrix.* As Edmund Potter says (and countless anthropologists could be cited to the same effect), "a l'origine *tout representation graphique repond a une pensée:* . . . Plus tard . . . *en bien de cas, le sens primordial est obscurci, attenué ou étouffé par l'élément decoratif*" (*Céramique peinte de Susa*, 1912, p. 52). Similarly Walter Andrae, in *Die Ionische Säule, Bauform oder Symbol*, 1933, p. 65, "*Sinnvolle Form, in der Physisches und Metaphysisches ursprünglich polarisch sich die Waage hielteb, wird auf dem Wege zu uns her mehr und mehr entleert; wir sagen dann: sie sei 'Ornament'.*" *Ours* is the world of "impoverished reality" and of forgotten meanings.

[1 H.L. Frankfort, "Cretan Griffin . . . ," *Ann. Brit. School at Athens*, XXXVII, 1936-37, pp. 106-122. — Ed.]

2 The one essential and distinctive quality of a "dragon" is his baleful glance, as the root (Δερκ = Sanskrit *drś*, cf. *drg-viṣa*, "poison-eyed," *dṛṣṭi-bana*, "eye-arrow," "leer," *dṛṣṭi-doṣa*, "evil eye") implies. We are apt to think of "dragons" as four-footed saurians rather than as snakes, and of any winged monster as a dragon; but in the Greek sources, "dragon" usually, if not always, means a snake (cf. *Iliad* XXII. 93-5, "terribly he glareth"; Eur. *Bacchae* 1017-26, *Ion* 21-6). The same "evil eye" is characteristic of the Indian *Nāgas*, whether we call them dragons or snakes; Arbuda has to be blindfolded (*AB.* VI.1), while the *Nāga* Campeyya "whose glance could reduce a city to ashes" closes his own eyes when he would be harmless (*J.* IV.457.460). Many philologists similarly derive ὄφις from [the] root οπ in of, ὄφ, ὄφις "aspect," "eye," on the analogy of δράκων.

3 In this connection, it is of interest that Dante (*Inferno* XXV.17-24) describes Cacus (the cave-dwelling robber who recovered some of the cattle taken by Herakles from Geryon, but was slain by Herakles, see Vergil. *Aen.* VIII.190 ff., *etc.*) as a centaur with many serpent tails and "over his shoulders, behind his head" (suggesting a bicephalous type) a winged dragon, breathing fire; thus almost exactly in the form of Marduk combined with Muśḫuśśū.

Descriptions of composite monsters abound in Greek sources. Amongst these, [that] Appolordorus (*Lib.* II.7.7) speaks of the centaur Nessus as a Hydra with venomous blood is important for our iconography, for it implies precisely that combination of human, equine and ophidian characteristics that we are investigating. Euripides, *Madness of Herakles* 880, 881) speaks of the many-headed

(Continued on following page.)

ending in a snake's or a dragon's head.[1] In some cases, (Hartner, Figs. 20, 21) the archer's body is leonine, and the trunk so turned that the arrow is aimed directly at the open jaws of the serpent that forms the tail; Hartner describes this form as a combination of the original Sagittarius centaur with "Jupiter as lord of the domicile, and the dragon's tail having its exaltation in this zodiacal sign": I hesitate to differ, but it seems to me that the lion is solar and that this is a Sagittarius descended from the Assyrian type of lion-bodied Defender. For in what is actually Scythian art of the 7th century B.C., but purely Assyrian in style, *viz.* upon a scabbard of the Melgunov sword[2] we find a sequence of four archers, all with lion-bodies and two with scorpion-tails but respectively with leonine (Fig. 14 [page 30]), human, bird and one unrecognizable head. These have a further peculiarity in that their wings are in the form of fish. All are shooting towards the hilt of the sword, on which there is represented a Tree of Life, and two smaller trees and a pair of winged *genii*; and it can hardly be doubted that the four leonine archers (whose types are rather suggestive of those of the Four Evangelists) are the Defenders of a garden.

In the great Zodiac at Denderah, of which one is now in the Louvre, Egyptian or the Roman period, Sagittarius is a winged, two-headed centaur, one of the heads being that of an animal (perhaps a leopard), and one of the tails that of a scorpion (Fig. 15 [page 30]). Hartner's Fig. 36, taken from Jeramias, has a snake-like rather than a scorpion's tail, but although no very good reproductions are available,[3] there can be no possible doubt that the uplifted tail is that of a scorpion. This Hellenistic-Egyptian archer is itself a reflection or survival

---

(Continued from preceding page.)

Lernean Hydra as a murderous "dog." Bull, polycephalous dragon, and flaming lion are forms of one and the same Dionysos (Eur. *Bacchae* 1017-19). Berosus, writing in Greek at Babylon, ca. 280 B.C., describes a great variety of primordial monsters, amongst them some combining the forms of men and horses with tails of fishes, and dogs with tails of fishes (by which we may understand, in all probability, tails of snakes, "snakes" and "fishes" being generally interchangeable in our mythology; but fish-tailed water-horses appear in India in the 2nd century B.C., see my *Yakṣas*, II, 1931, pl. 43, Fig. 2).

It is significant also that Dante's centaurs and serpents are proper to that part of Hell in which thieves and robbers are punished.

1 Classical references to the "knots" of serpents include Apuleius, *Met.* V.17, *coluber multinodis voluminibus serpens* and V.20 *noxii serpentis nodum cervicis et capitis* (here *nodus* must be "joint"); Vergil, *Aen.* V.279 *nixantem nodis seque in sua membra plicantem*; Athenagoras, two snakes knotted together). For Indian references see my "Sarpabandha" in *JAOS.* 62, 1942, pp. 341, 342 (add *S.* I.134, 135; and Vikramacarita in *HOS.* 26, p. xci; also *Manu* VIII.82, "Varuna's fetters," glossed "snake-bonds").

None of the foregoing references are proof that the body of a single snake has ever been thought of as actually knotted; neither can I cite any Classical or Early Indian representation of a single knotted snake but only of two snakes knotted together.

That Appolonius (*Lib.* II.7.7) speaks of the centaur Nessa as a Hydra, with venomous blood, is, however, rather important for our iconography, as it implies a combination of human, equine and ophidian characteristics, and it is precisely such a type that we are investigating.

2 From the Litój Kurgan barrow, opened in 1763, and now in the Hermitage Museum; see E. H. Minns, *Scythians and Greeks*, 1913, pp. 171-2 and Figs. 65-7.

3 The tiny photographic reproduction of the circular Zodiac in C. Boreux, *Guide-Catalogue, Antiquities Egyptiennes* (Musée du Louvre), 1932, I, p. xiv is better than the large drawing of the rectangular Zodiac in the *Description de l'Egypte* (generally known as "Antiquities"), 1822, vol. IV, pl. 21. For a general description of Denderah see Baedeker's *Egypt*, 1929, 261 ff.

Figure 14: Detail of one of four similar archers with various types of heads — lion, human and bird, *etc.* — all shooting towards the hilt of a sword on which is depicted a Tree of Life, flanked by two winged *genii* and two smaller trees. 7th century B.C., Hermitage Museum, St. Petersburg. The style reflects overwhelming Assyrian influence, but was found in the barrow of Litój Kurgan in 1763. From E.H. Minns, *Scythians and Greeks*, 1913, Figs. 65-7, pp. 171-2.

Figure 15: Sagittarius from the Denderah Zodiac ceiling, now in the Louvre, Paris. [Ananda Kentish Coomaraswamy's drawing. — Ed.]

of the almost identical type that occurs on the British Museum *kudurru* of Meli Śipak, ca. 1200 B.C. (Fig. 16);[1] here the two-headed centaur appears to be shooting at a bird on a pillar, at which the dog is also springing; the centaur has both horse and scorpion tails, as before, and a complete scorpion is represented below the forelegs. An almost identical type occurs on another *kudurru* of the same period from Babylon,[2] and a similar type, but with only one (human) head, one (scorpion) tail, and armed with a club instead of a bow, on a late Kassite or Assyrian seal [is] dated by Frankfort ca. 1450 B.C. (Fig. 17 [page 32]).[3] Here the Defender, a winged centaur with a single bearded human head and scorpion tail (one might as well say a horse-bodied scorpion-man) is driving off a number of deer.

Iconographic evidence at present available does not enable us to follow the type beyond, at earliest, the 14th or 15th century B.C. The form is unmistakable on a late Helladic seal from Prosymna.[4] What seems to be the oldest occurrence of the archer-centaur appears on a Kassite tablet from Nippur, ca. 1350 B.C.

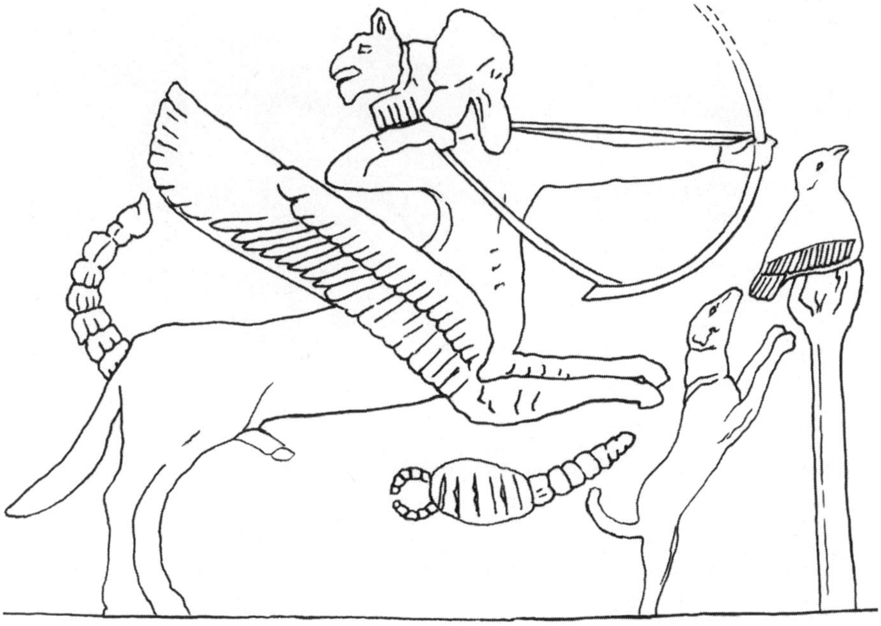

Figure 16: Sagittarius from a Babylonian (Kassite) *kudurru*, ca. 1200 B.C., reign of Nebuchadnezzar I. British Museum. [Ananda Kentish Coomaraswamy's drawing. — Ed.]

1 L.W. King, *Boundary Stones*, 1912, pp. 19-23 and pls. XXIII-XXX; *Babylonian Expedition of the University of Pennsylvania*, vol, 14; M. Jastrow, *Bildermappe . . .* , p. 17 and Fig. 33; A. Jeramias, *Altorientalische Geistesgeschichte*, Fig. 127.

2 Jeramias, *loc. cit.*, Fig. 146.

3 H. Frankfort, *Seal Cylinders*, pl. XXXI f. dated 1450 in his Chronological Index; W. Schaefer and W. Andrae, *Kunst des Alten Orients*, p. 548.

4 C.W. Blegen, *Prosyma*, 1937, p. 277 and Fig. 589. The seal is dated to "Late Helladic III," *i.e.* before 1100 B.C.

(Fig. 18);[1] the type is winged, the tail is divided up, and part of the equine body is covered with a panther skin; the head or heads are not clearly preserved; the arrow is aimed at a tree on which a bird may have been perched. Baur holds that while the centaur type of *kudurrus* is "the symbol out of which the Sagittarius of the Zodiac developed," the original function is apotropaic rather than astrological.[2] Hartner (p. 148) says that "one gets the impression that the centaur's body is thought to be fused with the body of a monster of which only the head and the scorpion tail are visible to the eye. Is this monster related to, or even a modified version of, the Mesopotamian double-horned dragon, well known from the *kudurrus*, which, when appearing on seals, is usually represented with a scorpion tail? The probability of such a hypothesis can hardly be denied." These two pertinent observations provide us with the clue to the mythological sources of our iconography; the archer's primary function *is* one of guardianship, and we shall be able to distinguish the component parts of the monstrous archer from one another, whose two heads, facing in opposite directions, already suggest the Marduk type of the Janus or Janitor.[3]

Figure 17: Winged centaur with a scorpion tail, the late Kassite period in Assyria. From Frankfort, *Seal Cylinders*, pl. XXXI f, dated to ca. 1450 [B.C.] in his Chronological Index.

---

1 W.H. Ward, *Seal Cylinders of Western Asia*, Fig. 21; *University of Pennsylvania Babylonian Expedition*, vol. 14, p. 15; P. V. C. Baur, *Centaurs in Ancient Art*, 1912, Fig. 2.

2 P.V.C. Baur, *loc. cit.*, p. 2. I cannot, of course, agree with Baur's view that the legends of Greek geometric art were "purely decorative" and that the legends "arose in connection with and in explanation of the art type." Primitive art is never meaningless, or merely "decorative" in our quite modern sense (cf. my "Ornament," *Art Bulletin*, XXI, 1939); nor are myths "poetic inventions," but much rather as Euripedes says, "the myth is not my own, I had it from my mother." As even Frankfort is aware, "divine symbols . . . are based on something more definite than a poetical simile" (*Seal Cylinders*, p. 95)!

3 For Marduk as Janus, four-eyed, *etc.*, see Langdon, *Semitic Mythology*, pp. 68, 69-294. Just as in India the Sun is also Death (*ŚB.* X.5.2.3, 13) so is Marduk with Nergal, Death who, like the Indian Yama "is often called the twin god" and has for symbol "two lion heads, *dos à dos*, looking right and left." In the building of the Indian Fire-altar, the gold plate (with 21 knobs, representing rays) representing the Sun (solar disk) is laid face downwards, for the Sun shines downwards; and upon it is laid the figure of the Golden Man, the Person in the Sun facing upwards, "the one so as to look hitherwards, and the other so as to look away from here" (*ŚB.* VII.4.1.10, 17, 18) — thus, and more naturally looking outwards and inwards rather than to the right and left, though the Sanskrit sources emphasize that the Solar watchman really faces every way and sees all things.

For the Janus type cf. also P. le Gentilhomme, "*Les Quadrigal Nummi et le dieu Janus*," *Rev. Numismatique*, IV, 1934, Ch. III. "*Les doubles tetes dans l'art asiatiqu*"e; G. Furlani, "*Dèi e démoni bifronti e bicefali dell'Asia occidentale antica*," *Analecta Orientalia* 12, 1935, pp. 136-62; René Guénon, "*Le symbolisme solstitial de Janus*," *Études Traditionelles*, 43, 1938, pp. 273-77. [Reprinted in *Fundamental Symbols* by René Guénon, Fons Vitae, 1995.]

Figure 18: Archer-centaur from an impression on a clay tablet from Nippur, Kassite period, ca. 1350 B.C. In P.V.C. Baur, *Centaurs in Ancient Art*, Fig. 2.

We shall now have to consider a series of seals, mostly Assyrian and of average date about 1000 B.C., on which the conflict with Marduk (Ninurta, etc.) with Zū (Imugud) is represented in various ways, but more often than not as that of a dragon with an eagle or griffin. Rather near to the *kudurru* type is Ward's seal No. 631 (Fig. 19) where the Defender is a winged archer centaur, with one bearded human head and two tails, one equine and the other a scorpion, the latter shifted forward to the middle of the back; and three forelegs, of which one is human and two seem to end in scorpion-claws.[1] The main body, hind legs and true tail are unmistakably equine. Of the same sort is Ward's No. 632 ([our] Fig. 20).

In other versions of the same subject the figure of the bearded archer is separated from its winged draconian vehicle, now lion-faced and horned, and breathing fire, and scorpion-tailed and without any recognizably equine features.[2] Our

Fig. 19

Fig. 20

Figures 19 and 20: Archer-centaur and winged lion from Ward, *Seal Cylinders of Western Asia*, Figs. 631 and 632. Fig. 631 is from an agate cylinder-seal, dates from the Neo-Babylonian period (mid-first millennium B.C.) and is from the Pierpont Morgan Library, N. Y.

---

1 This "cloven hoof" might be more significant than it appears at first sight. P.D. Krieschgauer ("*Die Klapptore am Rande der Erde in der altmexikanischen Mythologie und einige Beziehungen zur Alten Welt*," *Anthropos*, XII-XIII, 1917-18, pp. 272-312) shows, with reference to the figure of a scorpion-tailed quadruped with cloven feet (p. 278 and Abb. 2a) or, in his own words, "*mit deutlichen Symplegaden-Höckern ausgestattet*," must be regarded as significant of the Active Door.

[2 The type is to all intents and purposes an illustration of the text of *Psalms* XVIII.10, "He rode upon a cherub and did fly, yea he flew swiftly upon the wings of the wind."]

Figure 21: "Marduk and a dragon," as described in Langdon, *Semitic Mythology*, Fig. 81. Cf. also Frankfort, XXXV b and Moortgart, *Vorderasiatische Rollsiegel*, Fig. 595.

Fig. 21 illustrates a fine example in Philadelphia; and very like it are Moortgart's No. 595,[1] Ward's No. 575, and Weber's No. 295.[2] In the last mentioned the tree which the archer is defending against the aquiline robber-hero is clearly shown. In one of the finest seals extant, now in Berlin (Fig. 22),[3] the bearded archer is dismounted and preceded by his draconian vehicle or attendant, a horned monster whose hind-quarters are decidedly equine; the tree is again clearly shown, and the Defender's draconian assistant is taking part in the battle. On still another seal[4] the Defender and his vehicle are again compounded.

It will be observed, too, that our type of Marduk approximates that of the Chimera and that of the bicephalous Cerberus with the serpent's tail (Figs. 23 [and] 24). We know that all these, together with Geryon and others, are from one lineage (Hesiod, *Theog.* 270-86). The composite type of the monstrous archer corresponds, in fact, very nearly to that of the composite man whom Plato compares to such syncretic figures as those of the Chimera, Scylla or Cerberus: The outer form of a man, he says, embodies at the same time a many-headed

Figure 22: Archer with dragon-vehicle and Zū from Babylon, Assyrian ca. 1000 B.C. In Moortgart, *Vorderasiatische Rollsiegel*, Fig. 616; and Franfort XXXIV a. Staat. Museum, Berlin.

---

1 A. Moortgart, *Vorderasiatitische Rollsiegel*, 1940, No. 595; seal of Ninurta-bel-aṣur; S. Langdon, *Semitic Mythology*, Fig. 81.

2 O. Weber, *Altorientalische Siegelbilder*, 1920; in the Pierpont Morgan Library, not the Metropolitan Museum of Art. Ward, No. 565.

3 Moortgart, No. 616 (note that Moortgart always confuses the aquiline Zū with Tiamat).

4 Frankfort, *Seal Cylinders*, pl. XXIV a, cf. d.

and various beast, a lion. The Inner Man we think of [as] a man, a just man and master of himself when the latter is in full control of the beast (appetites), and has made an ally of the lion (boldness, courage), the beast and the lion in this context (*Rep.* 580 B f.) corresponding to the two horses that elsewhere represent, in the bodily team, the worse and better parts of the mortal soul. We can state the parallel at once from the Indian and Plutarch's point of view, if we say that Marduk himself is the Inner Man of the Sun, or Person in the Sun, or "Apollo as distinguished from Helios"; and that he is also our own Inner Man, to be distinguished from the composite psycho-physical vehicle of which he is the rightful lord and Master.

A double parallel with Indra can be recognized here. For, in the first place, we must suppose that Marduk or Ningśzida has originally, like the man who is master of himself, subdued the dragon on which he rides or sits[1] or with which he is

Figure 23: Chimaera, drawing by Lindsley F. Hall of a Corinthian plate. Metropolitan Museum, New York, MM9946.

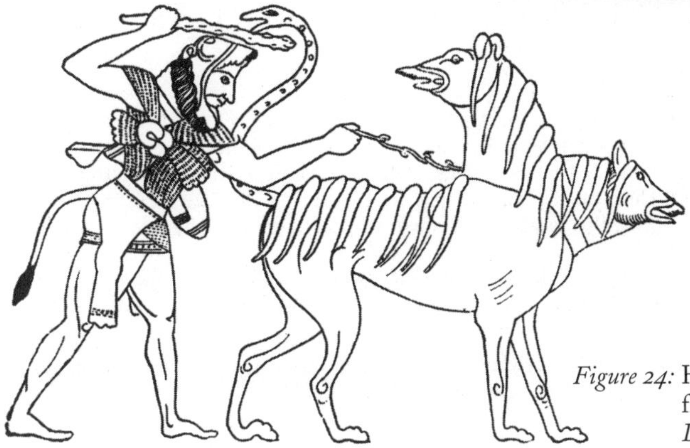

Figure 24: Herakles and Cerberus from Daerenberg *et* Saglio, *Diction. Ant.*, T. III, p. 98.

[1] On the *kudurru* of Meliśipak "the throne of Marduk with spade is supported by the dragon which he subdued in his victory over Tiamat" (Langdon, *Semitic Mythology*, p. 137).

Figure 25: "Ninurta (Marduk, Ashur) pursuing Muśḫuśśu" in Langdon, *Semitic Mythology*, p. 131; cf. Ward, 1910, No. 579. First millennium B.C. In the British Museum 89589, serpentine.

incorporated; these two expressions amounting to the same thing where, as in Indian and Platonic contexts, the body is precisely the vehicle and standing-ground of the Spirit. There survive, in fact, several early (Sargonid, ca. 2500 B.C.) seals representing the conflict of God or gods with a horned or seven-headed dragon. One of these (Fig. 25) is rightly described by Langdon as "Ninurta pursuing the Muśḫuśśu," though the principal deity might well have been called Adad, the god of storms whose distinctive weapon is the thunder bolt.[1] On the second seal of the same kind the dragon is seven-headed, and four of the heads have already been smitten, while the dragon's body is going up in flames.[2] A stone relief from Malatya (Fig. 26), dateable [to] about 1000 B.C., is of the same type.[3] I cannot but see the same conflict in the many representations of Marduk as an archer shooting at a horned dragon, evidently the protector of the tree that is seen between the combatants (Fig. 13 [page 26]); alternatively it is with the scorpion that Marduk fights,[4] and in both cases it is to be understood that what is shown is Marduk's

1 Langdon, *Semitic Mythology*, p. 129 ff., and Fig. 57; Frankfort, *Seal Cylinders*, p. 216; Moortgart's Nos. 680, 681 (*Vorderasiatitische Rollsiegel*, pl. 80) are of the same type. Langdon is altogether mistaken in equating Muśḫuśśu and "Azhi (= Ahi)" with Zū (!), who is certainly *not* the "poisonous tooth" of the Hymn to Ninurta, p. 129) but one of Tiamat's hosts (cf. BM. Seven Tablets, IV.53), and probably Muśḫuśśu himself. One can hardly identify the dragon with that very Zū against whom Marduk and the dragon fight together.

The God of Storms who, like Marduk rides the dragon or in a dragon-drawn chariot on so many seals is only another aspect of Marduk himself, who is expressly "the driver of the chariot of storms" (BM. *Babylonian Legends . . .*, Seven Tablets II.118, IV.50, pp. 46, 56) cf. Langdon Fig. 56.

2 Frankfort, *Seal Cylinders*, p. 122 and plate XXIII j; C.H. Gordon, *The Living Past*, seal 14, pp. 124-5; cf. Weber, *Altorientalische Siegelbilder*, No. 347; and J.H. Levy, "The Oriental Origin of Herakles," *JHS.* 54, 1934, Fig. 1 (hero in conflict with a five-headed Hydra and a scorpion-tailed dragon).

3 E. Herzfeld, in *Arch. Mitth. aus Iran* II, 1930, pl. XII; A. Moortgart, *Die Bildenden Kunst des Alten Orients*, 1932, pl. LXXXII.

4 For the types of Fig. 13 see Weber, *Altorientalische Siegelbilder*, No. 349; and Moortgart, *Vorders. Rollsiegel*, pl. 82 (where the scorpion-man of No. 696 corresponds to the horned Muśḫuśśu of Nos. 689-95.

original conquest of the deadly powers that he subsequently rides or incorporates. These types form, accordingly, the only exception to the truth of Frankfort's observation that "the scorpion tail is never quarry but always support" (*Seal Cylinders*, p. 216), a proposition that holds good absolutely for the conflicts of Marduk with Zū, who can never be equated with the scorpion-man.

In these representations of the fight of a god with Muśḫuśśu, the dragon whom he afterwards rides or incorporates, many scholars have recognized the archtypes or equivalents of "the Grecian myth of Heracles and the seven-headed Hydra,"[1] of the Hebrew myth of Yāw's (Yahveh's) battle with Leviathan (a "serpent" in *Isaiah* XXVII.1), and of Indra's victory over Ahi-Vṛtra[2] and it would be remarkable if this entire Indian and Iranian legend was not ultimately Sumarian.

We have stressed the words "rides or incorporates" above, because it is just in this connection that some of the oldest parallels are to be found in the Indian accounts of Indra's fight with Ahi-Vṛtra. It is true, indeed, that we do not find Indra actually riding a dragon. But we do find that his vehicle, especially as a Storm-god, is the elephant Airāvata (Erāvana); and here it is not at all insignificant that the word for "elephant," *nāga*, is also the word for "dragon." For Airāvata is Dhṛtarāṣṭra, the Regent of the East, originally a King of the Dragon-*Nāgas* but sometimes also king of the Gandharvas;[3] and there can be no

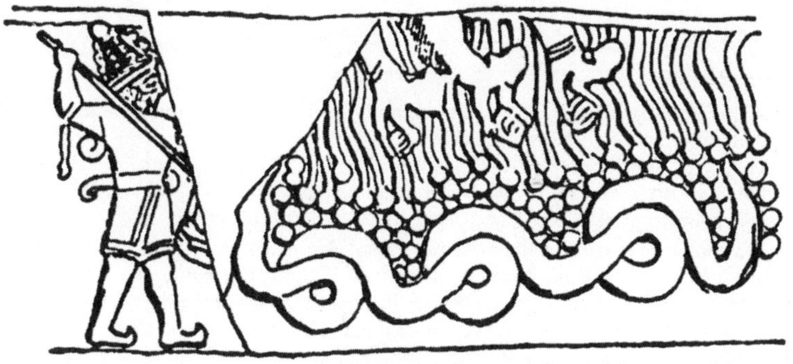

Figure 26: The slaying of the serpent Illuyankas by the Sky or Weather God, Malatya. Present Turkey, Hittite orthostat, 1050-850 B.C. In the Archeological Museum, Ankara.

1 C.H. Gordon, *loc. cit.*, p. 125.

2 Langdon, *Semitic Mythology*, pp. 129 ff. Cf. E. Siecke, *Drachenkämpfe*, 1907; my "Angel and Titan," *JAOS.* 55, 1935, p. 390, note 24; L. Von Schroeder, "Heracles and Indra," *Denkschriften d.k. Acad. Wiss.*, Wien, 28, 3 and 4, 1914; Von Schroeder (3, p. 92); in connection with Atlas who, in that he holds apart Sky and Earth (Pausanias), corresponds to the Indian *skambha* (*AV.* X.8.2. *etc.*) and *ātman* (*CU.* VIII.4.4), and plays the part of Indra in this respect, remarks that "*Alle dieser Mythen weisen, wie nir scheint, auf einen Urmythos zuruck.*" It is, in fact, only to the extent that this oecumenical *Urmythos* has been grasped that the iconography of its widely *disjecta membra* can be fully understood. Cf. F.M. Cornford, "A Ritual Basis for Hesiod's Theogony," reported in *JHS.* LX, 1940, p. xi ("The opening of the Gap (Chaos) reappears in Hesiod's myth as the forcing apart of Ouranos and Gaia by Chronos . . . the incidents, though blurred, are recognizably parallel to the exploits of Marduk in the Babylonian hymn (miscalled 'Epic') of Creation." References to the separation of Sky and Earth, who were originally one, abound in *RV.* and in many other mythologies.

3 Notably in D.II.257-8, where Dhattarattha is the king of the Gandhabbas, but also (with Erāvaṇa) classified amongst the dragons (*nāga*) such as eagles prey upon. On the other hand in Sn. 379 *nāgarājā erāvaṇo nāma*, "*nāga*" remains ambiguous.

possible doubt that all four Regents of the Quarters were originally dragons and only later "elephants";[1] and so it is that Indra's vehicle is, after all, originally a dragon. Again, it is true that Indra is hardly ever represented with ophidian parts,[2] but always anthropomorphically, though he is said to assume all forms. Nevertheless, he certainly "incorporates" Vṛtra, whom he even "devours,"[3] or who enters into him "to kindle thee,[4] that thou mayest eat," so that "Vṛtra is the belly, hunger is man's enemy," and Vṛtra remains to this day the consumer of food within us, *viz.* the digestive fire;[5] and furthermore, having thus literally incorporated Vṛtra, Indra "is now what Vṛtra was" (*TS.* II.4.12.6; *ŚB.* I.6.3.17). The acquisition of powers and properties, and in fact of a new "character," by eating of the victim's flesh is, of course, a very familiar mythological formula, and one that underlies the philosophy of all eucharistic meals.[6] In the present case Indra, having devoured the lunar Vṛtra, is "born again of the sacrifice" and "becomes Mahendra." Is it not in the same way that Marduk "incorporates" Muśḫuššu?

It is in the present connection, that of the double sense of the designation *nāga*, that the explanation of the flying elephant with knotted serpent's tail (Fig. 27) is to be found. This literally elephantine bird paraphrases on the one hand the centaur with the knotted serpent's tail, and on the other the two-headed eagle type of Marduk[7] and the corresponding Indian

---

1 References are summarised in J. Ph. Vogel, *Indian Serpent-Lore*, pp. 212-14. Further evidence for the elephant and reptile can be cited in the fact that at Barhut and Amaravati the elephant, *yakṣa*, full-vessel and *makara* ("crocodile," Varuṇa's vehicle = Ea's "fish-ram") occur interchangeably as the source of life. See my *Yakṣas*, Pt. II, 1931 [second edition published by IGNCA and Oxford University Press, 1993], comparing pl. 11, Fig. 1 and pl. 37, Fig. 4 with pls. 38, 42, Fig. 1, *etc.*

2 The reservation is made with reference to the remarkable image from Mathura described by J. Ph. Vogel, *La Sculpture de Mathura*, 1930, p. 46 and pl. XXXIX; the figure is anthropomorphic and identified as Indra by the typical crown (*kiriṭa*) and the thunderbolt (*vajra*). A quiver full of arrows having heads of serpents is worn and, even more remarkable, the head and shoulders are surrounded by figures of semi-anthropomorphic *Nāgas*, one holding a cup, and two of which spring from the shoulders. It is, then, a representation of Indra as a draconian archer.

3 *RV.* X.113.8 (*vṛtram ahim . . . āvayat*); *TS.* II.4.12.3 (*anariṣyāvaḥ*; *ŚB.* I.6.4 (*grasitva*, Indra here being the Sun and Vṛtra the Moon — like Marduk and Tiāmāt, cf. Pauly-Wissowa s.v. Sterne, p. 121, and Jeremias, *Hdbk. Altor. Geistesgeschichte*, p. 29).

[4 The burning of Vṛtra by Agni, who thus consumes his "evil," in *ŚB.* XI.1.5.8 corresponds at the same time to the representations on the seals, and to the burning of the Lernean Hydra by Iolaus, in aid of Herakles. In some contexts the burning is expressly of the "sixteen coils" in which Vṛtra entangles Indra (*TS.* II.4.1.6, V.4.5.4).]

5 The meal is eucharistic, and in terms of cannibal philosophy, necessarily endows the eater with the powers of the eaten; and "what is eaten is called by the eater's name and not its own" (*ŚB.* X.6.2.1), for "whatever is received into anything is, thereinafter, of the recipient" (St. Thomas Aquinas, *Sum. Theo.* Suppl. 92.1). It must not be forgotten that "*Soma* was Vṛtra" (*ŚB. passim*), and is the sacrificial victim.

6 Hence, as "grace" before meals, one should say, "Kindle the fire" (*samintsvāgnim*). The reference is to that Agni who may not be safely touched, *i.e.* the Varunya Agni of *AB.* III.4 (cf. *TS.* V.1.6.1) who must be "*made* a friend" (Mitra); "and verily he of the gods is the most voracious, this Agni . . . Verily, if one eats while the voracious one does not eat, he would be likely to fasten upon him (*abhiṣaṅktoh*), like a snake." So, then, when the meal is announced, one would say, "Let our superior be ingested first (*pariveṣṭavai*, cf. *Mbh.* II.40 *agniṁ vastreṇa pariveṣṭayan*), even so it is" (*JUB.* II.15.1-3).

7 Langdon, *Semitic Mythology*.

gaṇḍa-bheruṇḍa.[1] We shall not discuss the motive here at any length, but only point out that in our picture (Fig. 27) the ophidian-elephantine-bird is attacked by the Sīmurgh, the Islamic equivalent of the Indian Garuḍa. We read, in fact, in *KS.* of a flying elephant attacked by a *garuḍa*; and it is evident that the conflict of the Sīmurgh with the flying elephant is really an exact equivalent of the conflicts of the Sīmurgh with a dragon, as illustrated, for example, in our Fig. 27; in both cases the battle takes place in a Paradise landscape, of which the ophidian-elephantine-bird must be regarded as the Defender.

Figure 27: Mughal carpet with the elephantine-headed lion attacked by Sīmurgh. Boston Museum 93.1890.

Returning now to a further consideration of the seals, we shall find another group of types on which the bearded deity, armed with a bow, club or sickle, and sometimes but not always winged, fights alone, unsupported by any vehicle or associate. In our Fig. 28[2] the Defender wields a club, and as Langdon remarks, "Zū has become a

Figure 28: Combat of Marduk and the dragon Zū, cf. Langdon, *Semitic Mythology*, p. 82. Here the Zū bird has become a Pegasus (Langdon, *ib.* p. 279) "[as] based on an ancient astronomical association" (*ib.* p. 283). Cf. Ward, Fig. 580.

1 Full references to the types of the flying elephant and to the literature will be found in my *Catalogue of the Indian Collections VI, Mughal Painting*, Boston 1930, pp. 90-3; to which should be added Dh.A. I.164 where a skyfaring elephant-bird (*hatthilinga-sakuno ākāsena gacchanto*) carries off a woman, and an incorporated glossary explains that "these birds" are as strong as five elephants, and can therefore carry off their victims through the air to be devoured at leisure, i.e. in the branches of their tree, in this case a *nigodha*; and that it is their custom to keep watch (*oloketi*) upon the road that leads to their home. The elephant-bird is a Defender, and not (as in my *Catalogue* mistakenly) to be identified with the Sīmurgh or Garuḍa, the Hero.

2 Ward, 580; Langdon, *Semitic Mythology*, p. 82.

Figure 29: Marduk and the winged-ox. In Moortgart, Fig. 706.

Figure 30: Marduk, Zū and the Tree of Life. In Philadelphia, Museum of Fine Arts.

Pegasus . . . the winged horse is a form of Zū, based on an astronomical identification";[1] while in our Fig. 29 the Defender of the tree is an archer, and Zū is a horned Pegasus or winged Unicorn or perhaps a bull.[2] In the case of two fine seals, one in Philadelphia (Fig. 30) and one from the Brett Collection (No. 129), now in Boston,[3] the bearded Defender (Marduk-Ashur) is winged, and the tree is a Pillar of Light, candelabra-like and supporting a flaming Sun. In these, and in most of the cases referred to above, it is clear that Zū is repulsed.

Figure 31: Scorpion-man on *kudurru* of Nebuchadnezzar I. Babylonian, 1300 B.C. [Drawing after Ananda Kentish Coomaraswamy. — Ed.]

1 Langdon, *ib.* pp. 279, 283. The "astronomical explanation" may be doubted. Zū = Pegasus, just as the Indian Śyena [and] Suparṇa = Dadhyañc.

2 Moortgart 706. Cf. Weber, *Altorientalische Siegelbilder*, 1920.

3 MFA. 41.479; H.H. von der Osten, *Ancient Oriental Seals in the Collection of Mrs. Agnes Baldwin Brett*, 1936, p. 55 and pl. VI, no. 129. For the candelabra types of the Tree of Light, cf. L. Legrain, *Culture of the Babylonians*, 1925, nos. 594, 598, 845; Frankfort, *Seal Cylinders*, pls. XXIII a and XXXV d; Weber, *Altorientalische Siegelbilder*, 1920, 328, 336, 475, 476, 477, 481, etc.

Our archer appears on some of the *kudurrus* (Fig. 31) and on many seals[1] in the form of the "scorpion-man" (*girtab-ili*). Where (Fig. 32)[2] the scorpion-man is accompanied and assisted by a dog, this dog is no doubt the same that accompanies the scorpion-tailed centaur (Fig. 16 [, page 31]). To have recognized at last that "Sagittarius appears in the . . . Kassiṭe period as a scorpion-man or centaur shooting with bow and arrow"[3] takes us far on the way to a solution for our problems, for we know a good deal about scorpion-men, whose forms already appear in the third millennium B.C.[4] We know from the Gilgamesh Epic that scorpion-men, or rather man and wife, are stationed at the ends of the Earth as guardians of the Sun — "Scorpion-men guard his gate . . . whose

Figure 32: Scorpion-man corresponding to Marduk. Ward 630.

1 The scorpion-man is one of Ummu-Khubur's brood of snakes and other monsters whom Kingu, her first born son, commands (British Museum, *Babylonian Legends of Creation*, 1931, 3rd tablet, ls.23-6). Kingu, cf. Frankfort, *Seal Cylinders*, p. 156, is later sacrificed for the creation of man (6th tablet, ls 19-26), and can be compared to the Indian Ahi (*Vṛtra*), "the first born of the serpents, or dragons," slain by Indra (*Ṛgveda* I.32.1-4).

Clay and wooden figures of scorpion-men, spotted dogs, Muśḫuśśu, Ugallu, etc. have been found buried beside the doorways of Babylonian houses, with evidently apotropaic intention (L.C. Wooley, "Babylonian Prophylactic Figure," *JRAS.* 1926, 689 f.). E. Pottier speaks of scorpions as "*fétishes protecteurs*" (*Délégation en Perse*, XIII, *Céramique peinte de Suse*, p. 58). The memory of a scorpion-archer certainly survives in σκορπίος, an engine of war for discharging arrows (Plutarch, *Marcell*, 15). Σκορπίο-μάχος (Aristotle, *Mirab.* 139) = ἀκρίς = Latin *gryllus* parallels the ὀφιο-μάχης of the Septuagint and Philo (see in *HJAS.* VI, 1942, pp. 393-8) and we suggest that the "scorpion-fighter," like the "snake-fighter," was not a "locust" or "grasshopper" but an *ichneumon*. For *grylli* in the mythological sense as magical symbols see A. Roes, "New Light on Grylli," *JHS.* 55, 1935; W. Fraenger in *Jahrbuch f. Hist. Volkskunde*, II 1926, pp. 128-30 (note especially Fig. 1); J. Hackin, *Recherches archéologiques à Begram*, 1939, pp. 21, 22 (Indian examples).

Dante (*Inferno*, XVII) makes Geryon "with the pointed tail" essentially "a scorpion-man"; he has the face of a just man, and the rest of him is ophidian, and "in the void glanced all his tail, twisting upwards the venomed fork, which, as in scorpions, armed the point."

Indian texts in which scorpions are associated with snakes include *Ṛgveda* I.191.16; *Atharva Veda* X.5.9, 15 and XX.1.46; *Śāṅkhāyana Āraṇyaka* XII.27.

2 Ward, 630.

[3 Frankfort, *Seal Cylinders*, p. 156.]

4 C.L. Wooley, *Ur Excavations* II, pl. 105.

Figure 33: Winged Ashur supported by scorpion-man with bearded Orants, Phoenician. Cf. Ward, *Seal Cylinders*, no. 1153, in British Museum. Frankfort XXXIII e.

glance is death . . . they guard Shamash at the rising and setting of the sun."[1] Scorpion-men with uplifted arms, guarding a solar shrine, are well represented on Frankfort's seal, p. XXXIII e [our Fig. 33], while on his seal, *ib.* b, a single scorpion-man with uplifted arms "supports" the solar winged disc; cf. Moortgart 598, 599, 709, 752. A comparison with Moortgart's nos. 692 and 696 (where the archer is the attacking hero, comparable to Herakles) will demonstrate the equivalence of the horned serpent and scorpion-man, these last being defenders of the Tree, from which it is clear that the scorpion-man has been driven off. In other cases the solar janitors appear in the altogether human forms of bearded deities; sometimes, however, of the Janus type (Frankfort XVIII a) [our Fig. 34]. The evidence adduced so far points to the conclusion that there is to be recognized a whole series of the types of the defender of the Tree, ranging from that of the bearded human-headed snake, or scorpion-tailed centaur, or dragon to others in which the component elements of the human and monstrous forms are completely separated and then either cooperate or act independently. We are dealing, in other words, with the personality of a deity whose special functions are indicated not only by his actions, but also by the weapons he employs and by the draconian monster with which he may be organically combined and which serves equally as his vehicle whether he is combined with it or rides upon it; one is reminded of

Figure 34: Samas [i.e. Shamash] rising with anthromorphic janitors opening his gates. Cf. Frankfort, *Cylinder Seals*, pl. XVIII a. Boston Museum 89110; serpentine; 3.8 by 2.45 cm.

[1] Langdon, *Semitic Mythology*, p. 209; cf. British Museum, *Epic of Gilgamesh*, 1920, p. 50. The scorpion-men here are man and wife; the man claims Gilgamesh as food for the gods, but the wife recognizes that he is two-thirds divine and only one-third human, and [the] final result is that Gilgamesh is allowed to continue on his way, still beset with dangers, until he reaches the Paradise garden in which the Plant of Life is growing.

the Indian theological dictum, that "the weapons and the vehicle of any deity are his fiery-energy (*tejas*) . . . he himself becomes his own vehicle and weapon."[1] The question is no longer "entirely unsolved," as to why this dragon was combined with the constellation Sagittarius.

We have referred to the solar Defender, so far, as Marduk (his name in the Babylonian theology), Ashur (his name in the Assyrian) and as Shamash (his name in Semitic). As Ashur he is, of course, the well-known bearded archer of the solar disc (Fig. 35); the type, reawakened and given new spiritual content after thousands of years, can still be recognized in William Blake's *Repulse of the Rebel Angels*.

The great variety of Marduk's forms is sufficiently implied by the text of the first of the Seven Tablets of Creation, where we are told that he has the double form of a god, and that his measures "are not fitted for human understanding, difficult to survey," that he is very tall, four-eared and four-eyed, and all-seeing Sun and Child of the Sun.[2] He is, in fact, a rebirth of his father, Ea, whose identity with the Assyrian Lahmu fully accounts for his ophidian characteristics. Marduk is also Ba'al, or Bêl, "the Lord," and like the Indian Indra to whom he corresponds, is the "King of the gods." But the iconography of the Assyrian seals is ultimately Sumerian, and it is an older Sumerian deity, Ninurta or Ningiśzida, that Marduk really represents.[3] Who are these, or Who is this? According to Frankfort, Ningiśzida, Ninurta, Ningirsu, Ab-u, Dumuzi (Tammuz) are all epithets, i.e. aspects, of "a god who personified the generative forces of nature and was

Figure 35: The sun god in the winged disc above a "sacred tree" flanked by two winged human figures with buckets, both standing on the backs of winged bearded sphinxes. Assyrian, pink jasper. British Museum 89415, cf. Ward 679 and Layard, *Culte de Mithra*, pl. XLIX.9.

1 *Bṛhaddevatā* I.74; *Nirukta* VII.4.

2 British Museum, *Babylonian Legends of the Creation*, 1931, p. 39; Langdon, *Semitic Mythology*, p. 294.

3 Mrs. Van Buren, "The God Ningizzida," *Iraq*, I; Frankfort, "Gods and Myths on Sargonid Seals," *ib.*, and *Seal Cylinders*, 119 f. and *passim*; Langdon, *Semitic Mythology*, pp. 131, 136 etc., and *Tammuz and Ishtar*, p. 116.

Ningiśzida corresponds to the constellation Hydra, Siru or Siris, and "inscriptions prove that by the serpent dragon and the lion, the constellations Hydra and Leo were intended" (Jeremias, *Altorientalische Geistesgeschichte*, p. 288, Fig. 133. Cf. Langdon, *Semitic Mythology*, Fig. 89; F.X. Kugler, *Sternkunde und Sterndienst*, 1909, I.125). An excellent example of the Leo-Aquarius, "solar lion with the dragon's tail" (Hartner, p. 144) type occurs on the fibulae of the 7th-6th century B.C. in Greece (Chr. Blickenburg, *Fibules grecs et orientales*, 1926, pp. 280-1, Fig. 319), and this type survives in the

(Continued on following page.)

therefore manifest in the fertility of the soil and of the flocks, who lived in the nether [*sc.* other] world and often assumed the shape of a serpent, who was exposed to dangerous encounters but succeeded in vanquishing monsters, and whose connubium with a goddess was an essential part of the annual ritual. If he was invoked by varying epithets, these do not seem to have obliterated, in the third millennium, at least, the consciousness of his one and single individuality.[1] As, however, there are many names, so there are many aspects; and if Ningiśzida is sometimes the Janitor and at the same time the Deity *ab intra*, this is no more surprising than [that of him who] says "I am the door," and "No man cometh to the father save by me," [that one who also said] that "I and the father are *one*."

We have said that Ningiśzida has ophidian characteristics, such as are, indeed, almost everywhere characteristics of the high gods of life and fertility.[2] He is a god of healing, a physician, Asclepios or Varuṇa.[3] He may be represented in the form of a serpent-man, with human torso and lower part ophidian (Fig 36);[4] or

Figure 36: Snake-god (Ningiśzida), worshipper, door and janitor. From O. Weber, *Altorientalische Siegelbilder*, No. 394; Bib. Nat. 78.III.

(*Continued from preceding page.*)

art of Islam (Hartner, Fig. 23). In the case of Islamic representations of the Four Evangelists (Hartner, Fig. 18 = *Survey of Persian Art*, pl. 853 b) it is St. Luke's bull, and not St. Mark's lion, that is given the knotted tail. The addition of the knotted serpent's tail to the winged elephant of the Mughal carpet (Fig. 27 [page 39]) is quite in order, as explained above. In C.J. Hynginus, *Poeticon astronomicon*, Venice, 1482, Capricornus has the knotted tail; Sagittarius is horned.

1 Frankfort, "Gods and Myths on Sargonid Seals," *Iraq* I, pp. 16, 17, cf. 27. On the early monotheism cf. *Seal Cylinders*, p. 112; Langdon, *Semitic Mythology*, p. 93; W. von Soden, *Götterspaltung und Göttervereinigung*, 1933; and more generally, W. Schmidt, *Origin and Growth of Religion*, 1935. In India also the appearance of polytheism is undoubtedly a secondary development; in *RV.* for example, Gandharva and Yakṣa are singular, and only later many; cf. my "Vedic Monotheism" in *JHI.* XV.

2 Cf. my "Sir Gawain and the Green Knight; Indra and Namuci," *Speculum* XIX, 1944, pp. 104-25.

3 For Asklepios see J. Harrison, *Themis*, pp. 381-4, and H.J. Rose, *Handbook of Greek Mythology*, 139 f.; Langdon, *Semitic Mythology*, pp. 79 ff. Varuṇa — *amṛtasya gopā*, *Ṛgveda* VIII.42.2; *bhiṣajam pati*, *Vājasaneyī Saṁhita* XXI.40; identified with Soma, *Ṛgveda* IX.77.5, IX.95.5, *Tait. Sam.* VI.1.11 (Sayana, *somo varuno bhavati*), and Langdon, *Semitic Mythology*, p. 77 f., and Egyptian forms of Asklepios.

4 Weber 394, cf. Moortgart[.]

Figure 37: Ninurta, god with bow and arrow and mace, attacking Zū, the bird of prey; Gibil (Agni), god with rays at shoulders; Dumuzu-ab-zu, with corn growing from robe; Ningiśzida, god with battle-ax under left arm; Ea, god with streams falling from shoulders or with water streaming from a vase; attendant holding post. Cf. Frankfort, pl. XXIII g, p. 135; E.D. Van Buren, *Iraq*, I, pl. IX a, pp. 70 f. Green-flecked black serpentine, 38 by 24 mm. In the Ashmolean Museum, Oxford, 1931. 105. Kish k 962.

in human form with a pair of crowned serpents springing from his shoulders;[1] or he may ride upon or be accompanied by the horned and crowned serpent-dragon, Ughu-Muśḫuśśu. On the large Ashmolean seal (Fig. 37) he appears with Gibil, Dumuzu, Ea and Ninurta (the archer) in a group of deities opposed to the Eagle Im-gig = Zū); on the British Museum seal of the Agade period (Fig. 38) he is seated upon Ug-hu (Muśḫuśśu) and receives an offering; on the seal of Gudea, his worshipper, he is conducting the king to the seated Ea-Anu (Fig. 39 [page 46]). Ningiśzida is described as "to all eternity the companion of Dumuzi." As Mrs. Van Buren says, "the legend of Adapa related how [the] two gods, Dumuti and Gizzida, stood as guardians at the door of Anu's palace,"[2] We have already

Figure 38: Ningiśzida on Ug-hu, inscribed: *To the god Iba 'um, Beli-pala has dedicated (this) . . . seal for his life and the life of his son, Ur-Nin-asu.* Agade Dynasty, black and white speckled diorite or gabbro. In the British Museum, 122125.

---

1 Ningiśzida is, accordingly, the archtype of the Persian epic *Zohak* (= Azhi Dahaka).

2 Cf. Langdon, *Sumerian Epic of Paradise*, 1915, p. 42, where the two janitors, Tammuz and Giśzida, see and question Adapa, introduce him to Anu and intercede for him. They are, of course, to be identified with the two scorpion-men, whose sting they retain. Elsewhere the same two janitors are represented in purely anthropomorphic "Gilgamesh" types, e.g. Moortgart, *Vorderasiatische Rollspiegel*, 1940, Fig. 99.

seen that the garden and the tree are primarily Anu-Ea's. *Giś-zi-da* means "tree of truth," *Nin-giś-zi-da* therefore "Lord of the Tree of Truth," i.e. Anu himself. Again, in Mrs. Van Buren's words, "the two guardians who stood at the eastern gate of Heaven were Gizzida, 'Tree of Truth,' and Dumuzi, 'Tree of Life,' either as custodians of the two magic trees, or as themselves embodiments of the trees." Ningiśzida was *the* God (as we should express it in India, *iṣṭa devata*) of Gudea. His famous vase (Fig. 7 [page 14]), is dedicated to Ningiśzida, "for the prolongation of his life"; and here the two Ugẖu, crowned and scorpion-tailed,[1] holding the door-posts, are evidently Giśzida and Dumuzi. They corresponds also to the *baśmu* and *muśḫuśśu* with which "Gudea adorned[2] the lock-blocks of the door of the temple of Ningirsu," i.e. Ningiśzida at Ur.[3] What we see through the door is a pillar, about which are wound two guardian serpents, forming a caduceus. There can be no doubt that the wand between the two snakes of a caduceus is the vestige of this tree,[4] i.e. of Ningiśzida (Tammuz Soma, [or] Dionysius) himself.

Every detail of the iconography of Gudea's vase is important to us. To begin with the door-posts are literally their *cardinal* elements; it will be observed that they are adorned with half-rings. Ring-posts of this kind, occurring in pairs or singly, and either beside a doorway or as structural parts of it, mark the entrance of shrines or other penetralia or of cattlefolds[5] (see Figs. 40-46 [pages 47-49]).

Figure 39: Ningiśzida leads Gudea to Ea, the dragon Ug-hu follows. Inscribed: *Gudea, governor of Lagash*; the personal seal of Gudea, from Tello (ancient Girsu). This figure is from an ancient impression on clay; the original seal had metal caps 3 mm thick. See also Frankfort, Fig. 37, p. 143; Wooley, *Sumerians*, Fig. 21 a; Van Buren, *Iraq*, I, p. 72, Fig. 1. In the Louvre, ca. 2120 B.C.

---

1 Or rather with the tails of snakes, ending in scorpion points.

2 "Adorned" is here perfectly *mot juste*, according to the original and proper meaning of the word. See my "Ornament" in *Art Bulletin*, XXI, 1939.

3 Langdon, *Semitic Mythology*, p. 127.

4 Cf. J. Boulnois, *Le Caducée et la symbolique . . . du serpent . . .*, 1939, pp. 46, 166.

5 Endeavoring to keep the length of our article within bounds, we have not considered here the point of view from which the other-world is also referred to as a "stable" or "fold" of "cattle," which the Hero releases and carries off from their original keeper. We shall only point out here that the cattle-raiding motif represented in the Greek tradition by Herakles' feat in carrying off the cattle of Geryon (whom we have elsewhere identified with the Indian three-headed Gandharva, see *JAOS*. 60.50, end of note 12) is highly characteristic of the Vedic tradition and even survives in Buddhism (see *JAOS*. 58, p. 680).

Figure 40: Figure with feathers holding one of the door-posts before a temple. Carved relief from Tello (ancient Girsu), ca. 2700 B.C. Limestone, 7 by 5 3/4 by 1 1/2 in. One of the oldest inscribed reliefs known. [Ananda Kentish Coomaraswamy's drawing. — Ed.]

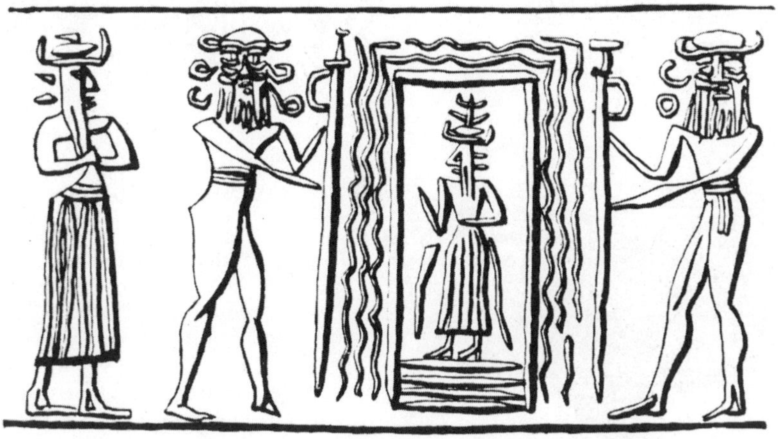

Figure 41: Ea-Anu with anthromorphic janitors holding the ring-posts of his Gateway. From Ward, *Seal Cylinders . . .*, no. 648. 1st Dynasty of Babylon. British Museum 89.771.

42 a

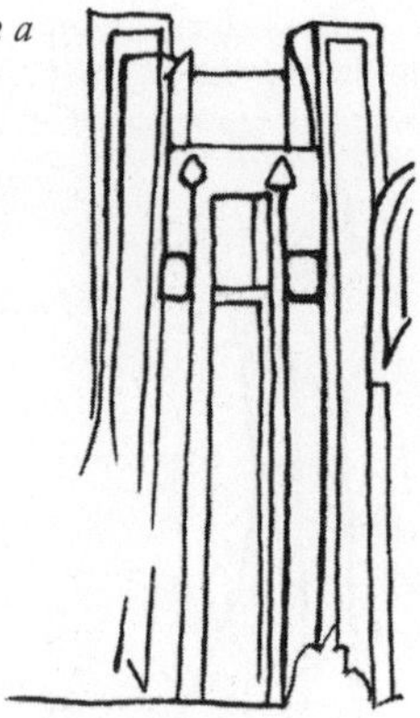

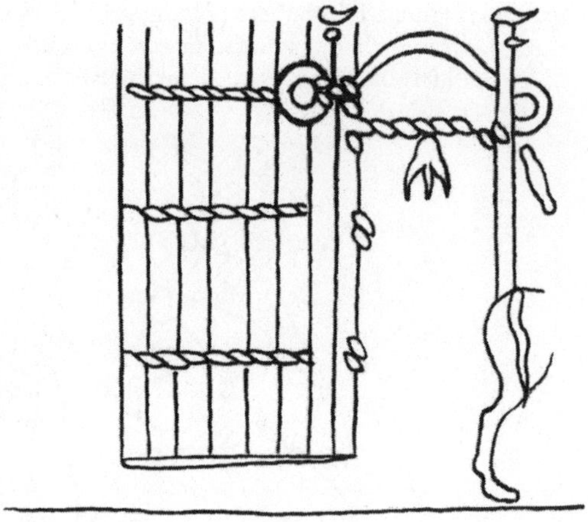

42 b

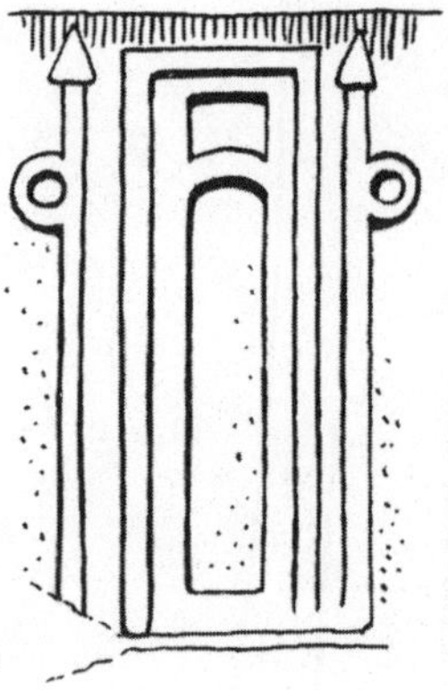

42 c

Figures 42 a, b and c:
Depictions of ancient Mesopotamian shrines with ringed gateposts. [Drawings after Ananda Kentish Coomaraswamy. — Ed.]

a and b: From Weber 430 and 405.

c: Andrae, *Das Gotteshaus* . . . , abb. 46, *Antiquities Journal*, VI, pl. LIII a.

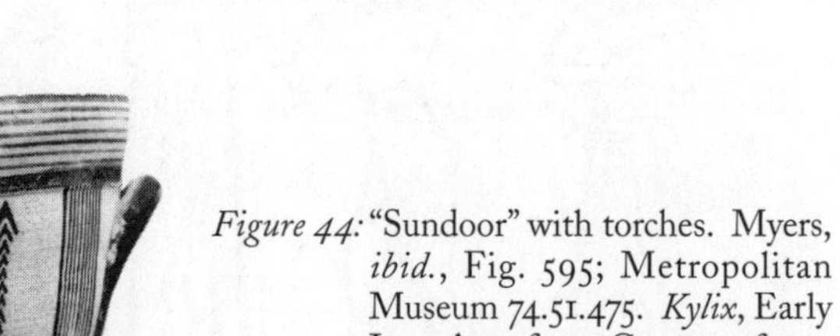

Figure 43: "Sun-birds" and Sundoor with swastikas, in J.L. Myers, *Handbook of the Cesnola Collection of Antiquities from Cyprus*, Metropolitan Museum, New York 1914, pl. XLIV, Fig. 34, 8th century B.C.

Figure 44: "Sundoor" with torches. Myers, *ibid.*, Fig. 595; Metropolitan Museum 74.51.475. *Kylix*, Early Iron Age, from Cyprus; cf. our Fig. 8 [page 15] for another depiction of addorsed torches, and [also] Fig. 56 a [page 54].

Figure 45: "Sundoor" white painted *kylix* from Cyprus. Myers, *ibid.*, Fig. 596; Metropolitan Museum 74.51.449, ca. 1000-750 B.C. [Ananda Kentish Coomaraswamy's drawing after Myers. Coomaraswamy also defined the ringposts here as "eyes." — Ed.]

In connection with a large votive ring-post found at Tello (Fig. 47), Conteneau remarks on the "symbolic significance" that the Sumerians attached to the constituent parts of doors, and especially to their posts.[1] In many cases the Janitor seems to be of the Gilgamesh type. In some cases Gilgamesh is almost certainly represented as entering the gateway of the western mountains, where he has gone in search of his ancestor Ur-napistim and to obtain the secret of immortality. In the [Gilgamesh] epic (IXth tablet) this way is guarded by the scorpion-men and leads to the Land of Darkness, through which he finally reaches the garden in which he finds "the Tree of the Gods." On a mother-of-pearl fragment from Tello (Fig. 48 [page 50])[2] we see the Hero entering a gateway, grasping its two ring-posts; on one of the Nimrud ivories (Fig. 49 [page 50])[3] alternatively, we find him grasping a pair of serpents who are either the guardians of the door or, what amounts to the same thing, its actual jambs, nor will it surprise [us] to find that the scorpions here are replaced by serpents. We cannot but regard as an identical theme that of another seal (Fig. 50 [page 51]) on

Figure 46: "Sundoor" with rings. [Ananda Kentish Coomaraswamy's drawing, possibly after C.F.A. Schaeffer, "Archeological Discoveries in Toraleti, Caucasus Region," *JRAS.* 1944, pl. VI. 1500-1400 B.C., Late Bronze Age. — Ed.]

Figure 47: Votive door-post from Tello. [Drawing by Ananda Kentish Coomaraswamy after Conteneau, *Manual*. . . , II, p. 588. — Ed.]

1 *Manual d'Archéologie Orientale*, 1927, pp. 588, 589; cf. 321 and 622-3[.]

2 L. Heuzey, *Cat. des. Antiquitiés chaldéenes*, Musée du Louvre 1902, No. 232, cf. 1, 125.

3 Weber, *Altorientalische Siegelbilder*, No. 275, in Assyrian style. Cf. in *Iraq*, II, p. 189, Fig. 2, a Nimrud ivory iconographically similar, but in the quasi-Egyptian style.

Figure 48: Figure holding door-posts with lion protomas. Cf. Weber 275 and Van Buren, *Iraq*, II. [After Ananda Kentish Coomaraswamy. — Ed.]

which the Hero in aquiline form is grasping a pair of serpents in his claws; they are the guardians of the Plant of Life, on the right of which a figure of the Gilgamesh type is contending with a buck. An equation of the animated door-posts with the snakes that protect them will hardly surprise us. For apart from the literary references, there exists a whole series of representations of the Sundoor (Figs. 51-56 [a and b] [pages 51-54]),[1] guarded by paired snakes, often winged and horned (Fig. 57 [page 54]). We must not forget that we are dealing with trees that can also be thought of as dragons. Mrs. Van Buren's words "either as custodians of the two magic trees, or as themselves embodiments of the trees" acquire a new significance if we reflect that actual gate-posts must have been originally trunks of trees or bundles of reeds. The most significant explanation of the "rings" has been given by Andrae, who equates them with the volutes of Ionic columns, and sees in these volutes

Figure 49: Gilgamesh figure holding ring-posts. L. Heuzey, *Cat. des Ant. chald.*, 1902, No. 232. [Drawing after Ananda Kentish Coomaraswamy. — Ed.]

[1 In this series of figures, we include an exemplar, Fig. 54, from P.H. Lehmann's work, *The Heiron*, I, p. 27, a *stele* from the Sanctuary of the gods on the island of Samothrace in the northern Aegean Sea. Though this bas-relief is Late-Classical it reflects the survival of a much earlier Hellenic tradition, incorporating many of the themes Ananda Kentish Coomaraswamy is concerned with in this essay. — Ed.]

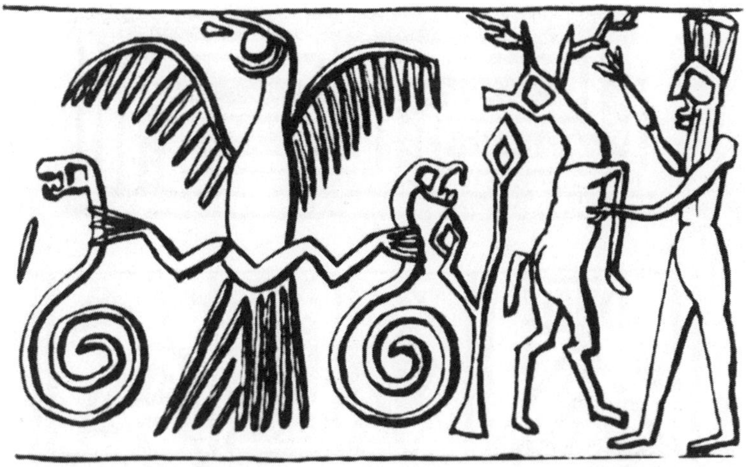

Figure 50: Aquiline hero grasping serpents. Cf. Apollodorus, *Lib.* II.4.8 where Herakles strangles the serpents. Weber 274. Black stone. Formerly Southesk Coll., British Museum 129473.

Figure 51: Guardian serpents and the Sundoor. [Ananda Kentish Coomaraswamy's drawing after Roes, *De Oorsprong der Geometrishe Kunst*, Haarlem, 1931, abb. 80. From an amphora in Leiden. — Ed.]

Figure 52: [Rampant serpents flanking doors with labyrinthine motives. Ananda Kentish Coomaraswamy's drawing from B. Schweitzer, *Herakles*, Tubingen, 1922, abb. 10, p. 35 f. Part of the decoration of a cult vessel from Rhodes, with photograph also from A.K. Coomaraswamy's file, Berlin Museum No. 4563 (0). — Ed.]

53 a

53 b

53 c

53 d

Figures 53 a, b, c and d: Band designs from R. Eilmann, *Frühe Griechesche keramik im Samischen Heraion*, Mitth. des Deutschen Arch. Inst. 58, 1932. [Drawings by Ananda Kentish Coomaraswamy of details of painted pottery, mostly from 6th century B.C. — Ed.]

a: Abb. 15.

b: Abb. 22.

c: Abb. 17 b combined with Abb. 18 a.

d: Band design after Hampe, R., *Sagenbilder*, pl. 33. Geometric period bowl, Nat. Mus. Athens 772.

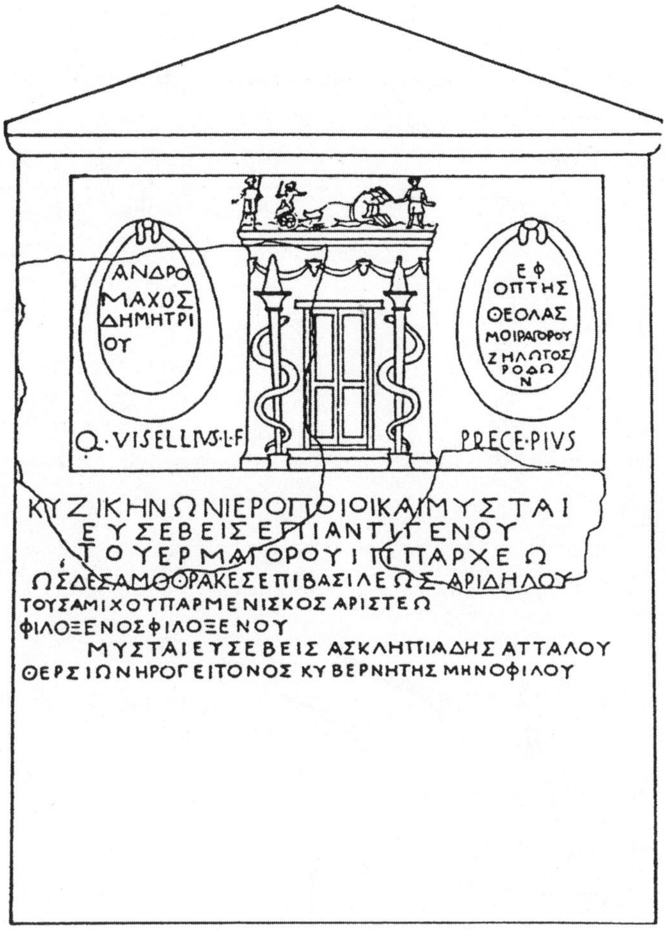

Figure 54: Serpents twined around torches flanking the double doors of a shrine. *Stele* from Samothrace, Roman period. Samothrace Museum, 39.16 and 39.23. From P.H. Lehmann, *The Heiron*, I, p. 27.

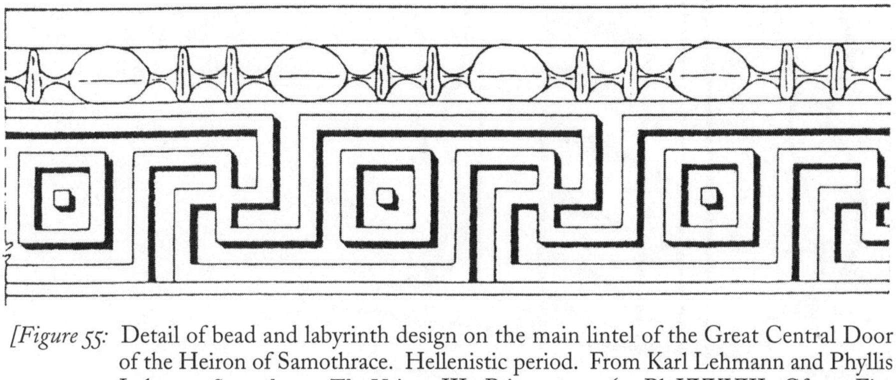

[*Figure 55:* Detail of bead and labyrinth design on the main lintel of the Great Central Door of the Heiron of Samothrace. Hellenistic period. From Karl Lehmann and Phyllis Lehman, *Samothrace: The Heiron*, III. Princeton, 1969, Pl. XXXVIII. Cf. our Fig. 8 (page 15). — Ed.]

Figures 56 a and b: [Two of A.K. Coomaraswamy's drawings of the *Adyton* of the Heiron.]

a: The *Adyton* of the Heiron, with central *bema* and *torchéres*.

b: Floorplan of the *Adyton*, with *bothros* behind the *torchéres*.

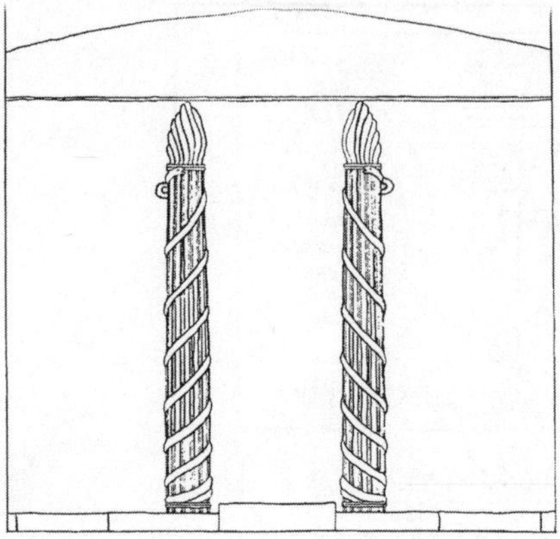

56 a

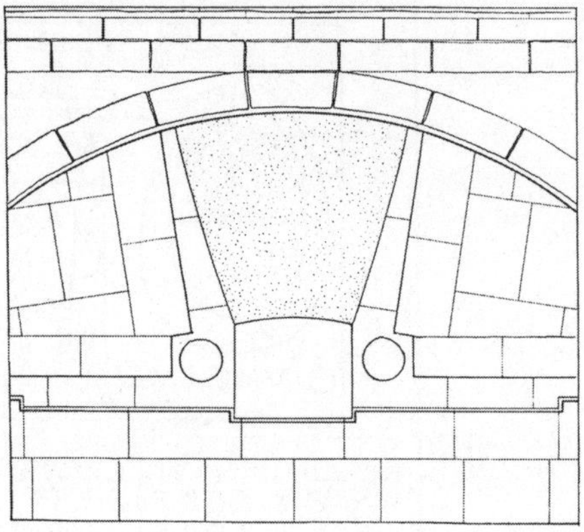

56 b

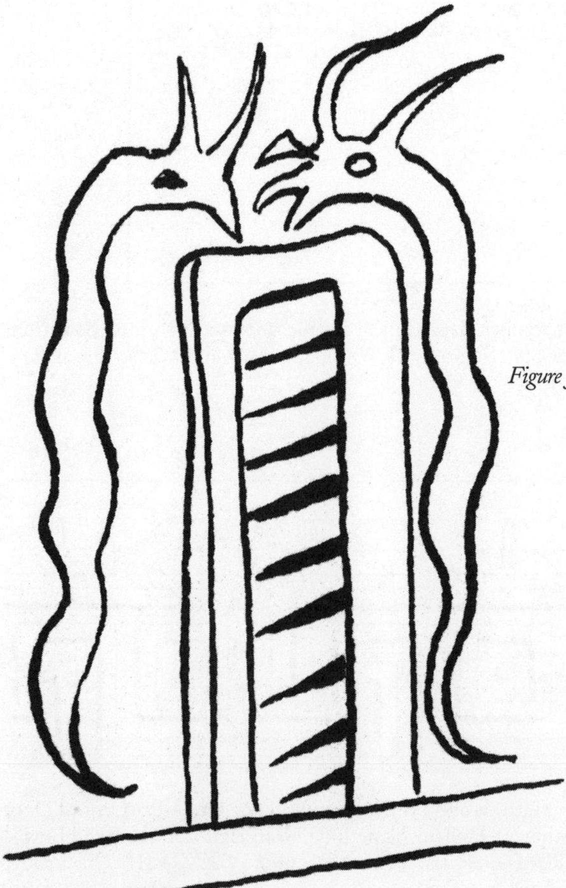

Figure 57: Horned serpents flanking door. [A. K. Coomaraswamy's drawing after P. Toscanne, "*Études sur le serpent figure et symboles dans l'antiquities elamite*" in *Delegation en perse*, XII, 1911, Fig. 357; cf. also Ward 491. — Ed.]

themselves the floral branches or pendant fruits of palms;[1] but the form can also be otherwise developed, e.g. from the Cretan cuttlefish (Figs. 58a-d [page 56]).[2] In one of the most remarkable representations of Dionysos Dendrites or Perichioios (Fig. 59), the two rings attached to the herm on opposite sides are, so to speak, the deity's arms; and Andrae, who sees that the two ring-posts taken together are conceivably the constituent parts of a single pillar with rings on both sides could well have used this Dionysos in confirmation of his theory. In the single pillar with rings on both sides Andrae, further, sees a symbol of the polar biunity, male and female, of the Supreme Identity; in his own words, "*Die Verschmelzung zweier Ringbundeln in Eines ist also eine Notwendigkeit. Sie kann nur die Polarität: Mann-Weib, die androgyne Einheit, meinen.*"[3] We have, indeed, already seen that the Scorpion-"men" who keep the Sundoor are of opposite sex, and this is a very important indication, one that applies to the two sides, right and left, of the door or tree, and all to "pairs of opposites," positive and negative, in whatever terms they may be stated; it is because the contraries actually meet, or clash, one beginning where the other ends, without interstice, that the Way that leads between them is the "strait" gate, and that whoever passes by it is "in straits" and will be crushed if he is not adequately tenuous and nimble, as he can only be who is "in the spirit," *atmani carati.*

The door-posts and their guardians are, then, the outwardly distinguished aspects of the one inwardly conjoint principle that can be seen beyond and between them, *ultra coincidentiam contradictoriorum*, as Nicolas of Cusa expresses it. We must now, then, consider the caduceus itself and above all in its trinitarian aspect, since it is a composite of two snakes wound about a single pillar. The two snakes are of opposite sex, and the "third" between them is their child in whom their natures are combined. Such, at least, are the explicit or implicit Assyrian, Greek[,] Indian, Chinese, Islamic and Christian interpretations. To begin with the Assyrian: The primordial serpents Lahmu and Lahamu (his wife) beget Ashur, the Solar God of wisdom; or to say the same in terms of Babylonian theology, Ea (Enki, Oannes) and his wife Damkina begat Marduk.[4] In the Greek version, as told by Athenogoras, Zeus and his daughter Rhea (Persephone) assumed the forms of male and female dragons (serpents), and

---

1 W. Andrae, *Das Gotteshaus und die Urformen des Bauens*, Berlin, 1930, pp. 49, 50 and 55-6; *Die ionische Säule, Bauform oder Symbol*, Berlin, 1933.

Andrae's interpretation need not be taken to exclude the practical use of the (metal) rings, as deduced by Alexander zu Eltz, "Nomadic Tradition in the Prehistoric Near East," *Bull. A. Inst. for Iranian Art and Archeology*, V, 1937, pp. 63-70.

2 On this theme see my "Tantric Doctrine of Divine Biunity," *Ann. Bhandarkar Or. Res. Soc.*, XIX, 1938, pp. 173-83; *Spiritual Authority and Temporal Power . . .* , 1942; H.R. Zimmer, "Srī-Yantra and Śiva-Trimūrti," *Rev. of Religion*, Nov. 1943.

"Not that the One is two, but that these two are One" (Hermes Trismegistos, XVI.3).

3 W. Andrae, "*Schrift und Bild*," in *Analecta Orientalia* 12, Rome, 1935, p. 5.

4 Seven Tablets of Creation, I.78 f., *British Museum Babylonian Legends of Creation*, 1931, p. 38; Langdon, *Semitic Mythology*, 1931, pp. 103 and 291-3. In earlier Sumerian and Accadian texts the parents of Ningiśzida are Ninazu (the Sun-god about to decline) and Ereshkigal (the Earth-goddess), or Nergal (the Sun as Death) and Ereshkigal, whose form was ophidian and who, like Ningiśzida himself, was identified with the constellation Hydra; the story of Nergal's quarrel and subsequent marriage with his sister Ereshkigel corresponds to the Indian myth of Yama and Yami (*RV.* X.10, *JUB.* I.53 f.), the sister in both cases being the wooer (Langdon, *ib.* 163-5). All these stories of the marriage of Heaven and Earth are variants of the one "*Liebesgeschichte Himmels.*"

Figure 58 a:
Late Helladic III. P. 183, No. 708.

Figure 58 b:
Late Helladic III. P. 178, No. 696.

Figure 58 c:
Late Helladic III. P. 179, No. 699.

Figure 58 d:
Spiral and "door" from a crater, No. 53, Side 1, found in Tomb XV. Late Helladic III. P. 187, No. 719.

Figures 58 a-d: [The spiral form in Hellas, ca. 1600-1300 B.C. Ananda Kentish Coomaraswamy's drawings after C.W. Blegen, *Prosyma*, 1937, Vol. II. The cuttlefish in the text is our Fig. 58 c. — Ed.]

Figure 59: Dionysos δενδίτης, Attic red-figured vase. From Langlotze, *Griechische Vasen im Wurzburg*, 1932, No. 520.

"tied themselves together in what is called 'the knot of Herakles,' and so mingled (συνήσας αυτήν τῷ καλουμίνȏυ ἤοακλεωτικῷ ἄμματι ἐμίγυη); and the symbol of the pattern of their mingling is the 'Wand of Hermes'."[1] The product of their union was Zagreus, i.e. Dionysos. In A.B. Cook's account, "Zeus consorted with his own mother, Rhea, both he and she being in the forms of snakes, and had by her a horned, four-eyed, two-faced daughter Persephone or Kore, with whom he, again in snake form, consorted and had for offspring a horned babe, the chthonic Dionysos or Zagreus"[2] — in whom Euripedes saw an Asiatic deity, and whom we identify with Ningiśzida, Tammuz, Dumu-zi, the "faithful son," an archtype of Christ.

In India, Soma is the "Son of Sky" (*divaḥ śiśu*, *RV.* IX.38.5), and in Sayana's words, "That is his sonship." The child of Heaven and Earth is begotten of his parents in the form of footless (snakes): "The two immobile, footless ones (*apadī*) bear the mobile footed germ of multiplicity; as it were their eternal son in his parents' womb — May Sky and Earth protect us from un-being (*rakṣatuṁ no abhvāt*)! Co-mingling (*saṁgacchamāne*), young (unaging), conterminous (*samante*),

---

1 Athenagoras, *Supplication pro Christianis*, 16.5. The text is cited, together with others, by L. Stephani in *Compte-Rendu de la Commission Archéologique* (for 1880), St. Petersburg, 1882 and discussed by B. Segall, *Katalog der Goldschmiede-Arbeiten, Museum Benaki*, Athens 1938, pp. 86, 118 ff., in connection with a bracelet on which the subject is represented; J. Boulnois, *loc. cit. supra*; A.L. Frothingham, "Hermes, Snake-god, Caduceus," *AJA.* 1916, 179f; Van der Osten, "The Snake Symbol and the Hittite twist," *AJA.* 30, 1926, pp. 405-417; P. Toscanne, "*Études sur le Serpent*" in *Mem. Délégation en Perse* XII, 1911; J. Ph. Vogel, *Indian Serpent-Lore*, 1926; A.B. Cook, *Zeus*, II.1929 f; Daremberg and Saglio, *s.v. nodus*; Rischer, *Lexicon*, *s.v.* Zagreus; and de Waele, *The Magic Staff in Graeco-Roman Antiquity*, The Hague, 1927 (the last is too much given to aesthetic interpretations of the form, ignores Athenagoras, and overlooks that, as B. Segall says "*in der Antike noch keine Moden ohne Sinn gab*"). It is significant that in Homer the herald's wand is not a *kerukeion* or *rhabdos* but a "sceptre" of magical efficacy, given directly or indirectly by Zeus, hence probably a *keraunos* (= Sanskrit *vajra*) and for this reason called *tripetalos*.

2 A.B. Cook, *Zeus*, II.1029. Cook further equates Zagreus with Zeus Chthonius — of whom Hermes Trismegistos (*Ascl.* III 27 C) says that he rules Earth and Sea, and "He it is that supplies nutriment to animated mortal creatures, and to all fruit-bearing trees; and it is by his power that the fruits of the earth are produced." Marduk = Tammuz = Gilgal. Langdon, *Semitic Mythology*, p. 156-7.

Figure 60 a: Fu Hsi and Nü-Wa; cf. also British Museum *Babylonian Legends* and p. 38 from Stein, *Innermost Asia*, III, pl. CIX.

Figure 60 b: Fu Hsi and Nü-Wa; cf. also British Museum *Babylonian Legends* and p. 38 from Stein, *Innermost Asia*, III, pl. CIX. [Drawing by J. Buhot for *Études Traditionnelles*, August-September 1932, p. 485. — Ed.]

the brother and sister twins are kissing in his parents' lap, the Navel of the Universe — May Sky and Earth protect us from un-being" (*RV.* I.185.2 and 5).[1] Unquestionably, the words "co-mingling" (i.e. sexually) and "conterminous," the reference being to serpents, can only imply a mutual embracing in the pattern of the well-known Indian *Nāga-kals*, which is also that of the Caduceus.[2]

In China, Wang Wen K'ao, writing in the first half of the 2nd century A.D., and doubtless repeating a much older tradition, says that in the beginning, when Sky and Earth were first divided, Fu Hsi (T'sang Tsing) and Nü-Wa made their

1 The "germ" may be here either the Sun, Fire or Soma. In some versions of the story, Agni and Soma are liberated together from Vṛtra's mouth (*TS.* II.5.2). Almost everything that can be said of Agni can be said of Soma, with this fundamental distinction, that what is dry pertains to Agni, and what is moist to Soma (*ŚB.* I.6.3.23). If "Earth's dry food" be "fire" this corresponds exactly to the distinction drawn in Euripedes, *Bacchae* 277 f.

2 See J. Ph. Vogel, *Indian Serpent-Lore*, pp. 265-75 and pls. XXIX, XXX. The Indian *Nāga-kals* are placed at the foot of trees, and represent two snakes, whose sex is sometimes clearly differentiated by a difference in the number of hoods, in sexual embrace. The [serpents] are never, however, in *this* context, tied together in a knot, but are simply braided or interlaced so as to form three rings; the analogous symbol, consisting of three vertically superimposed circles, occurring commonly on the old Indian punch-marked coins, is termed by numismatists the "caduceus symbol." The great Indian serpent-deity Gūgā, worshipped by Hindus and Muslims alike in the Punjab, is represented in human form as a horseman, but is accompanied by two snakes, one of which coils about his staff or wand. In general, the serpent deities are worshipped either for rain, for healing (especially of snake-bite and leprosy, a disease traditionally connected with the scaliness of snakes), or for offspring.

appearance, he with a body all covered with scales, she with a woman's bust and serpent below. In the later art of the 7th-8th century [A.D.] (Fig[s]. 60 [a and b]) these two, the first (mythical) Emperor and his consort, are represented in these semi-divine, semi-ophidian forms (like Indian *Nāgas*), tightly entwined and embraced; Ts'ang Tsing is the "essence of vegetation" and reigned as Chavannas says, "*en vertu de l'element bois*," while Nü-Wa represents "metal," the element that in the Chinese scheme corresponds to what is elsewhere "air." Between their heads, as Stein remarks, "is the sun disc"; other constellations surround them. If Fu Hsi is in reality the Sky, and Nü-Wa Earth, the Sun is presumably their "child." In some other representations the rulers are not entwined, but only approximated and held together by the arms of a kneeling man, again, perhaps, their Son.[1] What is essentially the same appears on a Chinese sword-hilt, perhaps of the Han period (Fig. 61), the representation is of a horned mask, which Jacobsthal rightly calls a "gorgoneion," between a dragon and a tiger.[2] Yetts quotes a mirror inscription (no. 28, p. 117): "Dragon on the left and Tiger on the right ward off ill-luck; Scarlet Bird and Sombre Warrior accord with Yin and Yang; may descendants in ample line occupy the centre." More precisely, the supporters are the Green Dragon of the East and the White Tiger of the West, correspond respectively to the elements wood and metal; and the Green Dragon, when it appears in the Sky, is the power that "presides over the revitalisation of nature"; Yetts is inclined to equate it with

Figure 61: Chinese sword hilt, Han Dynasty. Louvre, Paris. From P. Jacobsthal, *Imagery in Early Celtic Art*, 1941, Pl. V a and p. 8.

[1] For Fu Hsi and Nü-Wa see Chavannes, *Mission archéologique dans la Chine septentrionale*, I, pp. 32, 126 and Figs. 75, 156, cf. 123, 134; and A. Stein, *Innermost Asia*, Ch. XIX (pp. 664, 708, 709 and pl. CIX).

[2] P. Jacobsthal, "Imagery in Early Celtic Art," *Proc. Brit. Acad.* XXVII, 1941, p. 8 and pl. 5a. On the Chinese T'ao T'ieh as Gorgoneion cf. my remarks in the *Art Bulletin* XXII, 1940, pp. 52-5, and further discussion below p. 8: "The East was the chief factor in the origin of Celtic imagery."

the "scorpion."[1] It is clear, in any case, that the Dragon and the Tiger of the sword-hilt are male and female principles, and that they can be correlated with Fu Hsi and Nü-Wa.

In Islam we have only the iconography to depend upon. Referring to the representation of Gemini on the British Museum *qalamdan* of A.H. 608 (our Fig. 62), Hartner (p. 137) remarks that "if we recall that Gemini is the sign in which the dragon's head is exalted, the curious object between the two human figures in the Gemini medal [medallion] takes on a very strange significance. It looks like a mask or monstrous head mounted on a staff."[2] It is, apparently, horned. Hartner identifies it with the dragon's head, which is represented as an astrological sign by ☊. The meanings are further clarified if we also recall that Tammuz and Ningiśzida "the two gods who guard the portals of heaven," are almost certainly to be identified with Castor and Pollux in Gemini. We hold, with Langdon, that "perhaps the Babylonians located the gateway of heaven in the constellation Gemini.[3] The dragon's head detached from its body, and mounted on a pillar, would be, of course, the Sun; and one cannot but think of the Indian Pravargya ritual, with its repeated "For Makha's head art thou," with reference to the heated bowl that is the "head of the sacrifice," and equated with the Sun; it is precisely as the Sun that the dragon's head naturally takes on the form of a human face. The Indian Asvins, the "marvellous" twin-gods who are "children of the Sky" (*RV.* I.182.1 etc.), have been plausibly equated with the Dioskuroi.[4] They are, as pupils of Dadhyana (Vedic Dadhikra, Sun-horse or

Figure 62: Gemini medallion from the *qalamdan* of A.H. 608 (1211-12 A.D.). London, British Museum.

[1] P. Yetts, *The Cult Chinese Bronzes*, pp. 117, 125, 135, 136 and 138-9; on page 135 he refers to "our common debt to the Chaldeans." With this and Jacobsthal's remarks, cf. W.A. Nitze, "The Fisher King in the Grail Romances," *PMLA.* XXIV, 1909, pp. 365-418, where he connects the Fisher King, principle of moisture and fructifying power in nature, with the Gaulic deity Cernunnos (the "Horned") and with Zagreus, the "horned serpent."

[2] What is the heart-shaped support on which the "staff" rests? And why the ribbon held by the Twins and probably to be understood as fastened to the staff or twisted around it? The entire composition, when we take account of these two features, becomes curiously reminiscent of the Egyptian representations of the union of the Kingdoms (Fig. 63), where paired affronted deities hold the ends of cords that are knotted round the "windpipe" of the *sema* sign for "union" (the knot having at the top the characteristic form of the *nodus herculaneus*); the royal cartouche is at the top of the "windpipe." Such reminiscences of Egyptian iconography in Islamic art are just as possible as the survival of the psychostasis in Christian art.

[3] Langdon, *Tammuz and Ishtar*, 1914, p. 37.

[4] A. Weber, *Indische Studien*, V, p. 234; A. Macdonell, *Vedic Mythology*, p. 53.

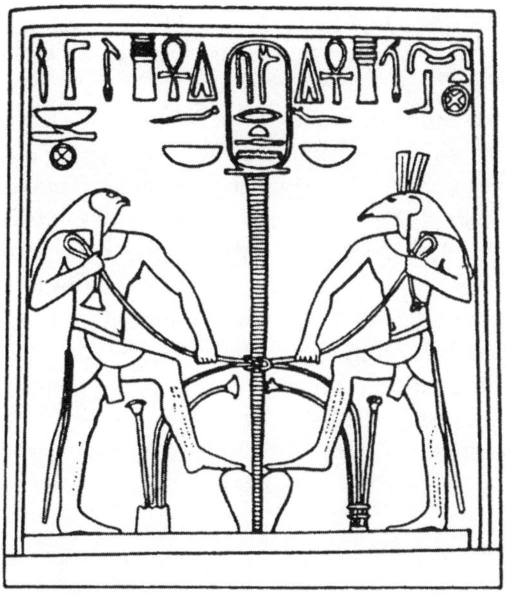

Figure 63: Horus and Seth uniting the two lands. After a drawing in D. Norman, *The Hero Myth, Image, Symbol*, New York, 1929, Fig. 24. From a bas-relief tablet of Sesostris I, Middle Kingdon, Egypt, 12th Dynasty, ca. 1191-1786 B.C. Cairo Museum.

Soma) versed in the mysteries of Soma, and referred to as "guardians or Immortality — or Soma" (*amṛtasya gopau*), *TB.* III.1.2.11, as well as preeminently "the physicians of the gods." If, then, as Macdonell says, "the origin of these gods is to be sought in the pre-Vedic antiquity" it would be natural to equate them with Tammuz and Giśzida, the archtypes of Castor and Pollux, and, once more, to recognize mythical formulae common to Sumerian, Indian and Greek [traditions]. Islamic sources can also throw a light upon the related problem of Hermes, and why he bears the caduceus as a sign of his herald's function. For, on the same *qalamdan* (Hartner, Fig. 18, second from left) Mercury-'Uṭarid, "the scribe" (*al-kātib*) is represented with a scroll and pen. This conception of Mercury corresponds exactly to that of the Babylonian Nabū, the messenger and prophet of his father Marduk, whose symbol is a writing desk on a table and "whose oldest titles are Ur and Dubisak 'the scribe'."[1] He can be identified with his father, and is so much like him that both may be represented together each supported by Muśḫuśśu, as on Langdon's seal (his Fig. 64), where Nabū holds (amongst other attributes) a clay tablet, and has before him a mason's chisel, for he is also an architect. In view of the close relationship of Marduk with Ningiśzida, amounting to original identity, it is natural enough (although we cannot trace all the links) that Hermes should have been entrusted with the caduceus as the symbol of his functions; Hermes, who is at once Mercurius and Nabū, bears the wand as both the mark of his descent and the symbol of his authority. In late Hebrew and Jewish mythology, and, it may be added, in Christian angelology, Nabū becomes the "recording angel."

Like Dionysos, child of Zeus and Semele, Christ is the Son of God — and of Mother Earth, for there can be no doubt of the identity of the Madonna with

1 See for Nabū, Langdon, *Semitic Mythology*, pp. 158-161.

the Earth Goddess,[1] *Natura naturans.* As much as this is implied by the doctrine of the eternal birth, which "does not depend on a temporal mother," and that of the divine procession as a "vital operation from a living conjoint principle,"[2] i.e. the undivided biunity of an essence and a nature, of which the latter is "that Nature by which the Father begets,"[3] or "Nature as being that by which the generator generates."[4] We could hardly, indeed, expect to find in Christian contexts the concept of an Ophidian Savior, or that of his procession from a "conjoint principle" in ophidian form; for although the "brazen serpent" (*sāraph*) of *Numbers*[5] is at the same time, so to speak, an Asclepios and a type of Christ, in actual Christian symbolism the "serpent" is considered only as a symbol of evil. Yet it is with perfect justification that in Celtic art the Savior is represented in human form supported (in the heraldic sense) by affronted serpents (Fig. 64); and that, on the reliquary at Chur (Fig. 65) the Cross is represented between a pair of dragons, knotted and embraced. In the Irish representations, and still more in some of the forms that

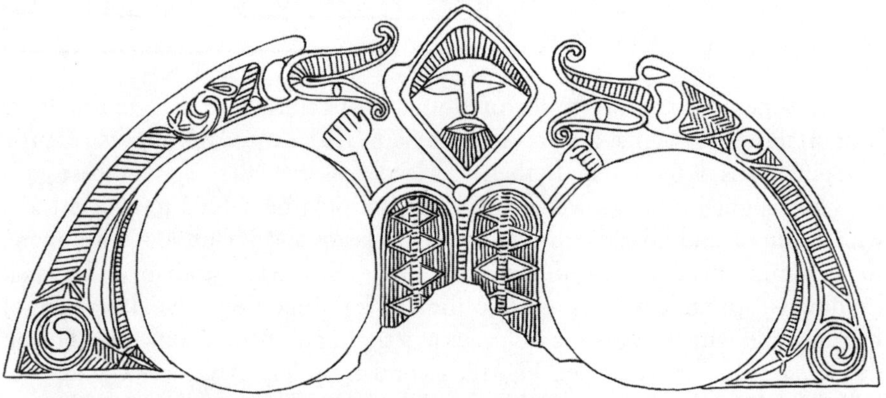

Figure 64: Christ between serpents. Drawing by Ananda Kentish Coomaraswamy after A. Mahr, *Christian Art in Ancient Ireland*, I, 1932, Pl. 36.1.

1 "For the Earth was Adam's mother . . . and God hath the likeness ta'en of the Son of the first Earth-Maiden" (Wofram von Eschenbach, *Parzival*, IX.549-60). "*Les Vierges Noires . . . sont la transformation chrétienne des divinités noires fécondes et plus spécialement de la Terre*" (M. Durand-Lefebure, *Étude sur l'origine des Vierges Noires*, 1937, Conclusion, p. 194. The ruined stable of the better known mediaeval Nativities is nothing but a rationalisation of the original Byzantine types in which the "stable" is a cave or grotto in what is obviously the World-mountain and the Madonna herself a Demeter; and as Professor B. Rowland has well said (in *Bull. Fogg Art Museum*, VIII, 1939, p. 63) "The original reason for the 'choice' of the mountain cave — or rather the 'necessity' for it — lies dead and buried in the minds of the creators of the Christian legend . . . [they] had the memories of the cosmological foundations of all the great religions of the Semitic world dating from Sumer behind them . . . The birth of the Christ in a cave as described in the Proto-evangelion and other Syriac and Arabic gospels [is] almost certainly derived from the same ancient Asiatic source as the iconography of the nativity of Mithras." That the Virgin of Lourdes is the Earth Goddess of the ancients is conspicuous.

2 St. Thomas Aquinas, *Sum. Theol.* I.27.2.

3 *Ibid.* I.41.5.

4 St. John Damascene, *De fid. orth.* I.18.

5 [*Numbers*] XXI.8, 9; cf. Philo[.]

Figure 65: Addorsed serpents, reliquary from the Cathedral of Chur. From C. Hentze, *Myths et Symboles Lumieres*, 1922, Fig. 109.

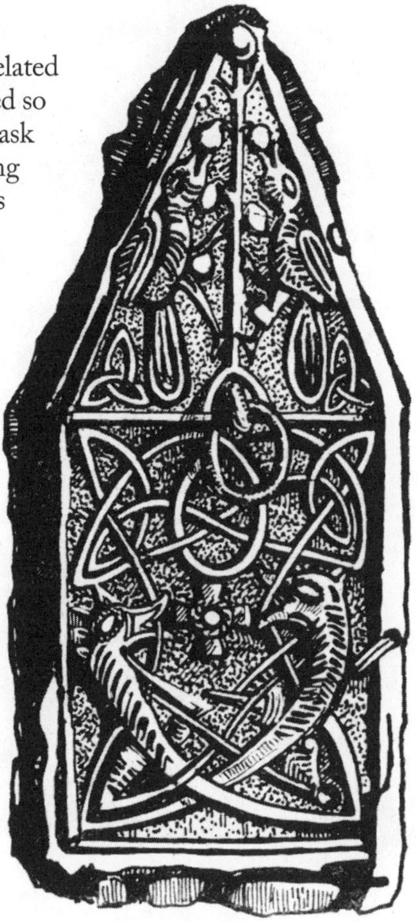

the motive assumes in Merovingian and related arts,[1] the central head is strongly emphasized so that the formula is reduced to that of a mask between or above affronted or interlacing serpents or fishes. The trinity thus represented is that of the Holy Family.

In connection with our Fig. 66 [page 64], a letter "Q" from the Bury St. Edmund's Gospels, E.H. Minns[2] remarks that "it shews the winged beasts affronted on each side of the sacred tree . . . going back through Sassanian and Achaemenian Persia to Sumerian Cherubim flanking the Tree of Life." The "winged beasts" might as well have been called seraphs or "cockatrices"; their tails are ophidian. On an archaic Ionian *revetment* in Boston (Fig. 67 [page 64]) the "winged beasts have leonine bodies: On one of the Nimrud ivories (Fig 68 [page 64]) they are "sphinxes *passant* or *couchant* guarding a sacred tree,"[3] that is to say, winged lions with human heads.

---

1 Cf. Karl Hentze, "*Minussinsker Steppenkultur . . . ein Beitrag zur Fruhgeschichte Nord-Europas*," *IPEK.* IX, 1934, pp. 51 ff.

2 In *Ann. British School at Athens*, XXXVII, 1936-7, pp. 192-3 and pl. 25. It will be observed, further, that the Tree springs from a dragon's mouth; the dragon is at once the root from which the Tree springs and the mouth by which it is uttered. In the same way in the old Indian iconography the vegetative principle of life so often springs from a makara's jaws (cf. my *Yakṣas*, II, 1931, pl. 12, Fig. 1, Figs. 4, 13 and [Figs.] 37-39). In fact, the iconography of the Bury St. Edmund's dragon-tree can be better explained by Indian sources than by any other way.

Brahma (root *bṛh*, to grow, wax) can be equated both with the Dragon (cf. *HJAS.* VI, pp. 39 f.), and *Taittirīya Āraṇyaka* II.19 (where Brahma is invoked as *siśumāra*) and with the Tree (*Taittirīya Brāhmaṇa* II.8.9.6; *Śaṅkhāyana Āraṇyaka* XI.2) of light and life that suspires (root *śvas*) and rise up like smoke (*Maitri Upaniṣad* VII.11); the Dragon is that being (*bhūta*) that is called the igneous "root" of all beings (*Chāndogya Upaniṣad* VI.9.4) and from which they are breathed forth (root *śvas*) like smoke from fire (*Bṛhadāraṇyaka Upaniṣad* II.4.10 and IV.5.11); and that is the same thing as the Dragon's (Vṛtra's) breathing out of fire and smoke when Indra "forced the Glutton (*jigarti*, root *gṝ*, swallow, cf. *mukhena nigirati*, Sāyaṇa's gloss on the *siśumāra* Brahma, as cited above) to disgorge and smote the Dānava that breathed (root *śvas*) against him" (*RV.* V.29.4, cf. I.54.5), making him gape (*Taittirīya Saṁhitā* II.5.2.3, 4).

3 R.D. Barnett, "The Nimrud Ivories and the Art of the Phoenicians" in *Iraq*, II, [1933,] p. 190 and Fig. 3.

Figure 66: The letter "Q" from the Bury St. Edmund's Gospel, 12th century [A.D.] In *Ann. British School at Athens*, XXXVII, 1936-7, pl. 25, pp. 192-3.

Figure 67: Addorsed griffins from an Archaic Ionian terra cotta *revetment*. In the Museum of Fine Arts, Boston.

Figure 68: Affronted sphinxes with Phrygian caps guarding a sacred tree. Nimrud ivory, probably Phoenician, ca. 7th century B.C. In Barnett, "The Nimrud Ivories in the Art of the Phoenicians," *Iraq*, II, [1933], p. 190.

Chapter III

Concerning Sphinxes

ΠΕΡῚ ΤᾺΣ ΣΦΊΓΓΑΣ

Τὴν δὲ τοῦ κόσμου ἁρμονίαυ ἡ σφίγξ . . . μηνύει.
— Clement of Alexandria[1]

Introduction

In the course of some two years of intermittent work on "The Early Iconography of Sagittarius," and on "The Concept of 'Ether' in Greek and Indian Cosmology," both of which I still hope to complete and publish, it has been necessary to study the guardian Cherubim of [the] Old Testament (particularly *Genesis* III.24), the sphinxes by which they are represented in Western Asiatic and Palestinian art, and the single Greek Sphinx; and as this study is more or less complete in itself, it can be, with advantage, published separately. It must be understood, however, that I shall not discuss here the equation of sphinxes with other types of the guardians of the *Janua Coeli*, and that, but for one allusion, I shall have nothing to say about the Egyptian "Sphinx" which has only been so called on the basis of a rather superficial analogy and is of another descent than that of the Western Asiatic and Greek sphinxes. Our Sphinx, of Oriental origin, combines the body of a lion (or sometimes a dog) with the face of a man or woman (in Greece it is always the latter[2]) and the wings, and sometimes the talons, of a bird of prey.

Figure 69: Affronted sphinxes and palmette. Detail from an Argive-Corinthian *pinax*, Archaic. Chr. Blickenberg and K. Frilis Johansen, *Corp. Vas. Antiq. Danemark*, fasc. 2, pl. 90 A.

[1 The title and introduction to this essay were not translated by Ananda Kentish Coomaraswamy in manuscript. The foreword can be rendered, " . . . by the Sphinx is meant the harmony of the world . . . " and is from Clement's *Stromata*, V.5.31. — Ed.]

2 Always, that is to say, when we are speaking of single sphinxes; paired sphinxes are sometimes male in late Cretan and early Corinthian art (Figs. 69 [and] 70 [a and b] [page 66]).

70 *a*

70 *b*

Figures 70 a and b: Two sphinxes from the same vase. In the upper figure (Fig. 70 a), he wears a Corinthian helmet. Geometric-orientalising style from Crete, 7th century B.C. After Doris Levi, "Early Hellenic Pottery of Crete," *Hesperia* XIV, 1945.

[Sphinxes]

The Western Asiatic sphinxes are usually represented in "*Wappenstil*" as affronted pairs, guarding the Tree of Life, or Truth, or Light, or an equivalent column with Ionic volutes; and it would be superfluous to argue here that tree and pillar are interchangeable symbols of one and the same referent.[1] Above the tree or pillar there is often shown the winged disc of the Sun. In Sumerian, Assyrian, Phoenician and some Cretan and Cypriote representations the types may be either male and bearded or female, and may wear either the feathered κίδαπις or a Phrygian cap, or fillet or plume as a sign of their royalty. In their capacity [as] defenders [of] or attendants upon the third principle that stands between them, and with which they form a trinity, the paired sphinxes may be replaced by griffins (with heads of eagles and bodies of lions), winged serpents, winged scorpion-men, or other *genii*; a discussion of these relationships pertains to the history of Sagittarius. In some cases the "Promethean" hero who forces his way in is shown between them, holding them apart at arms' length;[2] and in any case their primary function is that of the guardianship of the Sundoor. They are, in fact, its living and dangerous jambs; they represent all those contraries of which the Symplegades are a symbol, and between them runs the narrow path that leads to all that lies between them.

It has long been recognized that in Palestinian art the Cherubim of *Genesis* III.24 ("to keep the way of the tree of life") and *Ezekial* XLI.18 ("so that a palm tree was between a cherub and a cherub")[3] are actually represented by

Figure 71: Winged *genius* ("Borhead") separating female sphinxes. Mid-Corinthian. After H. Payne, *Necrocorinthia*, p. 307 and pl. 28.10.

---

1 With the concept of the Pillar as at the same time "performing a structural function" and being an "aspect of the Sun God" (A.J. Evans, "Mycenean Tree and Pillar Cult," *JHS.* [1901], pp. iii.173), cf. *Jaiminīya Up. Brāhmaṇa* I.10.9 "they call the Sun a sky-supporting pillar"; and *Taittirīya Saṁhitā* IV.2.9.6 "in it there sitteth an Eagle." More generally[:] [A.J.] Wenslick, [*Tree and Bird as Cosmological Symbols in Western Asia*, Amsterdam, 1921]; U. Homberg, *Der Baum des Lebens*, Helsinki, 1903 and *Finno-Ugarian and Siberian Mythology*, Boston, Chs. III. V[.]

2 Cf. Fig. 71; and in Greek Orientalising art from Crete, Doro Levi, "Early Hellenic Pottery of Crete," *Hesperia* XIV, 1945, pl. X.1 ("winged deity dominating two sphinxes").

3 The Cherubim of *Ezekial* XVI.18 are described as having two faces, those of a man and of a lion; a logical conception, since the Sphinx combines the bodies of these two. No Palestinian or Greek examples of two-headed sphinxes can be cited, but there is a Hittite example of ca. 1000 B.C. in which a sphinx has the two heads of a man and a lion, and, it may be mentioned also, a serpent's tail (Fig. 72 [page 68]).

Figure 72: Sphinx or cherub with a man's and a lion's head, and a snake-tail. Carchemish, ca. 1000 B.C. [In] Moortgart, *Bildewerke und Volkstum Vorderasiens zur Hethiterzeit*, Fig. 35 [and] O. Weber, *Die Kunst der Hethiter*, [no date,] pl. 14.

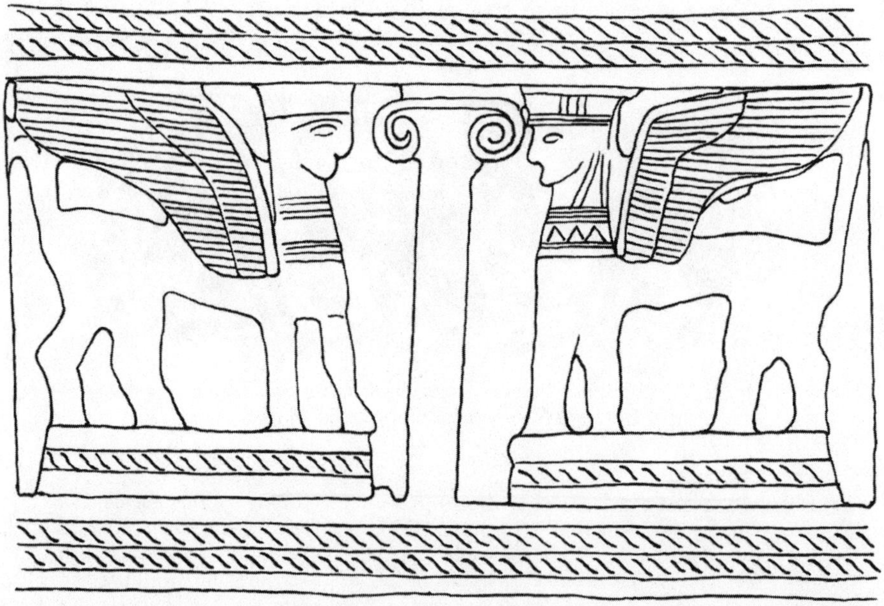

Figure 73: Cf. E. Cohn-Weiner, *Die Jüdische Kunst*, 1929, Abb. 20. "Stylized tree between Cherubim . . . and . . . Sphinxes . . . *Auf den Zargen stehen jedesmal zwei einander zugewandte* Sphingen *zu seiten eines Baumstammes säulenartiger Form . . . eine gute Vorstellung von phönizischen und damit auch salomenischen Stil.*" [He] says [that] cherubim understood as angels is a "late idea. In the Bible they appear as *Dämonen-Gestalten . . . neben Lowen und Rindern.*" Solomon's style is essentially Phoenician rather than Egyptian. [The illustration is a] detail of a side [panel] of a bronze basin-stand from Larnaka, Cyprus. Berlin Antiquarium.

pairs of affronted Sphinxes having a tree or pillar standing between them,[1] and that those of *Exodus* XXI.18 ("two cherubim in the two ends of the mercy-seat") and *Isaiah* IV.4 ("the Lord of hosts . . . between the two cherubim") are represented by similar sphinxes forming the sides of the thrones of earthly monarchs;[2] examples of such representations are given in Figs. 73, 74 [and 75 (page 70)]. It may be observed that in the *Book of Enoch* (LXXX.4-7) Seraphim, Cherubim and Ophannin (Wheels) "are they who sleep not, and guard the throne of His glory," and that in many traditions this sleeplessness is a marked characteristic of the guardians of the *Janua Coeli*.

Figure 74: "A cherub of Biblical times, supporting the throne of King Hiram of Byblus." After W.F. Albright in *Biblical Archaeologist* [, 1938] I.1, pl. 1.

---

1 E. Cohn-Weiner, *Die Jüdischer Kunst*, 1929; with reference to our Fig. 73: "*Baum zwischen Cherubim . . . zwei einander zugewandte* Sphingen *zu seiten eines Baumstammes säulenartiger Form . . . eine gute Vorstellung von phönizischen und damit auch salomonischem Stil.*"

2 W.F. Albright, "What were the Cherubim?," *Biblical Archaeologist* I.1, 1938 (with our Fig. 74). Inasmuch as the Deity can be represented as well (or better, Philo, *Somn.* I.240-242) by a pillar, the occurrence of paired sphinxes (in Hittite art, E. Wasmuth, *Hethitischer Kunst*, pl. 45, ca. 800 B.C.) forming the pedestal of a column should be noted; the column is, in effect, enthroned upon them.

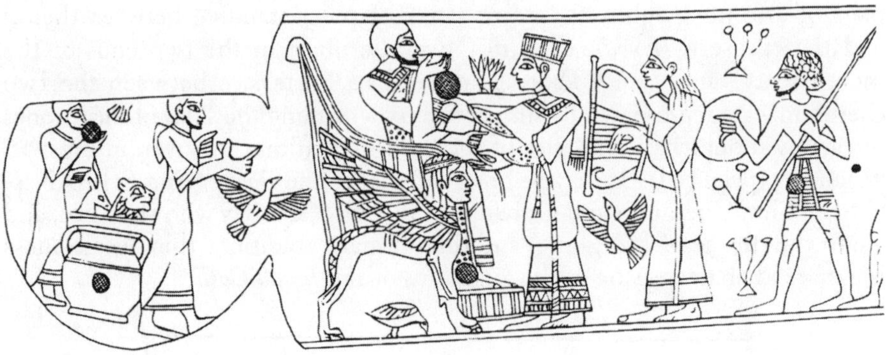

Figure 75: [Sphinx throne, ivory from Megiddo, 13th to mid 12th century B.C. From G. Loud, *Megiddo Ivories*, Chicago, 1939, p. 13, pl. 4. — Ed.]

My main intention in the present article [, or chapter,] is to discuss the meaning of the Sphinx in Greek art. We have to consider for this purpose the original meaning of the archtypes and of related forms, in which the function of guardianship predominates, the significance of the Cherubim in [the] Old Testament, chiefly as expounded by Philo, and what can be gathered both from the Greek types themselves and from references in the Greek literature, and more particularly from the senses in which the verb σφίγγω, from which Σφίγξ derives, is employed in the literature from Empedocles to Philo. Finally, Clement of Alexandria's interpretations will be cited.

Philo's position may be summarised as follows: The Cherubim are discussed in pairs, in connection with *Genesis* III.24 as keepers of the way of the Tree of Life, and in connection with *Exodus* XXV.21 as the guardsmen of the royal throne. In both cases they are regarded as the representations of the primary and elder Powers (δυναμεις) of the *Logos*, the Charioteer of the Universe, who stands between them, at once dividing and uniting. Invariably, the two Powers taken together with the *Logos* from which they proceed form a trinity; in *Genesis* the *Logos*, superior, median and "third," is represented by the "flaming sword" that turns every way, while in *Exodus* there is no visual conception. Elsewhere the *Logos* is represented by the living image of the High Priest, and by the intellectual and ruling principle within you, the Man of Truth, and Priest, in every man.

Chapter IV

The Concept of "Ether" in Greek and Indian Cosmology[1]

Quinque sunt corpora mundi simplicia,
scilicet quatuor elementa et quinta essentia.
— St. Bonaventura, *De. red. art. ad theol.* 3.

Sa yas ākāśa indra eva saḥ.
JUB. I.31.1

"Ether" in Plato

Without attempting an exhaustive comparative treatment of the five elements in the Greek and Indian traditions, though I have collected a very great deal of material for this purpose, it seems at least desirable to correct the statement made by E.R. Lamb in the Loeb Library *Epinomis*, p. 450, that Plato "does not allow ether (*Timaeus* 40 A, 81 B) as one of the elements." As to this, one cannot suppose him to have been ignorant of the earlier uses of the term in Greek literature; but in any case, in *Cratylus* 410 B he [Plato] speaks of ether as "so called because it always runs and flows about the air"; and however atrocious this *hermeneia* may be if treated as a serious etymology, all that matters for present purposes is that he distinguishes the ether from the air.[2] Again, in *Phaedo* 109 B-111 B, where Plato is describing "the true Heaven and the true light and true Earth" as a veritable Paradise he says that this is only to be seen by those who wing their way to the top of the air and lift their heads *above* it, for this is not just the aerial "sky," but the "pure heaven" in which the stars move. Of this heavenly world he says that it is "that which those who discourse about such matters call the 'ether',[3] of which water, mist, and air are only the 'dregs'"; and, further, of the dwellers there, that "what air is to us, ether is to them," all of whose conditions are "as much superior to ours as air is purer than water or the ether purer than the air." We ought certainly to bear this passage in mind when in *Timaeus* 28 B he speaks of "the heaven, or however it likes to be called." Plato's use of language, however apt, is never deliberately

---

[1 The title, not found in the manuscript, is taken from the opening of "Concerning Sphinxes." — Ed.]

2 Here it may be the proper place to remark and complain that again and again throughout the Loeb Library in versions of Greek texts a direct translation of the word αἴθχρ by "ether" seems to have been carefully avoided, and any circumlocution preferred; which places quite an unnecessary burden on anyone who wishes to study the Greek doctrine of the elements. [One] must read through many long texts in the original, as I have had to do so, [in order to] find out where the word actually occurs. The same holds good in other connections also, e.g. Euripedes, *Alcestis* 1003 where Euripedes has "Now is she a blessed Daimon," but A.S. Way (a "literary feller") [puts it]: "With the Blest now abides she on high"; which is really a travesty, and certainly worse than useless from the point of view of a student of religion.

3 For Euripedes, *Helen* 34 and 584, "wrought of οὐρανός" and "wrought of αἰθήρ" are synonymous.

Cf. Cicero, *De. nat. deor.* 2.29.40 "There remains . . . the all-engirdling, all-confining circuit of the sky, also called the ether" and 2.45 "the highest part of the sky, called the ether."

pedantic, and as he says himself elsewhere, "I presume we shall not dispute about names" (*Republic* 534 D).[1]

It will be convenient to start with Plato's account of the constitution of the world in *Timaeus* 49 ff., where he describes the four elements (fire, air, water, earth) and their continent ὑποδεχή, etc.). It is true that he does not explicitly call this all-containing (πανδεχής) space a fifth element,[2] but that is because he is starting from the concept of the two kinds, that of the primary (paternal) Form (εἴδος) and that of its (begotten) imitation (μίμημα)[3] and proceeding to a third Form, that of the (material) vessel (τιθήνη)[4] in which the variable sensible forms compounded of the elements appear, circulate[5] and disappear; and though he only refers incidentally to αἰθήρ as a purer kind of air; his "all containing nature" is actually that of the αἰθήρ, *ākāśa* and fifth element of other accounts, both Greek and Indian.

This space (τόπος, χώρα, etc.), in which all things live and move and have their being, participates in the intelligible; it is imperceptible, indestructible, formless, void, and cannot be defined by or compared to any of its sensible contents.[6] The all-receiving nature is thus like a plastic medium, soft linen or wax (ἐκμαγεῖον)[7] on which the copies of the ever-existent types are to be imprinted or drawn and a support or throne (ἕδρα) for them; and though it is naturally and properly void of all these forms, it assumes all sorts of different appearances at different times,

---

1 For this position in Plato, cf. *Laws* 864 A "We are not now concerned with a verbal dispute." All that Plato cares about is to make himself understood; he is not writing for those who do not want to understand, or whose demand is for a "closed system" of thought.

2 This is nevertheless implied by 55 C where of the five solid figures (32 c; four elements and φιλία; cf. Ritter and Preller 80) described, four correspond to the four elements, and "the fifth, which is to receive over all of it always the likenesses of the intelligible and eternal forms, of all which it is properly and naturally void," *ib.* 51 A, on which these forms are to be imprinted (50 C), their support or "throne" (ἕδρα, 52 B).

3 It may be observed here that μίμημα, "imitation," has been correlated with Sanskrit *māyā* which, however, may rather belong to *mā*, "measure," and correspond to Greek μαῖα, μῆτις, μήτηρ, μήτρα, "moon," and "mind," and "measure" in the sense of "vessel." To measure (*ma-nir-mā*) is to make; the image (*prati-mā*) is of the paradigm (*prama*). Agni's conception is that "he was measured in the Mother" (*anīmata mātari*), *RV.* III.29.11), i.e. as a "created form" (*nirmāṇa-kāya*), cf. my Nir*māṇa-kāya*" in *JRAS.* 1938, 81-4. In the same way the Buddha's "created body" (*nirmāṇa-kāya*) was born of his mother Māyā. Māyā is, then, the maternal measure, art, artifice and guile by and of which as means or material (*ulh, vana, materia prima*) all things nameable and sensible (*nāmarūpe*) are "materially-made" (*māyā-maya*); which "things" (originally "unmeasured," cg. *Timaeus* 50 B) (whereof the measurer is the solar Self of all, *RV.* VIII.25.18 etc.) are the quantitative "matter" (*mātrā*, i.e. *materia secunda*) of this all-embracing world" (*BU.* IV.3.9). Māyā corresponds with *Natura naturans*, *mātrāh* to *Natura naturata*.

4 *Spec.* 1.266; with Plato's τιοήνη, cf. *AA.* II.3.1 where "the ether is a vessel (*āvapanam ākāśaḥ*), for therein all this is collectively sown" (*samopyate*).

5 Plato's description of the elements as "revolving" and as a "cycle of birth" (*Timaeus* 49; cf. Philo, *Heres* 283), like St. James' "wheel of birth" (III.6) and Meister Echhart's "storm of the world's flow" in which the soul "goes round in an endless chain," corresponds with the Indian concept of the "wheel of becoming" (*bhava-cakra*) and "vortex" or "confluence" (*saṁśara*).

6 "The measure of all measures cannot be one of them" (*Tripurā Rahasya, Jñāna Khanda* IX.87 . . . "The properties of the ether are too fundamental to be stated in terms of something else" (O.J. Lodge in *Encyclopedia Britannica*, 14th ed., *s.v.* Ether).

7 Cf. *Heres* 181 wax, ἐκριανειον πρὸς αἴσοησιν; *Aet.* 1, wax for sensibles to be imprinted.

because of their coming and going.[1] Plato calls this empty and recipient Nature (φύσος) — which is that of the metaphysical "void" (Sanskrit *śūnyata)* — the "Nurse and Mother of all Becoming"; the totality of all things intelligible and sensible being that of these three, the father, the Mother and their offspring.[2]

Now, in the first place, as to the "wax" or other "support" on which the sensible copies of the eternal realities are imprinted, and without which they would not become at all: This corresponds to the "tablet,"[3] "wall,"[4] and "mirror"[5] of the Spatial-Self (*ākāśatman*), on which the World-picture (*jagac-citram*) is painted or in which it is reflected. Plato's recipient Nature is thus, in other words, the *speculum aeternum*, "in which the minds of those who gaze perceive all things, and better than elewhere."[6] "There, indeed, everything shows as if reflected in a mirror, without circumscription by time and place (*kāla*, κρονος, *desa*). For how could there be a circumscription by time and place, since both of these are comprised in the reflection in the mirror itself?[7] This is the mirror of our "own true form," in which, when thought has been smoothed out, the world is shown[8] . . . It is only when *that* is ignored that the suchlike-world is produced . . . Just as when space (*ākāśa*) is ignored, one sees only what is taking place in it,"[9] i.e. what is taking place around us, rather than in what we are. The mirror-vision is simultaneous, just as in actual mirrors however small, one sees innumerable things at a single glance.[10] Nothing is more significant than that

---

1 Cf. Plutarch, *Mor.* 382 C. Robe of Isis [was] variegated, of Osiris of shadowless light.

2 *Timaeus* 50 D. "The Father, the Mother, and the Son, the perfect Power" (*Apocalypse of John*, cited in Baynes, *Coptic Gnostic Treatise*, p. 14); "All that is declared to be One. For the Mother and the Father and the Child are this All" (*SA.* VII.15). Plutarch, *Mor.* 372 E, very naturally identifies Plato's "nurse" with Isis, who is indeed *Nutria Omnium.*

3 *Svatmanirupana* 95.

4 *Tripurā Rahasya* XI.25-7 *svātuiani bhittan jagacertvam . . . kalpitani svena kevalan . . .* etc.; Vinuklatura, *Iṣta siddhi* as [discussed] by Das Gupta, *History of Indian Philosophy* II.203. Wall and future reveal one another, but are entirely distinct substances.

5 *Trip. Ras.* IX.90. *Tatra sarvam bhāsate vai darpaṇa-prabhard avat*[.]

6 St. Bonaventura, I *Sent.* d.35, a unic. q.1, fund. 3 quoting St. Augustine; cf. Dante, *Paradiso* XXVI.106. *Kaus. Up.* IV.2, 11 *āditye mahat . . . adarse pratirupaḥ*; *KU.* VI.5 *yathādarśe tathātmani.*

7 The reflection is, then, "where every where and every when are focused," Dante *Paradiso*; *S. Th.* I.14.9, "Since eternity . . . " *Desa* will be distinguished as a dimensioned space as from the *ākāśa* in which the directions (*disaḥ*) acquire a meaning, cf. *S. Th. Sup.* 83.2.

8 "The mind of the sage, being brought to rest, becomes the mirror of the universe," Chwang Tzu.

God does not reflect the likeness of things, but they his likeness, and it is indeed in this sense that "He created man in his image and likeness." All things thus are to be seen in God as an intelligible mirror (*S. Th.* I.78.9), and the same judges according to this primary truth, reflected in the soul as in a mirror (*ib.* I.16.6 and 1.), cf. *Katha Up.* VI.5 . . . in itself its essence as if in a mirror (*yathā´ darśe tathātmani*) and *BU.* III.9.16 God is that Person who is the abode of forms, the Person in the mirror, life (*nıpāny eva yasyâyatanam . . . purusam . . . ādarśe puruṣaḥ . . . asuh*). There are then two mirrors, just as there are two images. In either case it is by mirror-knowledge that the knowing subject knows essentially, precisely because the mirror and the intellect are the same. The individual knowing subject, by the reflection of the eternal image in the mirror of his own intellect, the universal knowing subject, the divine Sun who "sees all things" (*viśvam abhicaṣte*, I.164.44 [. . .]) sees them in the mirror of his own intellect, or as it is expressed: "Painted by the Self, and simply as itself" (*Svatmaninipana*).

9 *Tripurā Rahasya*, *Jñana Khanda*, IX. 89-95, 85 b. The whole concept corresponds to that of Plato's "intelligible" and "sensible" worlds; the former in the mirror, the [latter] objectively with reference to things that we see around us. He sees indeed who sees all things in himself, cf. *BG.*

10 Cf. *S. Th.* I.14.9. Plato's "continental space" is the universal.

time and place themselves are a part of the reflection, and not a part of the mirror. This means that the *speculum aeternum* must not be thought of as a plane in two dimensions, but as an omnipresent and infinite support; i.e. as a "wall," as if we conceived that wall as an all-pervading surface.[1]

We can now examine a little more closely the proposition that Plato does not, in the *Timaeus*, know of ether as *quintessentia*. It will be remembered that he describes the five geometrical forms from which the whole living world, body and soul, is constructed; and that these are elemental forms. In *Timaeus* 53, 32 C and 48 B we are told that the visible and concrete universe has already been made out of the four elements, fire, earth, water and air, each having its own geometrical form; and then in 55 E that "there remained still one form, the fifth," *viz.* the dodecahedron, and that God [Zeus] made use of this "to trace the forms of living beings throughout the world." It is hard to see how anyone familiar with the Greek tradition, in which sensible bodies as such are always thought of as made of the four elements only (*Timaeus* 82 A), just as in Buddhism bodies as such are always *caturmahabhutika*, "four-elemental," can fail to recognize that Zeus is here described as using the quintessential, etherial principle, wherewith to animate what would have been otherwise a soulless and inanimate world, "not yet having within itself all living things, and in this respect still unlike its perfect paradigm"[2] (*Timaeus* 39 E) in which there preexisted the Forms or Ideas of the Celestial Deities, of the winged kind that traverses the air, the watery kind, and that which moves on dry land (*Timaeus* 39 E, 40 A), all that, as St. John says, "was life in Him." The "depiction" of life in 55 B is, of course, the same thing as the impression of the moulding figures made upon the recipient material that is thereby to all appearances diversified or patterned as if by a seal stamped on wax (50 B)[,][3] and to which Plato refers as an adorning delineation of forms (διασχηατίσατο ἐ̑ιδΣσι, 54 B). The net result is that, besides Zeus himself, and "all the gods," these are brought into being three kinds of mortal living creatures, those that fly in the air, or live in the water, or move on land (40 A, 41 B, C). An almost identical account of the creation of living beings is given in *Epinomis* 981 E ff., where, however, the elements are explicitly five: Fire, water, air, earth and ether, the "fifth"; the Soul, immutable and invisible, senior to the unintelligent body, and its ruler, is the efficient power that moulds all living things from the elements (of which one predominates in each

---

1 Cf. the Self as all-pervading.

2 That Zeus worked from a paradigm of himself, as the *Timaeus* says, is necessarily implied whenever God is thought of as Maker, since no one can make anything unless he has in him some idea of what it is that he wants to make. So that it is perfectly natural that whenever God is regarded as a "Maker by art," we meet with the concept of an intelligible "world picture" after which the actual world is modelled.

3 This well known conception of the divine *signature* to which all things owe their existence has a notable corollary, beautifully stated by St. Bonaventura who points out that nothing would continue to exist (*esse*, i.e. *esse hoc et vivere*) were it not for the continued presence of the Giver of their life, and illustrates this by the figure of "the impression of a seal in water, which does not last for a moment, unless the seal *remains* in the water" (*I Sent.* d. 37, p. 1, a. 1, q. 1, conclusion). There is an Indian parallel, expressed in terms of *vestigium pedis*: the Solar Gander, i.e. the Sun, "the Self of all that is in motion or at rest" (*RV.* I.115.1), when he rises, i.e. proceeds as in *RV.* X.90.2, "does not remove his one foot from the sea; and verily, were he to remove it, there would be neither night nor day, nor ever any dawn" (*AV.* XI.4.21).

kind), and so fills the whole world with beings "participant in life"; so that, apart from Zeus and Hera whose real nature can hardly be described, there are five kinds of more or less visible living things: First the fiery stellar gods, second and third the etherial and aerial Daimons (mediators between Heaven and Earth), fourth the beings (nymphs) in the waters, and fifth men and other land animals.[1]

Now, that the Soul is prior to the body — composite of the four elements, and the prime mover and cause of life in all things — is Plato's well established doctrine (*Laws* 891 C ff.),[[2] and this distinction of the Soul from all that is made of "fire, water, earth and air" amounts to speaking of it as a "fifth" essence; and actually, if we return to *Timaeus* (34 E and 36 B) we find the Soul as described as "woven throughout the heavens (universe) from the midst to the extremity, enveloping it in a circle from without" and so "making a divine origin of incessant and intelligent life lasting through all time" — expressions that taken by themselves one might suppose to have been predicated of the ether that "binds all things together in its circle" (Empedocles fr. 386) equated with Zeus himself. So it seems to me that while Plato rarely makes use of the word "ether" itself, he often refers by other names to what, he says, the specialists call "ether." And, finally that this is what most Greek Platonists would have assumed is apparent not only from the *Axiochus* (366) where the soul is spoken of as "ever longing for its heavenly native ether," but also from Plutarch (*Mor.* 390 C and 423 A), who took it for granted that Plato, in the *Timaeus*, was discussing all five of the elements, of which the fifth is ether, and each of which can be thought of as a realm or world, although the world is really one. That the Greek tradition as a whole took account of all five elements, four the component of "bodies," and one immaterial, needs no detailed demonstration.

"ETHER" IN PHILO

PHILO'S REFERENCES TO THE ELEMENTS, OR PARTS OF NATURE, ARE ALONE almost sufficient for a correlation of the Greek and Indian formulae. Philo, indeed, speaks sometimes of only three or four elements,[3] but in such cases it is clear that these are only three or four of the full complement of five: Earth, water, air, fire and sky.[4] When only four are mentioned the fourth is either fire *or* sky;[5] but the sky is a mysterious factor of which it can

1 The detailed correspondences of the *Timaeus* with the *Epinomis*, despite slight differences of wording, seem to me to argue for the authenticity of the *Epinomis*, or to prove at least that the latter accurately interprets Plato's own point of view. However, our present purpose is only to show that he rarely employs the word αἰθήρ itself, Plato is perfectly aware of ether as *quintessentia*.

[2 This is paralleled in a most interesting way in connection with the making of the living image (εἴαδωλον) of Helen that was carried off to Troy while she herself was kept safe in Egypt (Euripedes, *Helen* 33 ff and 582 ff). When Menelaus protests, "Who can fashion living bodies?" Helen answers "Ether." It was, in fact, Hera who, as Helen tells [us], of heaven framed a living image like unto me" (ὁμοιοσαὸ ἐμοὶ εἴεωλον ἔμπνουν οὐρανοῦ ξυνθεῖσαάπο); and here again we find the equation οὐρανός = αἰθήρ — a synonymy of which, as we may already have seen, Plato himself was quite aware.]

3 E.g. *Moses* II.121; *Spec.* I.208.

4 *Moses* II.133.

5 *Spec.* I.45; *Dec.* 31; *Moses* II.37; *Somn.* I.16, 23, II.116. Nevertheless, in lists of the four, sky often takes the place of "fire," e.g. *LA.* III.101, cf. *BU.* IV.4, 5 *ākāśa* as fourth, *tejas* as fifth, as one might say, by invocation. [Cf. *Conf.* 135.]

be asked whether it be "crystalline, or purest fire, or a fifth, revolving body, not participating in the nature of the four elements."[1] These are not, in fact, mutually exclusive theories.[2] An apparent confusion only arises because, in fact, there is more than one kind of fire, in particular the "saving" and the "useful";[3] the former is Heracleitus' "everlasting fire, in measures[4] being kindled and in measures going out."[5] Light (φῶς) is a form of fire[6] and so can take the place of fire as a fifth element. Mind (ὁ νοῦς) which is that form of soul that is not elemental but corresponds to this "better and purer" factor "out of which the natures of things divine were made," and is the only indestructible, freely-ranging (ἄφετος)[7] part of us, gifted with a share (μοῖρι) in God's own free-will (ἄφετος),[8] can either be

---

1 *Somn.* I.21.

2 See the notes in *Philo*, Loeb Library Vol. V., p. 594; and cf. *Aetios* II.20 attributing to Empedocles the notion of a "crystalline Sun." [. . .] *Sup. Life*, p. 270.

3 *Heres* 136; the "saving" (σωτήριος) fire that is "the substance of the sky" is the "*non corruptibilis ignis . . . sed salutaris, per quem omnia artificiose facta sunt*" of *Deo* 6 and the "sacred and unquenchable celestial fire" of *Conf.* 156-7. Philo's saving and creative fire is the Stoic "constructive (τέχνιοκον = *artificiosus*) and preservative (τηρητικόν = *salutaris*, cf. *Synteresis*) fire" that is in living things and makes them grow, and that can be identified with nature and soul (H. von Arnim, *Stoic. Vet. Fraq.* I.34, II.24 ff.; and Cicero, *De nat. deor.* II.40, 57-58 and 115-116, and so virtually Zeus Soter and Tritos, the fiery *Logos*, and Vedic Agni *trātṛ* and *vaiśvānara*, and *RV.* IV.58.11 *hṛdy antar āyuṣi*. The other and "useful" fire is the one that serves our everyday purposes, but only does so by destroying. Equally in Greek and Vedic sources there is a clear distinction of Fire as an immanent and transcendent principle from the transient and destructive fires at which we warm our hands.

Ritter's and Preller's words, "Ζεύς, Δίκη, σόφον, λόγος; *res non diversa. Idem significat illud . . .* πῦρ αἰείξ ωον, *unde manat omnis motus, omnis vita, omnis intellectus*" (*Hist. Philosoph. Gr.* 40, note a) not only summarise the doctrine of Heracleitus, but would apply as well to Philo (for whom the *Logos* is a "burning" principle and Wisdom "etherial," *Fug.* 134-7, *Cher.* 27), and to Vedic theology.

4 In *Heres* 227, Philo speaking of the sky as a "measure" from which the elements are "measured out," must have had Heracleitus in mind. Cf. *RV.* V.81.3 where Varuṇa (Dyaus, Sky) "making the Sun his measure, measures out the earth." In a slightly different (moral) sense, the *Logos* is also the criterion (κριτήριον) of Truth (Heracleitus, Sextus Empiricus, *Adv. Dogm.* I.131); and the measure (μετρον) of all things, teaching us to choose the good and avoid its opposite, so that "to make God our measure" (μετρεῖν κατὰ Θεόν) in this sense is to use the fiery sword of Reason to cut away from ourselves all our mortal parts and free the immortal to fly upward to God "in naked understanding" (*Cher.* 31) a near parallel to *Hebrews* IV.12 on the "suffering of soul from spirit," and suggestive also of *TS.* VII.4.9, "They cut off . . . considering, 'More lightly may we attain the world of heavenly-light'." This cutting off what is mortal is the same thing as the crushing of the stern of the vessel as she passes between the Symplegades, as, e.g. in the *Argonautica*.

5 Heracleitus, fr. XX. Cf. *AB.* III.4, on Agni's distribution. For other Indian parallels see my "Measures of Fire" in *O Instituto*, Vol. 100 (Coimbra, 1942).

6 Cf. Plato, *Timaeus* 58 E; *TS.* II.2.4.8, etc. Also Averrohoes.

7 Ἄφετος amounts to *Kāmacārin*, *kāmaga*, and implies the liberty of one *emeritus* and no longer involved in worldly affairs, as in the fourth *āśrama*, of which Plato, *Rep.* 498 C ὅταν δὲ λήγη μὲν ἡ ῥώμη . . . ἀφέτοως, is virtually a description (cf. 591 A). "For it becomes the Mind to be led forth and *let go free* (ἀφίεσθαι), to stand from everything, the necessities of the body, the organs of perception, sophistries, wishful thinking, and ultimately *from itself*" (*LA.* III.41). Cf. Dante, *Purgatorio* XXVII.131 *Lo tuo piacere . . . duce*, and St. Augustine's "Love God, and do what you will" (*Confessions* 108) and *Deum diligis? Quid dicam, Deus eris* (*In. ep. Joh. ad Parthos* II.2.14), cf. Rūmī, *Mathnawī* II, *Argum.*, "What is Love? Thou shalt know when thou becomst me."

See [also] *Confessions* 108 and *LA.* III.41. Zeus Ἀφεσίος releases.

8 Ἑκοθσία, [the] root εκ [is] present in Sanskrit *vaś* and Latin *volo* and *victoria*. The closely parallel passages in *I Peter* 5.5 and *Philemon* 14 should be noted. Free will in Vedic contexts is expressed by *yathā vaśam*, *vaśam anu*, or simply *vaśam*, predicated of divinities and notably one of the Spirit (e.g. *RV.* X.168.4,

(Continued on following page.)

compared to light[1] or thought of as "hot and fiery"[2] like the *Logos* whence the "aetherial wisdom" streams,[3] [becoming the] "ethereal and divine food of the soul" (*LA.* III.161). The four elements, of which the Mind is independent, are "soulless (or lifeless) and material,"[4] whereas the intellectual soul is a slip, spark, strain (ἀπόσπασμα), part or patrimony (μοῖρα) of God's etherial nature,[5] and that is why alike in Philo and Plato only the four elements are mentioned when the reference is expressly to the material constitution of the body or the world,[6] and, as Burnet says, "they account for all the qualities presented by the world to the senses."[7] So, for example, when Dante lists the four elements,[8] he is not ignoring the *quintessentia*, but speaking only of the "four-fold texture" (*quaderno*)[9] of the material world beyond which contingency does not stand, though it is "mirrored"

(Continued from preceding page.)

AV. VI.72.1, [also] *anukāmam RV.* IX.113.9). In *TS.* II.1.7.6 *vaśam . . . carati*, "ranges freely," is said of a bull offered to Bṛhaspati, and so to say ἄφετος, cf. Xenophon, *Cyn.* V.14 ἀφιᾶσι τῆ θεῷ; add *ŚB.* XIII.6.2.13, Keith, *R PV.* 347. Even today such "free-ranging" bulls are to be seen in any Indian city and are regarded as *sannyasins*; they are exempt from all restrictions and indeed "find pasture" (*John* X.9), "eating at will" (*kamanni, Taitt. Up.* III.10.5). That the offering of living beings to a deity does not necessarily imply their death appears also in the connection with the Puruṣamedha, where the human victims that have been bound to the stake are "released," as stated in *ŚB.* XIII.6.2.13-14, where the "voice" that interdicts their slaughter parallels that of the angel of the Lord in *Genesis* XXII.11-12, commanding the release of Isaac; and in *ŚB.* III.7.2.8 where the male animal victim dedicated to Tvaṣṭṛ is released after the fire has been carried around it. [Cf.] *Mark* X.28.

1 *Immut.* 45-7, cf. *Opif.* 30.

2 *Fug.* 134, not in the bad sense [of] fiery as in *LA.* III.224!

3 *Fug.* 137.

4 *Cont.* 4, ἄψυχος ὕλη, cf. *Heres* 160; as in Sextus Empiricus, *Adv. dogm.* 115, ὑλικαι. Nevertheless, the four roots can be referred to by the names of the divinities to whose qualities they correspond, as in Philo, *Cont.* 3 (cf. *Dec.* 53 and Plutarch, *Moralia*, 377); and Empedocles, Ritter and Preller section 164. Philo's four are Hephaistos (fire), Hera (air), Poseidon (water), and Demeter (earth), and I assume (against Burnet, p. 229) that Empedocles' Titan Zeus, "life-giving" (cf. Philo, *Opif.* 30), Hera, Aidoneus and Nestis are likewise the correlatives of fire, air, water and earth in the same sequence. Titan Zeus corresponds to Titan Aether in another fragment of Empedocles (Ritter and Preller 170 a, or in the Loeb Library *Timaeus*, p. 142, note 2) and there can be no doubt that Ζεὺς ἐστιν αἰθήρ (Aeschylus, fr. 65 a). I see nothing to justify Burnet's equation of Hera with Earth in this context (Burnet p. 228, end of note 3), against Philo (*Cont.* 3) and the Stoics (Cicero, *De nat. deor.* II.66, air = Juno, ether = Jove); and I cannot too strongly deprecate Burnet's most *inconvenient* rendering of αἰθήρ by "air."

5 *Heres* 282-3; *LA.* III.161.

6 Soul; cf. *Timaeus* 56 C, 36 E, 34 B; as repeated in the *Timaeus*, e.g. 46 D where the soul is invisible, and 42 C, D, where the "greatness of soul is to adhere to the dominant Soul . . ."

7 J. Burnet, *Early Greek Philosophy*, p. 231. According to Philostratus, Apollonius was surprised to hear from the Indian sages [that] the world is made of not only four but of five elements, the fifth being the αἰθήρ from which the Gods are sprung (*Life of Apollonius*, III.34); but this surprise was probably feigned, since Apollonius was no materialist, and the doctrine of the luminous "ether in the soul" is elsewhere plausibly attributed to him (*ib.* I.8). A positive denial of the fifth element would have implied a philosophical materialism, and might have been expected from the Epicureans. Such a denial is certainly wrongly attributed to the Stoic Zeno of whom it is said that "in dealing with *the* four beginnings of things (*in quattuor initiis rerum illis*) he did not add this fifth nature, which his predecessors deemed to be the source of sensation and mind" (Cicero, *Acad.* I.39); wrongly, since he identified the source of sensation and mind with "fire" (*ib.* I.26) or, more precisely, "creative (*artificiosus*) fire" (*De nat. deor.* II.57) and regarded Ether as the "supreme deity, possessor of the mind by which the universe is governed" (*Acad.* II.126).

8 Cf. *Acts* XI.5.

[9 *Paradiso* VII.124.]

in the eternal aspect above;[1] referring specifically, that is, to the sublunary world as distinguished from the sky.[2]

One of Philo's fullest statements is made in *Heres* 282-3, where what is bodily in man is made of the four elements, earth, water, air and fire, the corresponding qualities being those of dryness, moisture, cold and warmth, and of weight (earth, water) and lightness (air, fire) all of which return to their principles at our death,[3] "but the immortal soul, whose nature is intellectual and celestial (νοερὸν καὶ οὐράνιον) will depart to find a father in ether, the purest of essences. For we may suppose that, as the men of old declared, there is a fifth essence (πέμπτη οὐσία), one that revolves [or circulates], and differs from the four by its superiority.[4] Out of this they thought the stars and all the sky had been made, and deduced as a natural consequence that the human soul was also an offshoot thereof." The *quintessentia* is our spiritual part; "spirit — the most life-giving breath of God — is the essence of the soul"[5] (πνευμα εστιν ή ψυχῆς οὐσία);[6] "the spirit in the heart" (τὸμὲν ἐγκάρδιονπνεῦμα) is the father of intellections.[7]

Philo proceeds to a convincing analysis of the parts of the temple and its ritual furniture, on the basis of the foregoing doctrines and the "philosophy of symbols" and "laws of allegory."[8] Just as man's body is a garment for the soul, so the *Logos* wears the world as raiment, "for He arrays himself in earth, water, air and fire and all that is framed from these;[9] and by the same token the High Priest, except upon the occasion of his annual entrance into the Holy of Holies, wears a long robe that represents the sublunary world. The robe itself represents the air, its flowered hem the Earth, its pomegranates water, and its scarlet fire, while the ephod worn over it represents the sky.[10] This representation (μιμησις) is by means of the colors

---

1 *Paradiso* XVII.37.

2 For the well-known distinction of the sublunary world from the etherial sky, cf. Cicero, *De nat. deor.* II.56, and Claudian, *Rape of Proserpine* 299.

3 Similarly *Post.* 5. As in *ŚB.* II.207, earth to earth, etc., but the powers of the soul (*indriyāṇi*) return to the ether (*ākāśa*), cf. *BU.* III.2.13.

4 Cf. *LA.* 161. Philo's revolving principle, of which the soul is an extension, corresponds to Plato's "soul" that is woven throughout and all around the sky (οὐρανός here = κόσμος) and is the divine beginning of life (*Timaeus* 36 E-37 A). "Father is ether," i.e. Ζεὺς πατήρ.

5 That is, "Soul of the soul" ψυχὴ χυχῆς, *Heres* 55 = "Self of the self" (*ātmano'tmā, Maitri Up.* VI.6) = *CU.* VIII.12.1, *amrtās aññātuan.*

6 *Det.* 82 with *Opif.* 30.

7 *Spec.* I.6. *Cathedram habet in caelo qui intus corda docet*, St. Augustine, *In epist. Joannis ad Parthos. Omne verum, a quocumque dicatur, est a Spiritu Sancto*, St. Ambrose.

8 These expressions appear in *Moses* I.23, *Abr.* 68, cf. 99, 119, *Fug.* 179, *Post.* 7, etc., and for the Alexandrian Jewish Allegorists, Goodenough, *By Light, Light,* p. 83. These are the laws of "*le symbolisme qui sait,*" and if such expressions seem strange to us whose "symbolism" is personal and psychological, it may be observed that Emile Mâle very properly speaks of the Christian symbolism of the Middle Ages as a "calculus," and that the traditional symbols are the terms of a precise and universal "language"; one in which — for example — the "gold" standard is always the same.

9 *Fug.* 110. As in the *Īśavāsya Up.* I (= *VS.* XL.1), "All this, whatsoever moves on earth, is for the Lord's apparel" (*vāsyam = ācchādanīyam*) — "Who as a mantle weareth these, and couches in every birth" (*RV.* VIII.41.7). Cf. *Maitri Up.* VI.6; Hermes Trismegistos *Lib.* XVI.5-7 and *Ascl.* III.34 c (*mundum . . . quasi vestimentum contexta*); also the symbolism of the parts of the initiate's linen robe, *ŚB.* III.1.2.18. Claudian describes a cloth embroidered with the "series of the elements"; the sea is purple, the stars are "kindled" above (*accendit*) in gold (*Rape of Proserpine* I.247 ff. — Platnauer's ridiculous rendering of *elementorum seriem* by "concourse of atoms" should be forgotten!).

10 *Moses* II.88, where the pomegranates form a tasseled fringe, *ib.* II.119.

proper to the elements:[1] The undyed linen (βύσσος) that grows on Earth, and the purple (πορφύρα) obtained from the sea, represent the corresponding elements; ὑακίνθινος, blue-black, is the color of air,[2] and κόκκινος, scarlet, that of fire; the whole is interwoven with gold thread,[3] denoting the etherial essence of the sky,[4] while the gems of the breastplate are set in gold, as the elements are enclosed by the ether.[5] In the same way, the veil of the temple, which separates the outer from the inner chamber, is adorned with the colors of the four elements; the outer chamber corresponding to the sublunary world and the inner to the etherial essence.[6] So also, when he is to enter the Holy of Holies, the inner chamber, the High Priest puts off the variegated sacrificial robe and [dons] one of diaphanous (διάλευκος) linen of purest white (βύσσος τῆς καθαροτάτης).[7] The symbolism of flax, of which Philo remarks that when carefully cleaned it has a "very brilliant and luminous aspect," parallels that of gold; "it is a symbol of tension (εὐτονία), incorruptibility, and most radiant light; it does not break (ἀρραγής), neither is it a product of any mortal creature."[8]

In the preceding context the word εὐτονία is significant. Εὐτονία (root τείνω, Sanskrit *tan*) "tone," "*ten*-sion," "in-*ten*-sity," is the opposite of the slackening

---

1 *Moses* II.88, *Spec.* I.85, 93-97, QE. II.85. Cf. Josephus, *Wars of the Jews*, V.4, 16-26. [In] Apuleius, *Met.* XI.10 [he] describes initiates wearing *linteae vestis candore puro luminosi.*

2 Blue-black, as in Homer, where "hyacinth" is the color of dark hair, and since Philo himself adds that the air is "naturally black," *Conq.* 117 as also *Opif.* 29, Colson's "dark red" is mistaken in the present context. The color meant is the deep blue or black (Sanskrit *nīla*, indigo) of the sky that is meant. Aristotle says that air when seen nearby is colorless but seen in depth, "blue" (*De col.* 794 a 9 f.). Whoever finds it strange that in antiquity the sky is always thought of as dark should look at a photograph of snow and clear sky taken on panchromatic film.

3 *Moses* II.111.

4 This is not explicit as regards the threads, but necessarily follows from all that is said elsewhere, where gold is always the symbol of the quintessentia, sky or ether; the seven-branched candlestick, for example, is made of gold, to represent the fifth element and to distinguish the lights from the rest of the universe composite of the four (*QE.* 73).

5 *QE.* 113; cf. Eur., *Phoen.* 805 χρυσόδετοις περόναμον ἐπίσαμον (δέω σωξω), *Ion* 1008 χρυσοῖσι δεσμοῖς.

6 *QE.* 91.

7 *Somn.* I 216-217. Observe that while the βύσσος of the cosmic robe was a symbol of earth by its origin, that of the extra-cosmic robe is a symbol of the etherial essence by its whiteness, or rather lack of color. Things are colored, God and the soul colorless (*Epinomis* 981 B, Hermes Trismegistos *Lib.* XIII.6); *avarṇa*, "colorless," (*Upaniṣads*, passim.), contrasts with the "colors" of the four castes (*varṇa*, *Manu* X.4 *etc.*), cf. Rūmī, *Mathnawī* I.2467-8 (creation, the imprisonment of colorlessness in color). So, "*du musst ganz wesentlich und* ungefarbet *sein*," Angelus Silesius, *Cherub. Wandersmann* I.274.

On white and white robes see E.R. Goodenough, *By Light, Light*, pp. 173, 178, 256, 265-6; also Philostratus, *Life of Apollonius*, I.8 [where] Apollonius wears linen raiment, not an animal product. Babylonian priests, in the presence of deity, are represented nude, and in our context the putting off of the cosmic robe is, so to say, a gymnosophic procedure, for as he says elsewhere, the High priest "shall not enter the Holy of Holies in his robe" (*Leviticus* XVI.1 ff.), "but laying aside the garment of opinions and phantasms of the soul, *shall enter naked* with no colored borders or sound of bells . . . and this is the noblest form of γύμνωσις" (*LA.* II.56 ff.).

As Goodenough very rightly points out, the two robes have close analogies in the Egyptian mysteries; the variegated robe of Isis is often worn by the initiate, the white robe of Osiris only once (Plutarch, *Mor.* 382 C, D [in] Goodenough, p. 119).

H.J. Massingham, *This Plot of Earth*, p. 180-1, [where] linen *sarochs* [are] weekday-colored and embroidered with symbols indicative of the wearer's trade, but Sunday smock[s] are always white.

8 *Somn.* 217.

(ἐπιχαλῶν) of the *ten*-dons (τόνοι) of the soul that Philo condemns elsewhere.[1] Εὐτονία presupposes the traditional ontology and psychology in which the *Logos* or Spirit is the bond (δεσμός) or chain (δειρά) or cable (ὁρμίσκος) or thread (*sūtram*) on which all things are strung and by which they are moved.[2] In this "thread-spirit" (*sūtrātman*) doctrine, God's omnipresence "is not locomotion . . . but an act of tension (τονική)[3] . . . by way of the mind's power of intension (τονική) which it extends (τείνας) through the perceptual functions (δἰαἰσθήσεως = *prānāḥ*, *indriyāṇi*) . . . [for so it is said that] God extends (τείναντος) His power through the median breath (διὰ τοῦ μέσου πνεύματος = *madhye prāṇe*) even unto the material-substance-of-things-perceptible" (ἄχρι τοῦ ὑποκειμένου)[4] "The Word of Him-that-Is (τοῦ ὄντος λόγος) is the bond (δεσμός) of all existence, and holds together and constrains (σφίγγει) all the parts, hindering their disolution and disintegration" in the same way as which the soul which maintains the harmony and unity of the parts of the body.[5] Thus "all things are constrained (σφίγγεται) by the Divine Word (λόγος θεῖος), which is a glue and a bond (δεσμός) that fills up all things with its being. He who fastens (εἴρας) and weaves together each separate thing is, verily, full of his own Self."[6]

The concept is of at least Sumerian antiquity,[7] but here it will suffice to observe that in Philo it derives, in the first place from Plato, for whom it is "the circumambiance (περίοδος)[8] of the All" that "constrains (σφίγγει) all things," i.e. that of Fire, since "it is Fire that most of all rushes into all things,"[9] or that of the sovereign and undivided, Same and Uniform,[10] within us that dominates "by

---

1 *Spec.* I.90; cf. Plato, *Phaedo* 98 D, χαλῶντα opposite of συντείνοντα.

2 Almost all the citations in the present context are additional to what will be found in my "Iconography of Durer's 'Knoten' and Leonardo's 'Concatenation'," *Art Quarterly*, Spring 1944. The universality and catholicity of the thread-spirit doctrine can hardly be overemphasized.

3 *Sacr.* 68.

4 *LA.* I.30-37. "He (*prāṇa*, the "Breath") placed himself in the midst of all that is," AA. II.2.1. Cf. Ascl. *Hermetica*, p. 419 [and] Plato, *Timaeus* 34 B ψυχὴδὲ εἰς τὸ μέσον αὐτοῦ θεὶς διὰ παυτός τε έτεινε κχὶ ἔτε εξ ωθεντοσαυς.

5 Fug 112. Note τοῦ ὄντος λόγος = *Timaeus* 34 C, ὄντος ἀεὶ λογοσμὸς θεοῦ.

6 *Heras* 188. Cf. *AA.* II.1.6 "So by His (Prāṇa's, the 'Breath's) Word, (*vāc* = *vox*, *verbum*, λόγος), as rope *tanti*), and by names as knots (*dāmani* = δεσμοί) this All is tied" (*sitam*). *Sitam* here is also to be correlated with the concept of the "Bridge of Immortality" or "Sacrificer's Bridge" that links and separates this and yonder world — *ātmā sa setuḥ*, *CU.* VIII.4.1.

7 "The word *markasu*, 'band', 'rope', is employed in Babylonian mythology for the cosmic principle which unites all things, and is also used in the sense of 'support', the divine power and law which holds the universe together" (S. Langdon, *Semitic Mythology*, 1931, p. 109). It is in the same way, also, that the Chinese Tao is called the "link (*hsi*) of all creation" (Chwang Tzu, Ch. VI; in Hughes' version, Everyman's Library No. 973, p. 193). The Babylonians had also a doctrine of the creative Word (*mummu*) of God (Langdon, *ib.* pp. 104, 290; *ERE* XII.749 ff. "Word").

8 For περίοδος (= περφφορά, *Timaeus* 46 D) the literal sense of "circumambulation" is more appropriate, in the present contexts, than that of "revolution," and the more so in that the extension of the pneumatic thread is essentially the divine and royal *procession*. The making of the circuit *in divinis* is reflected in the processions of kings and circuits of judges, and in the custom of the "beating of the bounds." Cf. P. Mus, "Has Brahmā Four Faces," *JISOA.* V, 1937, especially [the] last paragraph of p. 70, and the story of Jotipāla's *cakka-viddham* in *Jātaka* V. 125 f., see in *Ars Islamica* X, 1943, p. 111.

9 *Timaeus* 58 A, B. Διελήλυθε, "charges," like a horse; but other senses of English "charge," e.g. to charge with electric power, or to impose a charge upon anyone, are implicit in the concept of the "bond" although not suggested in this context.

10 *Timaeus* 36 D.

Reason" (λόγῳ κρατήσας) whatever is unreasonable;[1] and secondly from Empedocles for whom it is the Titan Ether (τιτὰν ἠδ' αἰθήρ) that encircles and "constrains all things" (σφίγγων περὶ κύκλον ἅπαυτα).[2]

A further consequence of the concept of the etherial and quintessential *Logos* as the "bond" (δεσμός) of all things illuminates the problem of *destiny* and *necessity*, and their distinction. Philo asks, "Whose is the cord (ὁρμίσκος), whose the ordering (κόσμος),[3] whose the destiny (εἱμαρμένη), the sequence and analogy of all things, with their ever-unbroken chain (εἱρμος)? Whose is the rod (ῥάβδος) . . . whose the kingship? Are they not God's alone?"[4] More specifically, it is the Royal Power of the *Logos* that enjoins what things are to be done, and what not to be done;[5] and accordingly, "the Law (νόμος) is nothing but the Divine *Logos*, prescribing what we are bound (δεῖ) to do, and forbidding what we may not do" and the man-of-culture[6] who "does" the Law is assuredly "doing" the Word of

---

1 *Timaeus* 42 C, cf. Sextus Empiricus on Parmenides, I.3.112.

2 Empedocles fr. 185. "Titan Ether," i.e. Ζεὺσ αἴθριος (Heracleitus fr. 30), Ζεὺσ πατήρ, Philo's "etherial father" to which the soul returns (*Heres* 282-3), Titan, if from τείνω (Hesiod, *Theog.* 207) would be the "Stretcher," a sense that would be most appropriate to the supreme and most ex-*ten*-sive power, cf. *AA.* I.4.3 *prāṇenenam lokaṁ saṁtonoti*; II.4.3 *sa etam puruṣam brahma* [*ta-*] *tatamam apaśyat* —root *tan* "*Grundbegriff spannen, strecken, recken, wie etwa einen Faden (Seil, Sehne), dann aber auch . . . ein Gewebe auspannen*," i.e. lay a warp (Grassman, *Wörterbuch zum Rig-Veda*). Cf. [Philo,] *Conf.* 136.

3 Κόσμος here as in *Protagoras* 322 C, πόλεων κόσμοι τε καὶ δεσμοὶ φιλίας συναγωγοί.

4 *Mut.* 135. The "cord" or "necklace" is a symbol of nature's (i.e. God's) operation, [but should] not [. . .] be confused with the "wheel of necessity" [, cf.] *Somn.* II.44 and *Joseph* 150, and so of keeping one's word [*Fug.* 150, cf. *RV.* IV.33.6, IX.113.4); the cord, together with the signet and rod, symbols of fidelity and training (πανδείκ), are gifts of God to the soul, and are for her adornment. Cf. *JUB.* I.35, where the necklace (*niṣka*), of which the ends meet, is a symbol of the Year and Endless Chant; and *KU.* II.3 where the *sṛnkā vittamnyī* that Naciketas repudiates corresponds to the "golden collar" that Joseph accepts in *Somn.* II.44. "Analogy" to be understood as in *Heres* 152 and *Timaeus* 32 C. On Destiny see V. Cioffari, *Fortune and Fate*, 1935 (Ch. 3, p. 35. Destiny, the cause of incarnation, but temporal instruments condition the body; p. 40, Destiny "the instrument by which Providence utilizes Free-will to ensure the well-being of the Universe, the triumph of Good, and the defeat of Evil"; cf. also Ch. 5).

The catenary nature of destiny is clearly stated in *Asclepius* III.39 (Scott, *Hermetica* I.363, 423, 434, 437, II.413, 423, 433): "*Quam* εἱμαρμένην *nuncupamus, O Asclepie, ea est necessitas omnium, quae gerunter, semper sibi catenatis nexibus vincta*," and its divinity also by the Stoics (Seneca, *De benef.* IV.7.2, *Hunc eundem [Jovem] et Fatum si dexteris, non menteris.*)

The Hermetic dictum (*Stobaeus* I.5.20) that "there is none that can escape from Destiny" suggests that of Rūmī, cited on [page 85,] Note 2. Destiny is an aspect of the First Cause, which is that of our being; Necessity is that of the operation of the mediate Causes, which determine the conditions of our becoming. The distinction is that of the *necessitas infallibilitatis* of an autonomous agent and the *necessitas coactionis* by which a heteronomous subject is governed. To the extent that we cooperate with Destiny we are becoming what we are, and are liberated from Necessity; our Destiny is nothing but a predication of our Destination, which must be reached if we follow its direction. The "own-law" (*sva-dharma*) that determines a vocation (*sva-karma*, τὸ ἑαυτοῦ πραττεῖν) is self-imposed; and since this own-work is "laid down by our own nature" (*sva-bhāva-niyatam*, κατὰ φύσιν) it is to our last end of perfection that it must lead (*BG.* XVIII.45-49). Nothing is more blessed [and] more literally eudaimonic, than the *destined* (*niyatem*) and co-born (*sahaja*) task, the *metier*, that is the very *raison d'etre* of a nativity.

5 *Fug.* 104. Just as the Buddha is both *kiriya-vādī* and an *akiriya-vādī*, a teacher of what-should-be-done, and of what-should-not-be-done, *Vin.* I.233 f., A.I.62. Accordingly, "He who sees the Law (*dhamma*, δικαιοσύνη) sees Me," *ŚB.* III.120.

6 Ἀστεῖος is the exact semantic equivalent of Sanskrit *nāgara*, both denoting a truly civilized elegance and polish and all that is opposite of boorishness. The man who merely "knows what he likes" is not in this sense "clever."

God.[1] The invisible powers which the Creator has extended (ἀπέτεινε = *vitanoti*, *vitate*, *saṁtanoti*, etc.) are "bonds unbreakable" (δεσμὰ . . . ἄρρηκτοι),[2] and "with [these] unbreakable bonds of self-mastery (τοῖς ἀρρήκτοις ἐγκρατείας δεσμοῖς) we should be in earnest to bandage up (κατασεῖν) the apertures of the senses" (τὰ τῶν αἰσθησεων στόμια), for only misery can result if the parts of the soul are left open and loose (λελυσθαί) to admit from without anything and everything without discrimination of quality or quantity,[3] while if their outlets are controlled and "constrained" (συνεσφίγχθαι) this will result in rectitude of life and speech.[4] We recognize, accordingly, a real as well as an etymological connection between the *bonds* (δεσμοί) that have been laid upon us and what we are in duty *bound* (δεῖ) to do; and also that this doing not "as we like" but of the Law, in accordance with the share of the divine free-will in which we have been made participants, is the fulfillment of our *destiny* (*destinare*, "bind" = δέω) — a very different thing from the necessity (ἀναγκη) by which our accidents are determined. And therefore, as Rūmī says, "to flee from that destiny and decree is like fleeing from our own essence, which is absurd."[5]

Winged tetramorph — the Four Evangelists borne on winged and fiery wheels. After Byzantine mosaic, 13th century [A.D.]

---

1 *Migr.* 130.

2 *Migr.* 181.

3 An echo of *Republic* 397-398.

4 *Det.* 100-103. The metaphor of "closing the doors of the senses" is very familiar, e.g. *Migr.* 188; Heracleitus is cited by Sextus Empiricus, *Adv. dogm.* 349, and *BG.* VIII.12 *sarva-dvarani samyamya*; *D.* II.70.

Note the use of σγίγγω, again implying a constraint for good. For "constrained" we might have said "guarded" — as if by sphinxes, for there is really a strict analogy between the doors of the senses and the gates of Paradise, the Kingdom of Heaven being "within you."

5 Rūmī, *Mathnawī* I.970, cf. V.1666. It is of the highest interest that Arabic *qismet*, "portion," is the exact semantic equivalent of εἱμαρμένη, not of αναγκη; and that just as εἱμαρμένη determines the existence or becoming of the soul, but not the manner of its becoming, for which our own constitution is responsible, so in Islam the Word of God, by which the creation is brought about, is only the command to "Be" (*kun*). For all its supposed "fatalism," Islam expressly asserts man's free-will (*qadar*) and responsibility, and is bitterly opposed to "necessitarianism" (*jabr*).

Chapter V

Philo's Doctrine of the Cherubim

PHILO NEVER SPEAKS OF *A* OR *THE* SINGLE CHERUB,[1] AND NEVER MENTIONS sphinxes, though he can hardly have been unaware of the traditional representation of cherubim by winged sphinxes. But the idea of a single "Holy Cherub" seated on the Merkabah (the throne-chariot of *Ezekial*, Ch. 1) appears much later in the writings of Eleazar of Worms, one of the leading lights of mediaeval Hasidism, and it has been recognized by G.G. Scholem[2] that this is "an echo of Philonic thought." This Cherub is an emanation of God's *Shekhinah* or invisible Glory (*kāvōd*), or Her "great fire" that surrounds the throne and from which the human soul also originates. The Cherub can assume every form of angel, man or beast,[3] his human form being the pattern after which God created Man — in other words, the form of Philo's *Logos*,[4] "the image and idea, His Word" that God impressed upon the whole Universe.[5] In any case, however, it will be evident that the nature of the superior principle, of which the Cherubim are aspects charged with delegated functions (those of creation and government, or of mercy and justice) can to some extent be inferred from that of its divisions.[6] This is inherent in the nature of an organic Trinity, to be also in some sense a unity,[7] participation implying kinship.[8] For example, the Cherubim denote ἐπίγνωσις καὶ ἐπιστήμη πολλή,[9] while the ἐπιστήμη θεοῦ is the particular property and domain of the *Logos*;[10] and they and the *Logos* are aspects of one and the same creative Fire.[11] And if we venture to translate these considerations into the terms of the symbols as visually conceived, it will be to say that the nature of the *Logos*, standing between the Cherubim, and however superior to them, will be

---

1 In [the] Old Testament, the singular occurs only in *Ezekial* X.4 "Then the glory (*kāvōd*) of the Lord went up from the Cherub." Philos's exegesis does not reflect *Ezekial.*

2 Gerschom G. Scholem, *Major Trends in Jewish Mysticism*, Jerusalem, 1941, p. 113.

3 Trenaeus (III.11.11) says that the cherubim have four appearances: Those of a lion, calf, man and eagle, representing kingship, priesthood, human nature and *logos*-and-protector. These are, of course, the types of the Four Evangelists; and that their winged symbols are really those of cherubim will be evident from a collation of *Ezekial* I.6 and 10 with X.14; in I.10 the faces are those of a man, a lion, an ox and an eagle, in X.14 those of a "cherub," a man, a lion and an eagle, whence it follows that "cherub" = "ox"; which equation, together [with] the attribution of bovine feet in I.6 supports the analogy of cherubim to the Assyrian *śedu*, whose forms are those of man-bulls.

4 *Opif.* 139. "Man was made a likeness and imitation of the *Logos*." This is not an assertion of man's superiority to women as such, but of the superiority of what is masculine or virile in either with respect to what is feminine or effeminate in either. That "Man" is the Immortal Soul, Soul of the soul, or Pure Mind in every man or woman, as distinguished from their mortal part. (*Spec.* III.207, *LA.* I.31, *Somn.* I.215, *Det.* 83, *Heres* 55 f.)

5 *Somn.* II.45, *Mut.* 135.

6 The distinction of the Powers (attributes or attendants) from their source is only apparent, not real. Cf. E.R. Goodenough, *By Light, Light*, p. 25 and *QE.* II.66-68.

7 *Heres* 213, cf. Plato, *Timaeus* 31 C.

8 *LA.* III.161, cf. Plato, *Protagoras* 322.

9 *Moses* II.97.

10 *Fug.* 76, cf. *Spec.* I.345.

11 *Deo.* 6, 7; Goodenough, *l.c.* p[p]. 31, 41.

that of a Power in some sense cherubimic, for example, winged. Or, if we translate into the terms of the actual iconography, in which the Cherubim are represented by sphinxes, it might have been expected that the third member of the Trinity would also have been represented by a sphinx.

Actually, however, the oldest and most universal form of the symbol that separates the affronted guardian *genii* is the sacred tree (or plant) or pillar. In the oldest examples the tree or pillar is often one of light, either supporting a solar wheel (Fig. 76) or more often having the winged disc of the Sun hovering above it, or even replacing it (Figs. 77 and 78). This winged disc appears in both Syrian and Assyrian art of the second millennium B.C., and notably in the kingdom of the Aryan Mitanni where, as Frankfort remarks, "the winged sun-disk supported by some elaborate pole is the most distinctive trait of the Mitannian glyptic"[1] as a symbol of the royal power of the Sun and Sky.

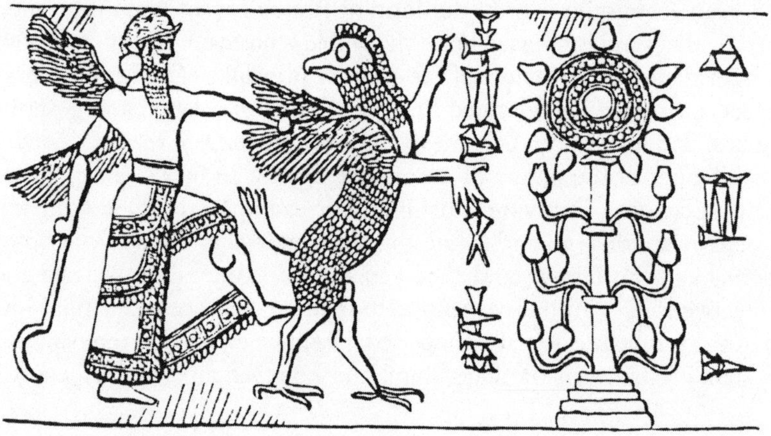

Figure 76: Marduk, Zū and [a] Tree of Light. Museum of Fine Arts, Boston 41.479 (Brett Coll. 129).

It has been thought that the winged disc in Assyrian art is of Egyptian origin and Semitic mediation, and this is possible since the motive occurs already in the art of the Old Kingdom. But as Frankfort himself remarks, "we should be on our guard against considering the Asiatic symbols too exclusively from the Egyptian standpoint," and actually, in the Eighteenth Dynasty, when the Sun-disc assumes its greatest significance, there is more reason to suspect an Asiatic influence on Egypt than the reverse. This occurs most conspicuously in connection with the concept of the life-giving "touch" of the Sun, represented in art by the hands of the Sun, radiating from the disc, and extending the *Ankh* symbol and Breath of Life to the nostrils of the Pharaoh and his Queen.[2] This conception, corresponding to that of *Genesis* II.7 on the one hand and to that of the Indian

1 [H.L. Frankfort, *Seal Cylinders*,] p. 264, 265.

2 A. Moret, *Du caractère religieux de la royauté pharaonique*, Paris, 1902, p. 46, Fig. 2. S. Bey, "Representation of the Solar Deity with human hands and arms," *Ann. des Services des Antiquitiés de l'Egypte*, 38 [1938], p. 53 f.

Figure 77: *Genius* separating sphinxes, guardians of a Tree of Light, below flying Ašur (wing[ed] disc with bearded head). Assyrian seal cylinder, MFA.45.215. Van der Osten, *Brett Catalogue* No. 127.

Sun-kiss on the other, reappears also in Greek mythology in the healing and life-giving "caress" of Zeus, from which Epaphos is begotten; and although the notion of the Sun's rays as extensions of his power and symbolized by hands or feet is characteristically Indian, that of the life-giving kiss is so universal that one would hesitate to suggest it for any precise time or place of origin.[1]

It is not, however, so much with the history of the motives as it is with their significance that we are concerned. It need hardly be demonstrated here that tree, pillar and bird are representations not of different but of one and the same solar, fiery and etherial principle of life and death. It will not surprise us to find that Frankfort thinks that both the sacred tree on Assyrian seals, and the winged disc (in which the archer god himself is sometimes represented) are representations of

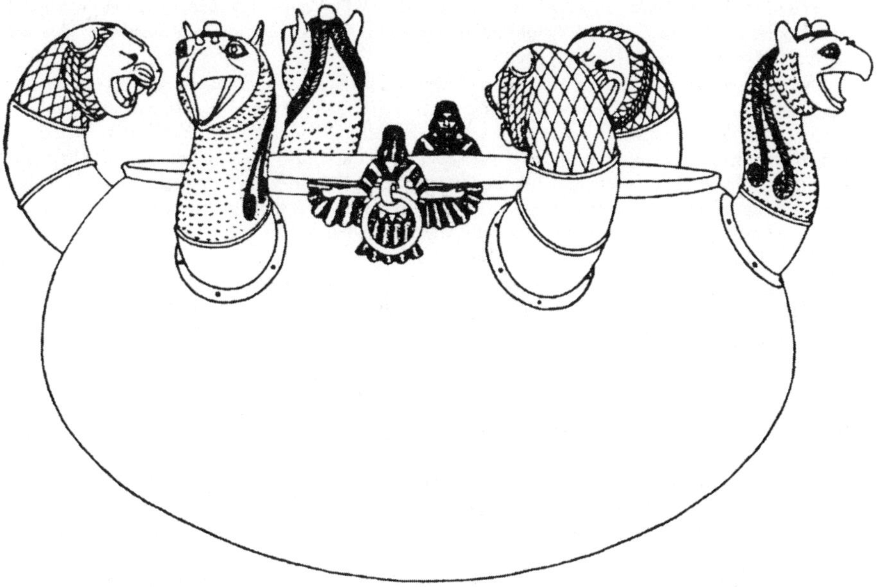

Figure 78: Symbol of the God Ašur on a bronze cauldron from Olympia. Orientalizing style (around 700-650 B.C.). After H.V. Hermann, *Olympische Forschungen*, IV, pl. 4.

[1] On the Sun-kiss see my "Sun-kiss," in *JAOS.* 60 [1940]; for Epaphos, [see] Aeschylus, Supplement 40 f., 312-315, 575 f. and *Prom.* 850; and for the hands of the Sun in Vedic scriptures and Egyptian iconography, [see] H. Güntert, *Der arische Weltkönig und Heiland* [1923], pp. 156-169, E.H. Sturtevant, "Indic speech and religion" in *Yale Classical Studies* I [1928], pp. 226-7 and E.R. Goodenough, "Hellenistic Kingship," *ibid.* pp. 80-82.

the "national god, Ašur";[1] or that in the Mediterranean area Evans should long ago have recognized in the cult pillar "an aspect of the Sun-God."[2] It appears that [the Mitannians] "or their ancestors" [were] speakers of an Indic language and worshipped well-known Indian deities. [These peoples] "exercised a powerful influence upon Assyrian religion" and "the god Ašur was borrowed from the Indic nation during their sojourn in or near northeast Mesopotamia" in or before the fourteenth century.[3] It will not be out of place to point out that in India Agni Vaiśvānara, the most universal form of the Fire of Life, King and Spectator of this entire Universe and often identified with the Sun,[4] is not only Lord of Trees (*vanaspati*) but also thought of architecturally as a "pillar" extending from the altar-navel of the earth to the sky[5] and as "a pillar of Life standing at the parting of the seven ways, in the nest of the Highest,"[6] and is described as "bird-like perched upon a tree, vociferous with light as priest with speech";[7] while in another text he is spoken of as a "golden disk (*rumka*) glorious with glory," and it is said with reference to the "Golden Reed,"[8] i.e. pillar of fire and *Axis Mundi* that "in it there sitteth the Eagle, and hath his nest,"[9] and so, indeed, "they do call the Sun a sky-supporting pillar."[10] Nor is it inconsistent with the fact that the Sun and Fire are powers both of life and death[11] that it should be said of the Goddess of Death, Nirṛti, that "like Savitṛ (Sun) of true laws, and like Indra, *she* standeth at the meeting of the ways."[12]

---

1 H. Frankfort, *Seal Cylinders*, 1939, pp. 205, 208. Cf. also W.H. Ward, "The Babylonian Representation of the Solar Disk," *Am. J. Theol.* II [1898] pp. 115-118 and B. Pering, "*Die geflügelte Scheiben in Assyrian*," *Archiv für Orientforschung* III [1932] pp. 281-286.

For representations of Ašur in the winged disc see seal no. 85 in G.A. Eisen, *Ancient Oriental Cylinders and Other Seals . . . Collection of Mrs. W.H. Moore*, Chicago 1941, pl. X, and the *faience* reproduced by W. Andrae, *Farbige Keramik aus Assur*, pl. 8 and by Frankfort, *Cylinder Seals*, Fig. 64, as well as the representation on the eleventh century "broken obelisk" in the British Museum illustrated by Frankfort, *l.c.* Fig. 63. In all such representations Ašur is armed, like Apollo, with bow and arrow, and is also a rain-god; but a comparison of Frankfort's two figures will show that he is wrong in regarding the feathered wings as clouds; in Fig. 63 only the pointed form on the right represents a cloud.

2 Arthur Evans, *l.c.* p. 173.

3 E.H. Sturtevant, "Indic Speech and Religion in Western Asia," *Yale Classical Studies* I [1928] pp. 225, 226.

4 *Ṛgveda* I.98.1; *Nirukta* VII.23.

5 *Ṛgveda* I.59.1, IV.5.1, IV.6.2.

6 *Ṛgveda* X.5.6, cf. *Chāndogya Upaniṣad* V.3.2. Cf. *Proverbs* VIII.2 "in the places of the path."

7 *Ṛgveda* X.115.5; cf. VI.3.5 "archer-like . . . and even as a bird that perches in a tree."

8 *Ṛgveda* IV.58; Atharva Veda X.8.41 (Prajāpati).

9 *Taittirīya Saṁhitā* IV.2.9.6. *Rukma*: "*Insbesondere wird die Sonne als das* Gold *oder* Goldschmuck *des himmels . . . bezeichnet*" (Grassman, *s.v.* in *Wörterbuch zum Rig-Veda*); notably *Ṛgveda* VI.51.1.

10 *Jaiminīya Upaniśad Brahmaṇa* I.6.10.

11 Agni's, Prajāpati's, Hiranyagarbha's "shadow" (*chāyā*: shelter, refuge) is both of life and death." God's shadow (σκίκ θεοῦ) is his Word (*Logos*) . . . the archtype for further imagery," and notably the image after which Man was made" (*LA.* III.96, cf. *Somn.* I.206), *viz.* the "Man in this man" (*Conq.* 97), Plato's "inner Man" (*Republic* 589 B) and the "God of Socrates" (Apuleius), *is qui intus est* (*II. Corinthians* IV.16), the invisible, ineffable (*anadiṣṭah*, literally ἀδεικτος as in *Heres* 130) "Inner Person of all beings," who is our real Self (*Aitareya Āraṇyaka* III.2.4, *Maitri Upaniṣad* VI.7), "Soul of the soul, its governing part" (*Heres* 55), "Immortal in the mortal" (*Conq.* 97), "thy Self, the *Logos*" (Marcus Aurelius VIII.40).

12 *Taittirīya Saṁhitā* IV.2.5.5. Nirrti ("dissolver," "separator," etc.), antithesis of *prārpaṇaḥ*, epithet of the immortal Agni in *Ṛgveda* X.45.5. But there are (as in the Greek traditions) "two Fires," friendly and unfriendly, sacerdotal and royal, sacrificial and domestic, opposed to one another (*Taittirīya Saṁhitā* V.2.7.6, *Aitareya Brāhmaṇa* III.4, *Śatapatha Brāhmaṇa* II.3.2.10 etc.), and to

(Continued on following page.)

The Sun, in Philo's third sense, is the symbol of the Divine *Logos*,[1] the Man who is both Mind and Word,[2] ὁ νοῦς, ἔνθιρμον καὶ πεπυρωμένον πυεῦμα i.e. *intellectus vel spiritus*[3] and Monitor of the soul,[4] and it is to this immanent principle of life and *gnosis* that he refers when he speaks of "the central pillar in the house, *viz.* the Mind in the soul, and its most healing remedy."[5]

It is said of the incarnate *Bambino* (Agni) that the body is his hearth, the head his roof, he himself is the central Breath (*madhyamaḥ prāṇaḥ*), the Breath is his pillar (*sthūṇā*).[6] This Breath, corresponding to Philo's θεῖον πνεῦμα or πνοή "the most life-giving Spirit of God,"[7] and repeatedly identified with the Sun ("the Spiritual-Self (*ātman*) of all that is mobile or immobile"),[8] Agni, Indra, Brahman, Sun, Life (*āyus*) and Death (*mṛtyu*),[9] is at the same time the

---

(Continued from preceding page.)

the destructive (*kravyat*, "flesh-eating") one of these are applied to the terms *nirṛtha* and *nirṛta* (masculine) as they are also to "Yama, Death, the archer" (*Atharva Veda* VI.9.1, 3, XII.2.14). Conversely, Yama's nature is also friendly, e.g. in *Ṛgveda* X.135.1, as *viśpati*, "Lord of the settlers"; and the two are often, and rightly, identified. Thus the powers of life and death are unified in both (cf. references in *JAOS.* 60.47), but necessarily divided in their operation, and when thus affronted can be regarded as contrasting in sex as well as other respects.

Nirṛti is the feminine counterpart of Yama *nirṛta*, and he being the King of Justice (*dharmā-rājā*) and the stern Judge of the dead, she is implicitly that Justice (*dharmā*, διακαιοσύνη) by which he rules, and so corresponds to Parmenides' "Penal Justice" (Δίκη πολύποινος, f.) who keeps the keys of the etherial gates to which "the road of the Daimon" leads, and opens them only to the true knower (σαφῆ . . . εἰδός), Parmenides in Sextus Empiricus, *Adv. dogm.* 111. With the admission of the "true knower," or perhaps "truth-knower," cf. *Jaiminīya Upaniśad Brāhmaṇa* I.5 where the Sun is the stern Janitor, and being himself the Truth, admits the sooth-sayer as like to like, and a *Bṛhadāraṇyaka Upaniṣad* V.15.1 where the dying man appeals to Yama, the Sun, to discover himself to be one whose essential quality is truth.

1. *Somn.* I.85.
2. *Det.* 83.
3. *Fug.* 133.
4. *Fug.* 131
5. *Migr.* 124, cf. *Maitri Upaniṣad* IV.3. In connection with the symbolism of the "house" in the traditional psychology it will be of interest to compare *Fug.* 212 where "the angels are members-of-the-house (οἰκέται) of God, and gods themselves" with *Bṛhadāraṇyaka Upaniṣad* V.14.4 where the Breaths (*prāṇaḥ*, sensitive powers of the soul, elsewhere often called gods, *devāḥ*, or sometimes gales, *murutaḥ*) are called the "household servants" (*gayaḥ*) of the Self, and *Satapatha Brāhmaṇa* II.5.3.4 where the Maruts are officiants-in-the-domestic-sacrifice, *gṛhamedhinaḥ* — for "the Breaths are gods, mind-born, mind-yoked, in them one sacrifices metaphysically" (*Taittirīya Saṁhitā* VI.1.4.5). Alternatively, the two cherubimic or many other Powers (δυάμεις = *śaktayaḥ*) that Philo generally calls "guardsmen" (δορυφόροι) are called in the Indian contexts "allies" (*āpayaḥ*) or are a regiment of the King's "own" (*svāḥ*).
6. *Bṛhadāraṇyaka Upaniṣad* II.2.1.
7. *Opif.* 29, 30. This πνεῦμα is "the substance of the soul," *not* the physical ἀήρ that we breathe, and to be distinguished from the "blood soul" or physical life that even irrational beings possess (*Det.* 81, 83; *Heres* 55 f., 61; *Spec.* IV.123); not the carnal soul (*nefeṣ*) but "*in* the soul" (Plato, *Axiochus* 370 C) as that by which it is empowered (*LA.* I.37, *Opif.* 67), and the fiery Mind (*Fug.* 133) — "spirit" as distinguished by St. Paul from "soul" (*Hebrews* IV.12). For the distinction of the Spirit of Life from the physical breath of life cf. *Kaṭha Upaniṣad* V.5, "it is not by his breathing in and out that any mortal lives, but by another (*Vāyu*, the Gale), on whom these two spirations lean."
8. *Ṛgveda* I.115.1.
9. References too many to be cited here. For Brahman, *Bṛhadāraṇyaka Upaniṣad* III.9.16; for the Sun and Death *Aitareya Āraṇyaka* II.2.4, *Śatapatha Brāhmaṇa* II.2.3.4, X.5.2.1-5, 13, 14, 16, 20, 23.

"hall-post" (*śala-vaṁśa*) or king-post (*sthūṇā-rājā*) of the cosmic house and the central principle of the microcosmic house that each of us inhabits; and all the parts and powers of the composite individual (Philo's σύγκριμα, [cf.] Plato's *Timaeus*) both rest upon and are derived from this primary principle in which they meet like the rafters of the house in its perforated roofplate which correspond to the Sun (-door) macrocosmically and to the bregmatic fontanel microcosmically.[1] The central or median position of the Breath in relation to the powers of the soul that arise from it is equally emphasized by Philo and in the Indian texts.

Philo thinks of all good, and indeed of the whole heaven and universe, as the "fruit of the Tree of God's eternal and evergreen nature,"[2] and also speaks of "the Tree of Life, that is to say, of Wisdom" (σοφία).[3] Nature and Wisdom are grammatically feminine, but there can be no question that the Tree or Column in Palestinian art, by its very position between the guardian powers, represents the *Logos*, grammatically masculine. I do not think that Philo ever expressly identifies the *Logos* with the Tree, unless in *Mut.* 140 cited above. For him the *Logos* is either invisible, and therefore not represented on the Mercy seat (*Fug.* 101); or anthropomorphically conceived, and represented by the living image of the High Priest,[4] or described as an "armed angel, the *Logos* of God, standing in the way, and through whom both good and evil (events) come to their fulfillment";[5] but also the mental presentation (φάντασμα) of "the image of God, his angel, the *Logos*" in the form of a pillar (στήλη), which is "the symbol of stability, dedication

---

1 References in my "Symbolism of the Dome," *Indian History Quarterly* XIV [1938] pp. 1-56; *Svayamātṛṇṇā: Janua Coeli*," *Zalmoxis* II [1939] pp. 3-51; "Sun-kiss," *JAOS.* 60 [1940] pp. 46-67 (pp. 58, 59, on the Breath as Kingpost); and for the Breath more generally. "On the One and Only Transmigrant," *JAOS. Supplement* 3 [1944].

2 *Mut.* 140; cf *Migr.* 125 οἷα φύτον . . . σοφία. Like *Śāṅkhāyana Āraṇyaka* XI.2 "As a great green tree with moistened roots, so Brahman stood," cf.*Ṛgveda* I.182.7 "What tree was that, that stood in the midst of the sea, to which Bhujyu clung?" X.31.7, and 81.4 "What was the wood, and what the tree of which they fashioned Heaven and Earth?" answered in *Taittirīya Brāhmaṇa* II.8.9.6 "the wood was Brahman, Brahman the tree . . . there stands Brahman, world-supporting." *CU.* VI.11.1.

3 *LA.* III.52, cf. *Genesis* III.6. Irenaeus, *Adv. haer.* I.27 "the Tree which is itself also called Gnosis"; Eriugena (cited, Bett, p. 79) "the Tree of Life, which is Christ." *Maitri Upaniṣad* VI.4, Brahman, "called the Sole of Asvattha ('Peepul') . . . man's Sole Awakener" (*eka sambodhayitṛ*), which is also the Bodhi Tree, seated under which, at the navel of the Earth, Gautama became *abhisambuddha*, "the Wide Awake" (*Dīgha Nikāya* II.4). It should be remarked that in the *Maitri* context the Branches of the Tree are the Five Elements, ether and air, fire, water, [and] earth.

4 *Migr.* 102, cf. *Fug.* 108 f. It is in imitation of the *Logos* that the High Priest wears in outward operation the variegated cosmic robe, and when he enters the Holy of Holies, the white (etherial) robe, corresponding to the etherial (*QE.* II.91) essence of the sanctuary.

In some cases the winged disc of the Babylonian seals is supported, not by a tree or pillar, but by a man, an "Atlas," with uplifted arms, e.g. seal 87 in G.A. Eisen, *Ancient Oriental Cylinders and Other Seals . . . Collection of Mrs. W.H. Moore*, Chicago, 1940, pl. X; or the figure between the *genii* may be that of a nude goddess (*ib.* seal 88).

5 *Cher.* 35-36. "Good and evil" here, not in the moral sense, but *kalyāṇa*, *papa* (pulcher, turpis), but *sukha*, *duhkha*. Such eventful goods and evils, occasions of pleasure and pain, are to be patiently endured; whereas the *Logos* teaches us to choose between the moral good and evil (*Cher.* 31, *Fug.* 130 and *passim*). The eventful goods and evils are not of the logical Destiny (εἱμαρμένη, *dharma*) but of irrational Necessity (ἀνάνκη, *karma*): The *Logos* is their permissive cause by the very fact of the creation of a spatial-temporal world that cannot but be conditioned by the "pairs" (ἐναντία, *dvandvau*), *Heres* 207 etc.

and inscription" [and] is a likeness of the Governor of all the Powers, the mighty *Logos* through whom the universe is ordered and on whom it rests securely better than the human or angelic forms."[1] Or the *Logos* is, obviously enough, symbolized by the turning (στρεφομένη in LXX) fiery sword of *Genesis* III,[2] by the central and highest light of the seven branched Golden Candlestick.[3] In the last two cases the symbolism is directly and explicitly solar, and the same is implied in *QE.* II.67 of which Goodenough remarks that "the solar character of the figure is at once indubitable."[4] In other words, the *Logos* is the Sun and Light of men; he who, being risen, draws all men unto him.[5] We have already seen that the Tree and Pillar are specifically solar symbols, and will only add that the seven-branched candlestick belongs to the "candelabra" type of the Tree of Light, so familiar on Assyrian seals and in the Indian iconography.

Actually, there is a good deal of evidence to show that the Tree or Column is often the representation of a goddess rather than a god. The pillar with volutes, Ionic column, which has lost in our eyes its symbolic value and has become a mere art-form, the index of a "style," when used as a written sign in combination with a divine determinant, denoted the Sumerian Goddess Innin, the later Ishtar and Anahita.[6] It has been shown also, rather conclusively, that in Palestinian art the sacred tree between affronted animals originally represented a Phoenician and Canaanite Mother-goddess of Love and Fertility, Asherah or Ashtoreth, evidently to be equated with Ishtar;[7] and there can be no doubt that in Egypt [the] sycamore and palm are aspects of the *Dea Nutrix*, for there are many representations of both in which the arms and bust of the Goddess issue from the trunk, holding forth

---

1 *Somn.* I.240-242, cf. 157, 158.

2 *Cher.* 26-28. The revolving fiery sword is a well-known type of the "active door," i.e. Sundoor or Sun-wheel; it is the two-edged sword of the Word of God that sunders the soul from spirit (*Hebrews* IV.12), all that is mortal from what survives the perilous passage.

3 *Heres* 215-226. The main stem of the Candlestick, which supports the Sun, corresponds, of course, to the *Axis Mundi*, the "straight light like a pillar . . . Heaven's bond" (σύνδεσμος) of *Republic* 616 B, C, rightly understood by Stewart, and *skambha* of the *Atharva Veda* X.7, etc., uniting and dividing Heaven and Earth, and which is also the "one foot" of the Ibex, *aja ekapād*, "prop of the sky and world progenitor" (*divo dhartā bhuvanasya prajāpatiḥ*, *Ṛgveda* IV.53.2, X.65.13), who with his pillar upholdeth the sky (VIII.41.10).

4 E.R. Goodenough, *By Light, Light*, p. 26 [; for] Hochma, see MacDonald.

5 *Ṛgveda* I.164.4, IV.54.4; *John* I.4, XII.32.

6 W. Andrae, "*Schrift und Bild*," *Analecta Orientalia* 12 [1935], p. 2. Note that the two halves of this pregnant form give rise to the paired doorposts (cf. *Proverbs* VIII.34) with rings; and that these doorposts being the *living* guardians of the Sundoor (as is often explicit in the iconography and the whole Symplegades concept), Andrae (p. 5) is perfectly correct in inferring [the] androgenous "Polaritat" of the primary form, which he identifies with that of the Tree of Life.

7 D. Nielsen, "*Die altsemitische Muttergottin*," *ZDMG.* 92 [1938]; H.G. May, "The Sacred Tree on Palestinian Painted Pottery," *JAOS.* 59 [1939], pp. 251-259; cf. Ilberg, *Die Sphinx* . . . p. 37. The Hebrews would naturally have repudiated these pagan goddesses, but in making use of an essentially pagan iconography [they] might very naturally have seen in the Tree a symbol of the "Wisdom" (Hochma, Sophia of *Proverbs* VIII "My fruit is better than gold . . . Blessed is the man that heareth me . . . watching at the posts of my doors . . . for whoso findeth me, findeth life," etc.). The parallel with Vāc, the Word, the *Dea Nutrix*, of *Ṛgveda* X.25 is very evident, and it should not be overlooked that this Word "indwelling sky and Earth, holds fast (*ārabh* = *labh* = λαμβάνω [εἰς χεῖρας]) all existence," a concept expanded in *Aitareya Āraṇyaka* II.1.6 where "with God's Word as cord (*tanti*) and names as knots (*dāma* = δεσμός) all this universe is tied."

Figure 79: Date palm with [the] Goddess offering food and drink, Egyptian relief, 18th Dynasty. Berlin. After Otto Puchstein, *Die Iönische Saule*, Leipzig, 1907, Abb. 15.

food and drink.[1] In fine, the Tree of Life is not in any systematic or exclusive sense of determinate sex, but rather the symbol of a divinity that may be thought of as either male or female, or better is the principle from which these differentiations are derived, male and female being the accidents rather than the essence of the "Man"; for it is not to him who became our Inner Man, but to the bodily and mortal nature only that the distinction of "man" from "woman" applies.[2] The "image" of God, the pattern of the *Logos*, after which the "Man in this man or that woman" was made is "bodiless and neither male nor female"[3] but a unity of both at once, for "to the image of God He created him; male and female created He them."[4] For all this there are many exact parallels in the Indian sources.[5] From Philo's point of view or, indeed, that of the whole traditional scheme of the divine procession — *a principio vivente conjuncto*[6] — [the] born image of the supreme God (ὁ θεός), to which he generally refers as θεός without the article,[7] presented

---

1 E.g., the relief in Berlin 90. Puchstein, *Die ionische Säule*, Leipzig, 1915, Abb. 15 (here Fig. 79), corresponding to the *Bharhut* and *Bodhgayā* illustrations (here Fig. 80) of the Story of the Treasurer (*Dhammapada Atthakathā* I.204), except that in this story the tree spirit is male. The Indian tree spirits are either male or female, but the Greek Dryad is always feminine.

2 *Heres* 139. Similarly St. Thomas Aquinas, *Sum. Theol.* I.47.3 ad. 3, "Man is the form; this man [or woman] is the form in matter."

3 *Opif* 134; *Galatians* III.28 "according to the image of Him that created him, where there is neither male nor female."

4 *Genesis* I.27. The biunity of the image is the ultimate basis of Plato's [myth, as well as others, cf. Philo, *Heres* 139,] of man's original androgyny. That the immortal part of human beings is called the "Man" also explains [the] conception of regeneration as "man," and the Islamic exclusion of "women" from Paradise; the real distinction from this point of view being not of physical sex, but of virility from effeminacy. Cf. also my "Tantric Doctrine of Divine Biunity" in *Ann. Bhandarkar Res. Inst.* XIX [1938] pp. 173-183, and "Ūnātiriktau and Atyaricyata" in *New Indian Antiquary* VI [1943] pp. 52-56.

5 Notably *Bṛhadāraṇyaka Upaniṣad* I.1-3 where the Self (*ātman*) as Person (*puruśa*, i.e. Prajāpati, Progenitor) is originally *agre* = ἐνάρχῇ) "like a man and a woman closely embraced . . . himself made to fall apart, thence arose 'husband' and 'wife'"; *Aitareya Āraṇyaka* II.3.8.5 where the immortal Breath (*prāṇa*) can neither be spoken of as female, male or neuter; and *Śvetāsvatara Upaniṣad* V.10 where the Lord of the Breaths (*prāṇādhipati*) "without beginning or end, in the midst of multiplicity, the omniform one by whom the universe is generated and circumvested" is neither feminine nor masculine nor sexless.

6 St. Thomas Aquinas, *Sum. Theol.* I.27.2.

7 *Somn.* I.229.

little difficulty. "Nature," for him and in earlier Greek philosophy,[1] even also in Christian theology,[2] does not always or even often mean now what the term means to us, our physical environment (*natura naturata, materia secunda*), but the divine power that "natures" everything, making, for example, a horse horsey and men human. It is only from this point of view that we can understand the conceptions of all sin as an infringement of the Natural Law, of all human law as "just" insofar as it is based on the Natural Law, and that all of art as "correct" insofar as it is "an imitation of Nature in her manner of Operation: For the *Logos is* this Law,[3] and Nature and Essence are one *in divinis*.

Another aspect of the problem already alluded to, is that of the coincidence of contraries in their common principle, of which very simple examples can be cited in the abstract concept of "time" which may be either past or future and that of twilight marking the conjunction of darkness with light. But it will be observed that such collective or middle terms, like the Sanskrit duals that denote a *mixta persona* are grammatically speaking designations not of unities but of composites; for the unity of past and future without composition we have to employ the "now" (of eternity) in which the past and future merge and

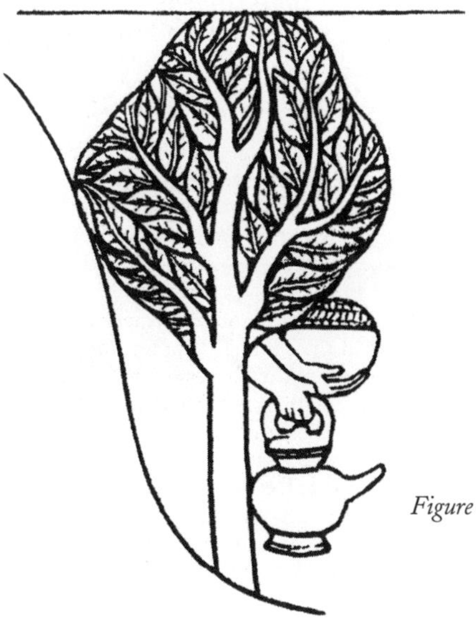

Figure 80: ["The Story of the Treasurer" in *Dhammapada Atthakatha* (Dh. A.I. 203 sqq.), after a bas-relief from Bharut. Drawing by Ananda Kentish Coomaraswamy. — Ed.]

---

1 *Heres* 115, that "invisible Nature" that is the beginning (ἀρχή) of all things"; *Fug.* 172 "God alone, the noblest Nature"; *Sac.* 98, the "unborn Nature" who yet gives birth, and is not to be distinguished from the "unborn God," *ib.* 101 — as in *Śvetāśvatara Upaniṣad* I.9, "She, too, is unborn." Plato, *Laws* 773 E "the ever-generative Nature," *Timaues* 52 C, "true and sleepless Nature." Sextus Empiricus reminds us, those whom the Greeks called "Physicists, from Thales down" regarded the evidence of the senses as unreliable, and "set up reason (λόγος, cf. Heracleitus frs. I, II) as the judge of truth as regards the real essences; and starting from this arranged their doctrines of first-principles and elements and the rest, the apprehension of which is by the power of Reason" (*Adv. dogm.* I.89, 9). In other words, the Greek "Physicists" were not at all in our sense of the word "Naturalists," but much rather philosophers, contemplatives or theologians who, like Socrates (*Phaedo* 79 C, D), held that the senses can never lead us to a knowledge of reality because their report is always of inconstants that can never be known because they never stop to be.

2 St. Augustine, *De trin.* XIV.9 "That Nature, to wit, that created all others." *Natura naturans, Creatrix universalis, Deus.*

3 Explicit in *Opif.* 1, *Migr.* 130; cf. *Opif* 143, where "the *recta ratio* (ὀρθος λόγος) of Nature is the Law of God." The *Logos* is thus the "Common Law" Heracleitus fr. XCI, XCII, Plato *Laws* 644) which to obey or "do" is to participate in God's Freewill (*Immut.* 47, *Confessions* 94, *Somn.* II.74, *Migr.* 130; *James* I.25; St. Thomas Aquinas, *Sum. Theol.* I.26 — "the soul is free insofar as it obeys reason"). So that, as Marcus Aurelius says "for a rational being the same act is both natural (κατὰ φύσιν) and deliberate (κατὰ λόγον, VII.11).

by which they are divided, while for a twilight shorn of its duality there is no term in English, though [we] have the very striking Sanskrit expression *brahmabhūti* (*theosis, deificatio*) as the analogical, *paramārthika* equivalent of *sandhi*, twilight.[1] In many ancient or heiratic languages, however, it is not unusual to find "polar" words which represent the common principle of pairs or contraries,[2] and without discussing this in detail, it will be pertinent to our present theme to cite the case of θεός, used in Homer and often also much later with prefixed ὁ to denote a masculine and with ἡ to denote a feminine divinity, the implication being that both are essentially "God," but only accidentally "God" or "Goddess."

Philo points out (what would be obvious to any student of Indian mythology[3]) that grammatical gender is not always a valid indication of actual functions, and expressly identifies the *Logos* of God with the Wisdom (Σοφία)

---

1 I cannot take up here the extremely important problem of the Symplegades and that of the "Golden Mean" (Webster, "the way of wisdom and safety between extremes" — *aurea mediocritas*, by no means in the modern pejorative sense "mediocrity"), and the *raison d'être* of ritual acts to be performed at dawn or dusk when it is neither Day or Night. [We] shall only refer to Parmenides (in Sextus Empiricus *Adv. dogm.* 111): "There are the gates etherial dividing Day and Night," to which "the road of the Daimon" leads, and to *Opif.* 33, 34 where Philo describes the opposition (ἐναντιότης) and clash (διαμάχη) of Day and Night, and how the incorporeal and intelligible barriers (ὅροι) of Dawn and Dusk were set in their midst (ἐν μέσος, the place of the timeless *Logos*, He of whom it is said that "no man cometh to the Father but through Me") to disdain them; for which there are many striking Indian parallels, notably that of *Jaiminīya Brāhmaṇa* I.11 where between the two great seas of Day and Night (the jaws of Time, the devourer of lives) there runs a bar or bridge for those who sacrifice at dawn and dusk; which is an imitation of the First Sacrifice, when Indra slew Namuci (Vṛtra, Death) "neither with anything dry or anything wet, and neither by day nor night" (*Maitreyanī Saṁhitā* IV.3.4, *Śatapatha Brāhmaṇa* XII.7.3.1 etc.). The "nows" of the twilights are momentous of Eternity in which all whens are one.

2 On the polarity of words see Karl Abel, *Über den Gegensinn der Urworte*, 1884; R. Gordis, "Effects of Primitive Thought on Language" *American Journal of Semitic Language and Literature*, 55 [1938] 270 f; B. Heimann, "Plurality, Polarity and Unity in Hindu Thought" in *BSOS.* IX [1937-39] pp. 1015-21 and "The Polarity of the Indefinite" in *JISOA.* V [1937] pp. 36-40 (especially Note 18); M. Fowler, "Polarity in the Rig-Veda" in *Review of Religion* VII [1942] pp. 115-123.

Conversely, abstract nouns can be formed by combining the pairs of which they denote the one essence: For example, in Chinese, "big-small" = "size," and in Sanskrit "dark-light" (*chāyā-tapau*) corresponds to Dionysius' "divine darkness, blinding by excess of light." These are illustrations of Philo's dictum, that "two opposites together form a single whole" (*Heres* 213) and that of St. Thomas Aquinas, "*contraria conveniunt in genere uno, et etiam conveniunt in ratione essendi*" (*Sum. Theol.* I.49.3 ad 1). It will be observed that every such group forms a Trinity corresponding to Philo's divisive and unifying *Logos* with any two of its contrasting powers. These contrasted powers are the "lions in the path," cherubim, or "clashing rocks" between which runs the "narrow way" of those who would be "delivered from the pairs of opposites" of which the wall of Paradise is built and after which the gate is called "strait" (*Bhagavad Gītā* VIII.28, XV.5; Nicolas of Cusa, *De vis. Dei.* IX, *Matthew* VII.13, 14).

3 Much of the pertinent material is summarized in my *Spiritual Authority and Temporal Power in the Indian Theory of Government*, New Haven, 1942, pp. 38-41, especially with reference to Varuṇa and Dyaus. There also [are] many references to "Prājapati as a mother-being" (Caland, *Pañcaviṁśa Brāhmaṇa*, 1931, p. 659), e.g. *Pañcaviṁśa Brāhmaṇa* VII.6.1, X.3.1 and even to his breasts and his milk (*ib.* XIII.11.18, *Śatapatha Brāhmaṇa* II.5.1.3, etc.). Cf. my "Tantric Doctrine of Divine Biunity" in *Annals of Bhandarkar Oriental Research Institute*, XIX [1938] pp. 173-183; also S.M.A., "God is Our Mother," in *Blackfriars* (Supplement No. 15, *Life of the Spirit*) May 1945.

of God,[1] notwithstanding that he knows that the one is the Son and the other the Daughter of God.[2] Of the Daughter of God, Sophia, the Mother of All things, whom he identifies with the "Rock" from which the soul can "suck honey" (*Deuteronomy* XXXII.13), he says that from her breasts she gives to all her children the nourishment they need, and thinks of her as the River of Life, as it were of honey for sweetness and of oil for light;[3] though he differentiates this motherhood from hers whom Adam named Eve (Ζωή), i.e. αἴσ θήσις,[4] who is the "mother of all living" only in the limited physical sense, whereas Sophia's motherhood is that of the "really and truly living" for whom the natural life is not an end but only the means to the end of knowledge.[5] So he says again of the Daughter of God, Sophia, that while her name is feminine, her nature is virile; and that she is not only masculine, "but a father, sowing and begetting in souls aptness to learn."[6] Nonetheless is God "the only true generator and sower," and "only truly wise (σοφός)."[7] Sophia corresponds in many ways to Athene, and to the Muse, or Muses collectively, who are the daughters of Zeus or Ouranos,[8] or of the Sun, as the

---

1 *LA.* I.65; Goodenough, *By Light, Light*, p. 23.

2 *Confessions* 146; *Fug.* 51,52. Just as the Indian Varuṇa, feminine to Mitra = Savitṛ, is nevertheless male to his own domain; and as the "great Brahman" (grammatically neuter) is feminine to Krishna (*Bhagavad Gītā* XIV.3, 4) and all beings are "its" children (*brahmayonini, ib.* VII.5, 6, cf. *Muṇḍaka Upaniṣad* III.1.3), that is to say are Krishna's, who is both "the Father and the Mother of the Universe" (*ib.* IX.17). Underlying all such formulations is the orthodox assumption that "Nature and Essence are one in God."

The explanation of the secondary development of "grammatical feminine formations" (A. Texeira-Barbaro in *Review of Religion* IX [1945] p. 229) is neither grammatical or sociological, but ontological, and parallels the secondary development of the Kingship, originally coincident with Priesthood. The grammatical development parallels that of the Nature which the Divine Essence separates from itself "as a mother of whom to be born" (St. Augustine, *Contra V. Haer.* v, like *Pañcaviṁśa Brāhmaṇa* VII.6.2-3). In other words, "primitive" man, the metaphysician whose traces survive even in modern speech, thought first and named the MAN in all men, and only afterwards and for practical purposes distinguished the categories of "this man" and "that woman." Even today, "man" often means the human being of either sex. It should not be overlooked that our current expression "the common man" originally referred not to the average "man," but to the *homo communis*, the immanent *Logos*, in everyman, and woman.

3 *Det.* 115-116; *LA.* II.49, 50. "Milk," as in *Atharva Veda* VIII.10.22-29.

4 Αἰσθήσις, always feminine as contrasted with νοῦς, masculine, and as Vāc (feminine) is contrasted with Manas (grammatically neuter but functionally masculine), these two forming a progenitive pair of which our notions are the "concept." But αἰσθήσις coincides with νοῦς when she follows him "forsaking the ways of woman" (*LA.* 49, 50, *Abr.* 99 f., *Fug.* 128 (*Genesis* XVIII.11): I.e. when the Mind is purified (*Maitri Upaniṣad* VI.34.6) and we "repent" (cf. my *Spiritual Authority* . . . , Note 40, and "On Being in One's Right Mind" in *Review of Religion* VII [1942] pp. 32-40).

5 *Heres* 53. The distinction of Sophia from Eve is that of the eternal from the temporal Theotokos; that of the Māyā (Μητις, Σοφία, Hochma, *kauśalyā*) of God, the *Māyin*, from the analogous Māyā of whom the Buddha is born on Earth; and that of the "divine" from the "human womb," the sacrificial and the domestic fires or hearths, from which the spiritual and the natural man are respectively "born again" (*Jaiminīya Brāhmaṇa* XVIII.1) in the sense of *John* III.6-8 and *Galatians* VI.8.

6 *Somn.* I.51, 52.

7 *Heres* 171, 172 and *Confessions* 94.

8 *Iliad* II.49; Hesiod, *Theog. passim*; Mimnermus in *Pausanias* IX.29.2.

Heliades or Helicon, daughters of Mnemosyne, without whose guidance none can follow the steep path of wisdom that leads to the etherial gates whose keys are kept by "Punitive Justice,"[1] and that are opened only for those whom *they* have led.[2] It is significant enough that the Muses are called "Reminders," and that they are, in fact, the different aspects or powers of their common mother Mnemosyne, "Memory"; since there is no salvation but for the soul that remembers.[3] [It is] needless to say that Sophia also corresponds to Isis;[4] and in almost every respect to the Indian Sāvitrī, daughter of the Sun, and like Sophia, the mother of every initiate.

An interesting parallel to Philo's conception of the two Guardsmen (δορυφόροι) of the Providential Power occurs in the Hermetic fragment, XXVI.3 (Scott, *Hermetica* I.516): "For there are (two) guardsmen of the Universal Providence. One of them is the Keeper of Souls (ψυχοταμίας), the other the Guide of Souls (ψυχοηομπός). The Keeper is in charge of the embodied souls, [while] the Guide is he who sends off (ἀποστολεὺς)[5] and assigns their places to (διατάκτης) [or] of those who are embodied. And both he that oversees (τηρεῖ) and he that dispatches (προίσι) act according to the mind of God."[6] It may be observed that these delegated and opposite powers are precisely those of Him who both "maketh alive and killeth" (*I Samuel* II.6, *I Kings* V.7, *AV.* XIII.3.3. etc.), and that they correspond to those of Philo's respectively "creative and regnant," or merciful and retributive" cherubim; the

1 Contrast Euripedes *Hipp.* 540 [re] Aphrodite.

2 Pindar, *Paean* VII and IX; Parmenides in Sextus Empiricus, *Adv. Dogm.* 111; H.J. Rose, *Greek Mythology*, p. 174.

3 Cf. my "Recollection, Indian and Platonic," *JAOS.* Supplement 3, 1944.

4 Apuleius, *Met.* XI.4 (Isis = Minerva, Venus, Juno, etc. *cujus numen . . . totus veneratur orbis*).

5 Scott's rendering of ἀποστολεύς by "he that sends down to Earth" is most unnatural, both as regards the "Psychopomp," a term elsewhere applicable only to such conductors of souls as Hermes [(cf.] Diogenes Laert. 8[)], Charon and Apollo, and because the souls referred to are, in fact, already embodied. Ἀποστέλλω is not necessarily to "send down," as in *Luke* X.16, but to "send away" as in *Luke* IV.18 ἀποστεῖλαι . . . ἐω ἀφέσει, "to set at liberty"; and there is nothing in the text to justify the words "to Earth." Διατάκτης refers to the ranking of the souls "according to their worth" as in the first paragraph of the excerpt; and προίησι is "dispatches" or "lets go," and actually a causal form exactly corresponding to the Sanskrit intransitive *pre* (*pra* + *i*) in *preta*, the regular designation of one "gone forth," "departed," "deceased."

The Keeper of Souls I would identify with the "Prophet" who in the *Republic* 617 D ff. lays before the souls about to be reborn the patterns from the lives from which they choose mostly in accordance with the habits of their former lives. Although I cannot discuss here Plato's doctrine of rebirth, I must point out that the periods of 100 and "1000" years correspond to the respective durations of the lives of men and of gods in the Indian *devayāna* and *pitryāna* (e.g. of *CU.* V.3.2); also that Plato's final prayer "that we may be dear to ourselves and to the gods," virtually identical with the prayer of *Phaedrus* 279 B, and Sophocles *O.C.* 309, corresponds to the Indian doctrine of true "Self-love" (*ātmakāma* = φίλαυτος), for further references to which see *HJAS.* IV p. 135 and *JAOS.* Supplement 3, pp. 40, 41 and Note 82.

[6 In any case, the two Guardsmen of the Hermetic fragment correspond to the two guides (ἡγεμών) of *Phaedo* 107-8, *viz.* the daimon of each soul who leads it to the place of judgment, and the "other guide" who brings it back here again after great periods of time; the latter is the same as the guardian daimon of the soul's new life in *Republic* 620 E. In other words, the two are both equally "guardsmen," "guides," and "daimons"; one of the past, the other of the coming life.]

concern of the Keeper being with the births of the unembodied, and that of the Guide with the lot of the departed. These two Guardsmen, the angels of Life and Death, and invested with the powers of Day and Night and Light and Darkness, conditions one and undivided in Him whose station is between them as their Divider, are the symbols of all those contraries (ἐναντια, *dvandvau*) of which the wall of Paradise is built; a wall that none can pass but those who are able to overcome the highest spirit of Reason — Cusa's *spiritus altissimus rationis*, ἀνώτατος λόγος — and truth in whom they coalesce and by whom they are divided.[1]

Male sphinx with flower offering, flanking the Wisdom-Tree (*Bodhi-duma*). Indian, Kuṣāna, 2nd century A.D. Museum of Fine Arts 26.241.

[1 Cusa *De vis. Dei.* I.10; *JUB.* I.5. For Day and Night cf. *Opif.* I.33, *TS.* VI.4.2 and 41, X.11.9.]

81 a

[Figures 81 a and b: Sirens and sphinxes from the tomb in Xanthos, ca. 480 B.C. British Museum. Ananda Kentish Coomaraswamy captioned his illustration (our Fig. 96, page 113) with a reference to Euripedes, *Rhesus* 890 f. — Ed.]

81 b

✦ Chapter VI ✦

The Greek Sphinx

It is a matter of general agreement that sphinxes, *kēres*, sirens and harpies are closely related and even equivalent types and conceptions; it may, however, be further observed that the verb ἁρπά ξω is at least as characteristic for the Sphinx as it is for the Harpy, and that the word is not always used in a wholly bad sense, but rather characteristically of the "rape" of a mortal by a god, a rape that may be a "rapture": It can hardly, I think, be overlooked that the derivative adjective ἁρπαλέος is not only used in the sense "voracious," but also in that of "attractive," "alluring," or "seductive." We have seen that the Sphinx, like the Siren, carries off her victims alive, and that they sometimes show no sign of distress. Discussing the sirens of the British Museum tomb from Xanthus [(Figs. 81 a and b)],[1] where they are carrying off diminutive mortals, Cecil Smith has remarked that "in the sculpture there is no sense of dismay shown in the figures who are carried off, nor yet in their companions; the graceful bird-women support their burdens with the utmost care, and there is no suggestion of rape or violence. The Siren here is the gentle messenger of death."[2] Much the same applies to the Harpies or Blasts as Homer conceives them; to be carried off by the Harpies (ἅρπυιαι) or Blasts (θύελλαι, ἄελλαι) is a translation and disappearance sharply distinguished from the normal death in which a body is left to be burnt or buried; and such a translation, as Rhodes points out, may even be desired.[3] The same verb (ἀυερειπομαι) is used of a rape by the Harpies or Blasts (*Odyssey* I.241, IV.727, XIV.371), for the rape of Oreithyra by Boreas (*Phaedrus* 229 B, C), for the Rape of Ganymede by the gods, to be the cupbearer of Zeus

---

[1 Ananda Kentish Coomaraswamy collected images of the "Sarpedon" legend as found in *Iliad* XVI.419-683 — see our Fig. 82 [page 98)] from the Cleveland Museum article of April 1945 — though he was never able to incorporate this important Hellenic story into his work. G. Nagy, in *The Hellenization of Indo-European Myth and Ritual*, p. 141, relates the "name Sarpedon . . . not only to the hero but also to various places associated with the mythological theme of abduction by winds or birdlike harpies. This theme is expressed by way of various forms containing the verb-root *harp* — 'snatch' (as in *harpuia* 'harpy' and *harpazo* 'snatch'), which may be formally connected with the element *sarp* — of *Sarpedon*." In this connection, I cite the following observation: "It is not too surprising that Homer makes Sarpedon the subject of the only big snatch in the *Iliad*, though he transformed the carriers from lady birds to Sleep and Death, to match more familiar configurations of epic mortality." (Nagy quoting E. Vermeule, *Aspects of Death in Early Greek Art and Poetry*, Berkeley, 1979, p. 169). Vermeule, herself, calls Xanthos: "Sarpedon's town where harpies are at home," *l.c.* p. 242. — Ed.]

2 Cecil Smith, "Harpies in Greek Art," *JHS*. XIII [1892-1893]; Smith points out also that the Harpies are called the "guardians" of the Apples of the Hesperides, and are certainly "guardians" as represented on a Cyrenean cup from Naukratis, now in the British Museum. In a representation of the Rape of Europa by Zeus (Smith's Fig. 2), there is an accompanying harpy or *Nikē* holding wreaths, as if to emphasize that this is a successful "rape."

3 Edwin Rohde, *Psyche* (edition 1925), Chapter III and Note 4, discussing "Translation." On page 56: "The belief that a god could suddenly withdraw his earthly favorite from the eyes of men and invisibly waft him away on a breeze not infrequently finds its application in the battle scenes of the *Iliad*," and such are not regarded as dead, but "the Harpies have carried him away."

[*Figure 82:* Sleep and Death holding the dead Sarpedon. Bronze *cista* handle, Etruscan, ca. fourth century B.C. Cf. *Iliad* XVI.671. Cleveland Museum of Art; see the discussion in the *Cleveland Museum of Art Bulletin*, April 1945.]

(*Iliad* XX.232), and by Hesiod for that of Phaëthon by Aphrodite, who carries him off (ἀναρεψαμένη) and makes of him a "divine *genius*" (δαίμονα δῖον, *Theog.* 990). Apollo himself plays the same part when, at the command of father Zeus, he saves (σεσωσμένη . . . ἐ ξέσωσα . . .) Helen from Menelaus' sword by snatching her away (ἥρπασα), to reveal her later "wrapped in folds of ether,[1] for as Zeus' daughter, she may not die" (Euripedes, *Or.* 1496 f., 1557, 1630 f.; cf. Lycophron, *Al.* 820).[2] Apollo carries off (ἥρπασε) Halcyone (*Iliad* IX.564); Eos carries off (ἥρπασε) Kleitos and Tithonus (*Odyssey* XV.250; *Hymn to*

---

1 In this and many other contexts ([i.e.] *Orestes* 1631, 1636) A.S. Way and others (notably J. Burnet) often render αἰθήρ by "air" (or by such poetical terms as "cloudland") far too freely, for if there is one thing certain it is through the air that one ascends to the Ether (equated with Zeus or with the Sky) above (*I Corinthians* XIV.288). On the other hand, Way inserts "etherial" where there is nothing in the text or sense to warrant it (Euripedes, *Rhesus* 533)!

Cf. Philo, *Mut.* 179: "from earth through air to ether"; *Speculum* IV.235: "Justice extends from sky or ether through air to earth." [In Philo there is] clearly distinguished [the] celestial etherial from [the] aerial. Cf. *Migr.* 184 [and] *Apollordorus* III.34.

[The Ether is the soul's "immortal covering" (Marcilio Ficino, cited in Kristeller, p. 371) or "subtle body" (*sūkṣma śarīra*), or "body of glory."]

2 Compare Euripedes, *Rhesus* 886 ff. where a Muse is seen overhead "conducting" (πέμπει) the body of the newly slain Rhesus (her son), intending to "set free his soul" (ψυχὴν ἀνεῖναι) and that he shall be a "human-*genius*, seeing light."

Aphrodite, 218); Athene and Apollo assume the forms of vultures, perched on an oak, whence they survey a council of warriors (*Iliad* VII.59). In the sense that all things are what they do, all these are "Harpies" (ἅρπυιαι), or "Seizers" (Sanskrit *grahāḥ*),[1] or Hades himself may be the raptor (Lycrophon, 65 s; Callimachus, *Ep.* III, ὁ πάντων ἁρπακτὴς Αΐδνς) [certainly of] Persephone [, cf.] *Anth. Pal.*, or Charon, [cf., again] *Anth. Pal.*

The Harpies themselves act only by divine command, and are much rather, like Valkyries, choosers of those who are to live with the gods, than murderers; angels of death, but emissaries of Him (or Her) "who slaying, doth from death to life translate." That they are, indeed, *Kēres* or *Moirai*, Fates, appears in the saying of Achilles, "My *Kēr* I will accept whenso Zeus willeth to fulfill it" (*Iliad* XXI.366) and that to "escape one's *Kēr*" is to save one's life (*Odyssey* XV.235; *Iliad* VII.254, XXII.202). Aeschylus calls the Theban Sphinx "a man-ravishing *Kēr*" (ἅρπα ξάνδπαω κῆρα, *Septerion* 759). These are the explanations of the associations of sphinxes, harpies and sirens with battle scenes and with the tomb. If all these winged winds are often, or even usually, regarded with fear and dread, and called by harsh names (as is Aphrodite herself, and sometimes even Apollo or Zeus), it is not because they are evil themselves but because the love of life is strong in everyone, and all men fear Death, who is welcome only under abnormal circumstances or in old age, and also because the fate of those who depart is both mourned and resented by those who remain. But, "unjustly men fear Death" (Aesch. fr. 191), and the true Philosopher is a practitioner of the *ars moriendi* throughout his life (Plato, *passim.*, cf. *Phaedo* 117 D "I wept not for him but for my own loss."), and at least in old age, a natural death is a "happy release" (*Timaeus* 81).

Miss Jane Harrison,[2] with less than her customary acumen, saw in the Sphinx only "the 'throttler', an excellent name for a destructive bogey, but she became the symbol of oracular divinity." Ilberg (*l.c.* p. 16) is much nearer the mark: " . . . *die Sphinx erscheint as Werkzeug einer hoherem Macht*," and the Theban saga is nothing but a local adaptation of a much older conception, and by no means its "*Kerpunkt*." Nilsson,[3] too, regards the Theban Sphinx only as the secondary development of the widely disseminated type of myth in which the Hero solves a riddle and therewith wins the hand of the riddler and her kingdom. Support for this point of view can be cited from Pausanias (IX.xxvi.2-4) who calls her "mountain" (i.e. the φίκιον ὄρος of the saga) [and] her "domain" (ἀπχή), which she protects with her sophistries against her brothers whom, if they could not answer her, she slew on the ground that

---

1 Cf. *Bhagavad Gītā* XV.8 where "when the Lord assumes a body and when he departs he *seizeth* (*gihitvā*) these (powers of thought and sensation, collectively 'soul') and goeth his way, even *as the Gale* takes scents from their lairs and departs." Cf. *Chāndogya Upaniṣad* IV.3.1; *Brahmaṇa Upaniṣad* IV; [etc.]

2 J. Harrison, "The Ker as Sphinx," in *Prolegomena to Greek Religion*, [p.] 270 f. G.M.A. Richter (in *Archaic Attic Gravestones*, 1945, p. 20), though she calls the sphinxes on Orientalizing vases "purely ornamental," finds it "hard to believe that a sphinx surmounting a gravestone was purely ornamental."

3 M.P. Nilsson, *The Mycenean Origin of Greek Mythology*, 1932, p. 105.

they "had no valid claim to the rule (ἀπχή) or to kinship"; but, he says, "it seems the answer had been revealed to Oedipus in a dream."[1]

The mention of Apollo, acting for Zeus (as the Theban Sphinx for Hera), and that of Ganymede carried off by unspecified gods on Zeus' behalf, reminds us that all these winged messengers of which we have spoken are really the powers of the gods or forms that they assume under given circumstances without ever ceasing to be themselves. All are *raptores* by whom men are "caught up," and "hounds of heaven"; and it is only to state this in other words to say that Zeus himself carried off (ἥρπασε) Ganymede or that it is a "God-bidden Blast that carried him off" (ἀνήρπασε θέσπις ἄελλα) whither his father knew not.[2] Ἄελλα here, is surely at once a Gale and the Eagle (ἀετός) of

[*Figure 83:* Cyprian cylinder in the Perseus-Gorgon group, Ward 643. Kaiser Friederich Museum, *Vorderasiatische Abteilung,* V.A. 2145 in C. Hopkins, "Assyrian Elements in the Perseus-Gorgon Story," *AJA.* 1934, pp. 341-358.]

---

[1] In other words, the Sphinx is an *Alakṣmī* who became a *Lakṣmī* for him who knows her secret, and can therefore overcome her. The motive is that of the "Loathly Bride" who, for the solar Hero who woos and wins her in all her horror, becomes a resplendent beauty, and is, in fact, the Sovereignty (see references in my "Loathly Bride," to be published soon in *Speculum* [20, 1945]). His connection provides a clue to the combination of beauty with horror that one finds in the concept and representations of sphinxes, gorgons and sirens. [In the Oedipus legend,] Jocasta [, the mother of Oedipus,] represents the Sphinx.

[2] Euripedes, *Rhesus* 530. Cf. *Revelation* VIII.30 ἑνὸς ἀετοῦ πετομένου ἐν μεσουρανήατι λέγουτος and *Atharva Veda* XIII.2.36, *patantam aruṇam suparṇam madye divaḥ*, "the Ruddy Eagle flying in the middle of the Sky," i.e. the Sun Collation of *Rhesus* 530 with *Iph.* 159 gives the equation, Sun in chariot = Sun as Eagle.

Ἄελλα, like ἀτμός, ἄηρ, ἄνεμος (*an*ima, Sanskrit *anila*), ἀετός, from ἄω, ἀήμι "blow," root Sanskrit *an* or *vā* in *Vāyu*, "Wind" and *Ātman*, "Spirit"). The concept of the Blast as *raptor* is exactly paralleled in India, e.g. *Chāndogya Upaniṣad* IV.3 where the Gale (*vāyu*) is a "snatcher-to-himself" (*saṁvargaḥ*, root *saṁvṛh*), and the corresponding immanent Breath (*prāna*) or Life in living beings likewise a "snatcher-unto-himself": How and in what sense is clear from *Bṛhadāraṇyaka Upaniṣad* IV.4.3 and VI.1.13 where, like a horse its hobbles, the Breath uproots the Breaths and departs with them; cf. *Bhagavad Gītā* XV.8, "When the Lord assumes a body and when he leaves it, he seizes these (powers of the soul) and departs, just as the Gale carries off scents from their seats."

Flight implies lightness, and wings unimpeded "motion at will"; the "*Knielauf*," Greek and Indian, may be combined with wings, or may alone suffice to indicate the flight of wingless figures.

Maidens attendant on Artemis and Athena are "wind-footed" (Euripedes, *Helen* 1314) like the steeds of Zeus (*Hymn to Aphrodite* 217): in the iconography of the Gorgon, Perseus and Hermes, this is represented visually by the sandal wings. The Gorgon (and Gorgoneion) requires a separate discussion, but two important points may be noted here: (1) that Roscher was perfectly correct in pointing out that the *Fratzenmaske* was originally the terrible face of the Sun, for which additional evidence can be cited in the fact that the Gorgoneion frequently occupies a central position with an unmistakably solar significance, as notably on the Attic sherd (Graef and Langlotz 923 A) referred to above; and (2) that in the remarkable composition of the late Assyrian seal cylinder reproduced by Ward (*Seal Cylinders of Western Asia*, no. 643 = Weber, *Altorientalische Siegelbilder* 269 and our Fig. 83, could only be described from a Greek point of view as "Perseus beheading the Gorgon" — note, for example, the Hero's winged feet and averted head.

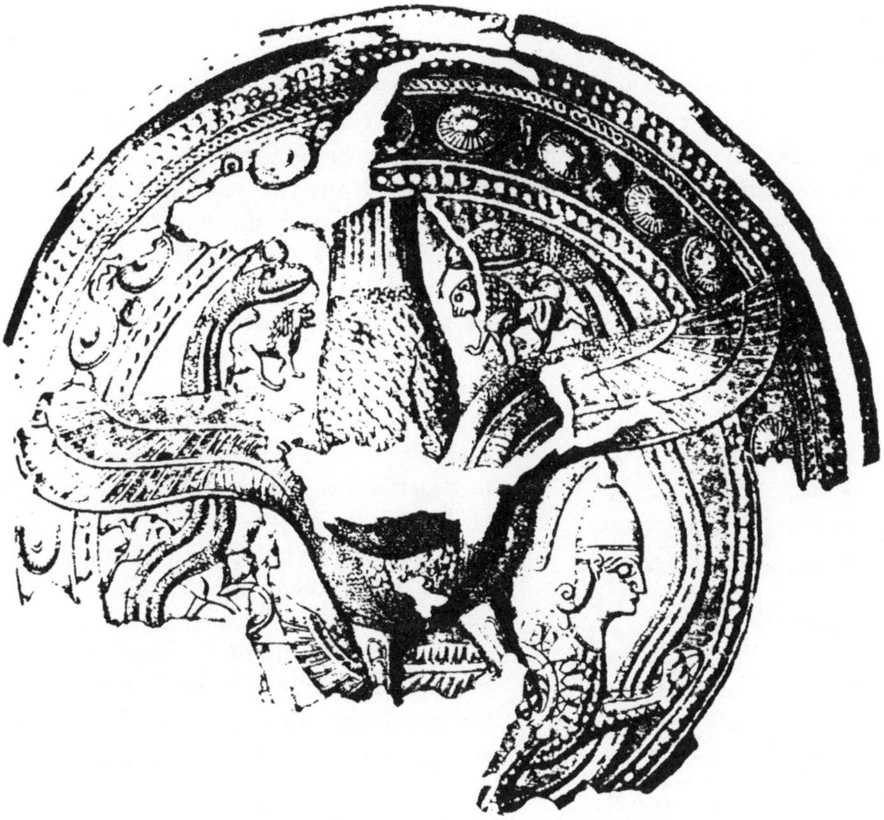

[Figure 84: Bronze shield with eagle of Zeus as blazon. Crete, Idean Cave, ca. 700 B.C. From H. Demisch, *Die Sphinx: Geschichte ihrer Darst. von d. Anf. . . . bis zur Gegenwart*, Stuttgart, 1877.]

Zeus, and perhaps Apollo himself in the form of the winged disc (μέσα δ'αἰετὸσ οὐρανοῦ τοτᾶται).[1] The distinction of his Power from Zeus himself is only a matter of describing his effects; just as the Biblical Cherubim are the Wings of the Wind, the Gale of the Spirit on which God rides, and as the Indian Garutman, Suparṇa, Śyena, is either the Sun-bird or the solar Vishnu's vehicle, on which he rides as Yāw rides upon the Cherubim, and as eagles are both the servants of Zeus, and himself an eagle (Fig. 84), as they are in the *Palentine Anthology* VIII.33 and 54, "the winged soul of Nonna went to heaven" and "an angel of dazzling light, O Nonna, carried thee off" (ἥρπασι), as Christ has carried off Alpius (*ib.* 103). The problem vanishes, in fact, in the light of self-knowledge, if we have been able to recognize ourselves not in the mortal outer man, but in the immanent divinity, "Our Self, the self's immortal Leader" (*MU.* VI.7), alike in life and at death; for if we had known Who we are, it is our Self that flies away with us, and

---

1 *Hymn to Aphrodite* 203-215. Ganymede is made "deathless and unaging, even as the gods"; cf. *Atharva Veda* X.8.44.

in our Self that we fly away (*AA.* II.6, *CU.* III.14.4, *ŚA.* VIII.7 giving the answers to *Prasna Upaniṣad* VI.3).

We are ourselves the Sphinx. Plato himself implies as much by his "etc." when he discusses the problem of man's relation to the Chimera, Scylla, Cerberus, and other composite animals (*Republic* 588 f., cf. 544). Plato equates the two parts of the composite creature with the two parts of the soul, the better and the worse, immortal and mortal: The composite represents the whole man, the human head the Inner Man (ὁ ἐντὸς ἄν θραπος) (*Republic* 441 A). He might even have gone further, and pointed out that the serpent tails of these creatures correspond to the appetites (ἐπιθυμια), equating the two animal forms, those of the lion and the snake, with the two parts of the mortal soul, as Philo assuredly would have done. In any case, Plato says, that man is one who can be described as *just* (or, in Christian terms, is *justified*), in whom the Inner Man prevails, and is not pulled about by the beasts, but makes an ally of the lion or dog, and so cares for the other beasts so as to make them friendly to one another and to himself. On this basis one might say that the composite animal [is carried] off at last, either to punishment in case the beasts have prevailed, or to the beatific life if the Man in the man has prevailed: The question is really just that of the *Prasna Upaniṣad*, "*In which*, when I depart, shall I be departing?"

The phraseology of the "rape" is taken over almost verbatim into [the] New Testament. In *II Corinthians* XII.2, 4, St. Paul speaks of himself as the man who was "caught up" (ἁρπαγέντα) to the third heaven, to Paradise; In *Acts* VIII.39, the Spirit of the Lord (πυζῦμα κυρίου) "caught away" (ἥρπασε) Philip, so that he was no more anywhere to be seen; in *Revelation* XII.5 the child of the Woman Clothed with the Sun was "caught up (ἁρπάσθη) unto God and unto His throne."[1] And in connection with the Resurrection and Last

Figure 85: Coptic *stele*; Jerpanion, p. 133, Fig. 31. In the Coptic Museum of Cairo. Cf. *Anth. Pal.* VIII.62. [Drawing by A.K. Coomaraswamy. — Ed.]

[1 In *Revelation* XXI.10 ἀποφέπω (ἐω πνεύματι ἐπ ὄρος μένα) only paraphrases ἁρπάξω elsewhere.]

Figure 86 a: Etana carried to Heaven by the Eagle, seeking the Plant of Birth. Accadian seal, ca. 2800 B.C. [From] H. Frankfort, *Seal Cylinders of Western Asia*, p. 138 and pl. XXIV h. [British Museum] 129480 (Southesk Collection); serpentine; 3.8 x 2.75 (2.65) cm.

[Figure 86 b: Garuda with a *Nāgini*, Indian ca. 500 A.D. MFA Boston 36.262. *MFA Bulletin*, June 1937.]

Judgment, in *II Thessalonians* IV.17 "we which are alive, and remain, shall be caught up (ἁρπαγησόμεθα) together with them, in the clouds, to meet the Lord in the air, and so shall we ever be with the Lord": There is an allusion to this in *Luke* XVII.37, "for wherever the body is, there will the eagles be gathered together" (cf. *Job* IX.26), and the whole conception goes back to *Exodus* XIX.4 where the Lord reminds Moses "how I bare you on eagles' wings, and brought you unto myself." So might Zeus have spoken to Ganymede! The Eagle, in fact, survives on Christian tombstones (Fig. 85), no doubt as an expression that the deceased will be "taken up" to heaven.

The motive is, indeed, worldwide, but in Greece and India it may have originated in Sumeria, where in the myth of Etana, the Eagle (*erū*) carries Etana, who is seeking for the Plant of Life, to heaven's gates. The myth is imperfectly preserved, but it is quite clear that Etana clings to the Eagle; and there is a corresponding iconography in which Etana either clings to the Eagle or rides on its back (Fig. 86 a).[1] Elsewhere, of course, there may be substituted for the "Eagle" any of the other birds, e.g. Gander (*haṁsa*) or Sīmurgh, that represent the powers of the solar *Spiritus*[2] (Fig. 86 b).

It hardly needs to be argued that Ganymede (who has actually a feminine counterpart, Ganymeda), whose boyish form is to be explained by the special character of Greek eroticism, is really a symbol of the Psyche. We actually find, in fact, that in art the living form that the Eagle soars away with is not always masculine, but may be altogether feminine. In a representation of the

---

1 For Etana and the Eagle see S. Langdon, *The Legend of Etana and the Eagle*, Paris, 1932 (especially p. 45); Karl von Spiess, "*Der von Vogel Gettagene*," *loc. cit.*, pp. 170-172, 182-184 and pl. 1. Langdon (p. 45, Note 2) points out that Etana "places his arms round the eagle's neck."

2 For the Gander as the vehicle by which the Himmelfahrt is accomplished see U. Holmberg, "*Der Baum des Lebens*," *Ann. Acad. Sci. Fennicae*, XVI, Helsinki, 1922-23; and my "*Svayamātṛṇṇā: Janua Coeli*" in *Zalmoxis* II, Paris, 1939, 13 f.

soul's ascent on the back of a lovely mirror of the fourth century B.C., in the Altes Museum, Berlin (Fig. 87), Ganymeda (if this name may be used) has flung one arm round the Eagle's neck and thrown back her head as if to kiss and be kissed. The expression of ecstacy is repeated in a slightly different way in the much later medallions of the gold flask of the treasure of Nagy St. Miklos, in the Kunsthistorische Museum in Vienna.[1] We meet, moreover, with exact parallels much further East in numerous representations of the Rape of the *Nāgī*,[2] whom the Eagle bears aloft; a visual representation of the words of the *Taittirīya Saṁhitā* (III.2.1.1), "Thou art the Eagle . . . I cling to thee, ferry me over in safety" (*suparṇośi . . . tvārabhe svasti mā sampāraya*), i.e. unto the Farther Shore, unto Brahma, whose abode is in the Ether, and in the last resort (*parāyaṇam*) of every self,"[3] that Brahma, silent and unmanifested, in whom contemplatives "go home," merging in him their individual characteristics,[4] even as sparks are carried away by the gale, and are no longer recognizable.[5]

It is just at this point that light is cast upon the concept of the Sphinx as a "devourer of raw flesh":[6] For while it is true that the Eagle likewise carries off the *Nāgī* to devour her,[7] and the Eagle's prey is often to be seen within him (cf. Fig. 88), this is a consummation devoutly to be desired, since, as Meister Eckhart says, "just as food in man . . . so does the soul in God turn into God";[8] and as I have remarked elsewhere, "if the act of solar violence is a rape, it is also a 'rapture' and 'transport' in both senses of both words."[9] The full sense of the representations of the flying Eagle's prey shown visibly within him — a motive of worldwide distribution[10] — can hardly be

Figure 87: Eagle with Ganymeda or Psyche; Greek, 4th century B.C. Altes Museum, Berlin. After Karl von Spiess, *Jahrbuch f. hist. Volkskunde,* V, pl. 2.

1 See Karl von Spiess, "*Der vom Vogel Getragene*" in *Jahrbuch f. hist. Volkskunde*, V, VI, [1937,] pp. 168-203.

2 My "Rape of a *Nāgī*; an Indian Gupta seal," *MFA Bulletin*, nos. 209, 210, Boston, 1937.

3 *Bṛhadāraṇyaka Upaniṣad* III.9.10-17; cf. *Chāndogya Upaniṣad* I.9.1, *ākāśah parāyaṇam.* Death is the magister (*ācāryo mṛtyuḥ*, *Atharva Veda* XI.5.14) and naturally appears as the exponent of the great transition (*parāyaṇam*, *Kaṭha Upaniṣad* I.29, II.6).

4 *Maitri Upaniṣad* VI.22.

5 *Milinda Pañha* 73 (*atthaṁ gatan = parinibutto*); *Sutta Nipāta* 1074-6 (*vimutto . . . atthaṁ paleti . . . na pamānam atthi*).

6 "Eating raw flesh" (ὠμόσιτος), Euripedes, *Phoen.* 1025; Aeschylus, *Septerion* 541; cf. Lycophron, 669).

7 "*Ne l'enlève que pour le manger,*" in Foucher's words (*L'Art gréco-bouddhique du Gandhara*, II, 1918, p. 37. If, indeed, the body were not consumed, the soul would not be freed; an immortality in the body is impossible (*Śatapatha Brāhmaṇa* X.4.3.9).

8 Pfeiffer, p. 331. It is asked in the *Ṛgveda*, "When shall I come again to be within Varuna?" *Ṛgveda* VII.8.62), of which the explanation is to be found in *Śatapatha Brāhmaṇa* X.6.2.1 where it is pointed out that when the eater and the eaten are united, the resultant is called by the name of the former. *"Con quanti denti Amor ti morde"* (Dante, *Paradiso*, XXVI.21).

9 My "Rape of a *Nāgī*; an Indian Gupta seal," *MFA Bulletin*, nos. 209, 210, Boston, 1937.

10 See Karl von Spiess, *loc. cit.*, and Karl Hentze, *Objets rituels de la Chine antique*, 1935.

Figure 88: Raven with swallowed prey, attacking the ophidian guardian of a door. After Fr. Boas, *Social Organization and Secret Societies of the Kwakiutl Indians*, 1897, pl. 41.

better stated than in the words of the *Bṛhadāraṇyaka Upaniṣad* III.2 where the Wind (man's "last home") puts into himself those who he conveys to the World's End.

We come now to one of the most cogent parts of the argument. We have seen that harpies are obviously so called because in fact they snatch away (ἁρπάζω, *rapio*) their prey. In the same way it is rightly assumed that the designation "Sphinx," corresponds to an activity denoted by σφίγγω, even though there cannot be cited a single text in which the Sphinx is actually the subject of this verb; and on this basis a majority of scholars have said that the Sphinx is the "Throttler" or "Strangler." As to this, it may be pointed out that the Sphinx as represented in Greek art has no members with which it could be imagined that she [could] strangle anything: The *Anthology* does afford us an instance of constriction or strangling by a snake (σφιγθεῖς δράκοντι, VI.333.1), and Oppianus speaks of a σφιγκτὸς μόρος, death by strangling, but such an activity on the part of a sphinx could only be conceived of in the case of the snake-tailed variety, for which there is some literary authority, although no example survives in Greek art. In any case, the use of σφίγγω to mean "strangle" is most exceptional; the ordinary word for that is ἄγχω, in connection, for example, with the strangling of the two snakes by the infant Herakles,[1] while the Sphinx is never the subject of this verb, but typically and almost always of ἁρπάζω, to carry off, and φέρω, to bear away.

We must ask, therefore, what are the senses in which the verb σφίγγω is generally and regularly used. The common sense is that of δέω, and the meanings those of binding, tieing, lacing, tightening or encircling things such as hair, a fillet, a girdle, band or garment, or persons, whether for good or for evil. We have, for example, σφιγκτά referring to a breast-band,[2] σφίγγε, "bind him fast,[3] κοσμοὺς ἐπισφίξας, "tightening the bridles" (of unruly horses, the

1 Pindar, *Nem. O.* I.33 f. Cf. *Anth. Pal.* VI.107.
2 *Anth. Pal.* VI.272.
3 Aeschylus, *Fr.* 58. There is no question of strangling Prometheus, but only of preventing his escape.

passions),[1] and most significantly σφίγγειν δύναμις, [the] magnet's power of attraction (ὁλκός).[2]

The last context introduces us to the most significant and very frequent use of σφίγγω = δέω = *destinare* in connection with the Quintessential, Etherial and Golden Chain or cord that holds all things together at once collectively and individually, enclosing and pervading.[3] For Empedocles (fr. 185) "Titan Ether [i.e., Zeus],[4] binds his circle fast about all things" (σφίγγων περὶ κύκλον

---

1 Philo, *Somn.* II.294, cf. *Plant.* 70. ὅλον ἀντεσπασε. I see no reason to emend κοσμούς to κημούς, cf. Hesychius, ἱπποκόσμικ. The particular κοσμούς intended may be the "curb-straps" (εὔρραθέα) described as "compressors of the jaws" (γεννύων σφίγκτορα) and mentioned after the κημούς in a list of trappings, *Anth. Pal.* VI.233.

Philo takes over from Plato the whole symbolism of the chariot, which is also characteristically Indian (cf. *Phaedrus* 246-247; *Fug.* 101; *LA.* I.40; *Plant.* 72 f.; *Kaṭha Upaniṣad* III.3; *Jātaka* VI.252; and *passim* in both traditions.

2 *Opif.* 141. Cf. *Abr.* 59 where ὁλκός is used again of God's attractive power, and *John* XII.32 (ἑλκύσω). In *Det.* 90 the mind's divine endowment by which it can range afar and be in contact with distant things is similarly one of "attraction" (ὁλκός).

3 For an outline of this "thread spirit" (*sūtrātman*) doctrine see my "Iconography of Dürer's '*Knoten*' and Leonardo's 'Concatenation'" in *The Art Quarterly* VII [1944], pp. 109-128. It is this pneumatic and luminous "thread" connecting all things to their source, this "Golden Cord" that we ought by all means to hold on to (Plato, *Laws* 644-645), "the 'Rope of Allah' which is to renounce self-will" (Rūmī, *Mathnawī*, VI.3942-3) that gives its meaning to the word *religion* (if from *religare* or even *relegere*), and imposes upon us an ob*lig*ation (*ligare*); this is our "Bond" (δεσμός), and the "leading string" that tells us what we "ought" (δεί, δέον, cf. *Cratylus* 404 A, 418 E) to do. Religion implies an alliance.

From amongst innumerable references additional to those that are given in the paper referred to above, I cite Cicero, *De nat. deor.* II.115 *vinculo circumdato*, etc.; Jacob Boehme's "the band of union . . . called the centri-power, being broken and dissolved, all must run thence into the utmost disorder, and falling away as into shivers, would be dispersed as loose dust before the wind" (*Dialogue of the Supersensual Life*); from the *Tripurārahasya*, "Without Him (the *prāṇa-pracaraḥ*, Proceeding Breath, the guardian of the 'city') the citizens would all be scattered and lost, like pearls without the string of the necklace. For He it is that associates me with them all, and unifies the city; He, whose companion I am, is the transcendent Holder-of-the-Thread (*sūtrah-dhārah*, puppeteer, stage-manager) in that city" (*Jñāna Khaṇḍam* V.122-123); H. Vaughn's

And such a knot, what arm dare loose
What life, what death can sever?
Which us in Him, and Him in us
United keeps for ever;

and finally Bayard Simmons'

That chain that bound and made me, link by link,
Now it is snapped: I only eat and drink.

The "emancipation" implied by this breaking of the links, if it could be effected absolutely, would imply "extinction"; to the extent that the tension can be relaxed or dissolved or loosened, the living being becomes at the same time "slack," "dissolute," and "loose," and is on his way to be dissolved or "lost." Philo therefore (*Det.* 89, 90) rightly emphasizes that the divine "spark" (ἀπόσπασμχ) is never cut off from or completely separated from its source; it is an extension and not a fragmentation ([cf.] correlation in *LA.* III.157). In the Loeb Library (Philo I, p. 409) "particle detached" is therefore a mistranslation.

4 The identification of Zeus with Ether is made repeatedly. Heracleitus, fr. 30, αἰθρίοσ Διός is expanded by Euripedes, fr. 386, τόνδ ἄπειπον αἰθέρα . . . τοῦτον νόμιξε Ζῆνα, τόνδ' ἡνοῦ θεόν; and Socrates in *Cratylus* 412-3, though he does not use the word Ether, calls that swift and subtle all-pervading "Somewhat" that is the generative cause of the becoming of all things, "Justice" (δίκαιον), as being that which is present to and through (δία) all things, and adds that

(Continued on following page.)

ἅπαντα); Plato is only paraphrasing when he says that "the circuit [or circumambience] of the All . . . binds all things fast" (σφίγγει πάντα, *Timaeus* 58 A);[1] and Philo continues, "the *Logos* is the Bond of all things (δεσμὸς . . . ἁπαντων) and holds together and binds fast all the parts" (συνέχει τὰ μέρη πάντα καὶ σφίγγει, *Fug.* 112). Composites (σύγκριμα, *Det.* 83, cf. *Timaeus* 37 A συγκραθεῖσα) such as "we" are naturally incoherent, but are held fast by the Word of God (λόγῳ σφίγγεται θείῳ), which is a glue and a bond (δεσμός) that fills up all things with its being (*Heres* 188), and the Powers of the All are bonds (δεσμοί) that cannot be broken (*Migr.* 181): Omnipresent by the extension of his Powers, the Lord "uniting all things with all, has bound them fast with invisible bonds, that they may never be loosed" (πάντα δὲ σθωαναγὼν διὰ πάντωγ ἀοράτοις ἔσφιγξε δεσμᾶς ἵνα μή ποτε λυθείν); that Power which made and ordered all things "holds the universe in its embrace and has

---

(Continued from preceding page.)

it is a secret doctrine that Zeus is Δία for the same reason. This "something" is also, of course, the same as the immortal Soul that is the source of life in *Timaeus* 36 E, 37 A, and which functions like the Ether as the unifying principle of all things. Aeschylus, fr. 34 (70) says explicitly Ζεύς ἐστιν αἰθήρ (as well as other things). Philo's point of view is the same when he speaks of the Soul, in her pure essence, returning to her source in God (*Abraham* 258), "to find a Father in Ether, the purest of the substances," (*Heres* 282-283), of which Etherial Nature she is herself a spark (ἀπόσπασμα) and part (μοῖρα, *LA.* III.161). That "Etherial Nature" is the particular subject of Abraham's investigations (*Gig.* 62). [Cf.] *Det.* 90. Cicero, *De nat. deor.* II.66 preserves the identification of Jove with Ether. The Quintessentia is still for St. Thomas Aquinas immaterial (*Sum. Theol.*, III., *Supplement*, 81.1).

Plato's "Somewhat" (τι), further emphasized by Socrates' persistent enquiry, "What (τί), after all, is this 'justice'?" — to which the answers Sun, or the Heat in Fire, or Intellect are given (much as in *Bṛhadāraṇyaka Upaniṣad* IV.3 in answer to the question "What Light?"), as being at once creative and all-pervasive powers, διὰ πάντων ἰόντα — reappeared in Philo, *Det.* 118 where "the Divine *Logos*, eldest of the essences, is called by the most general name of 'Somewhat'." An analogous Hebrew *Mi*, "Who?," is similarly the name of "God, as the subject of the mundane process" (G.G. Scholem, *Major Trends in Jewish Mysticism*, p. 217); and it is remarkable that [the] Sanskrit *Ka*, "Who?," etymological cognate and semantic equivalent, is similarly used throughout the Vedic tradition as a name of the Deity, especially in his capacity as Prajāpati, the Father-Progenitor. One is reminded also of Erigena's "God Himself does not know *What* He is, because He is not any what."

1 *I.e.* "exerts a centripetal force" (E.G. Bury, in the Loeb Library edition, p. 142); *ad medium rapit* (Cicero, *De nat. deor.* II.115). The "circuit" (Empedocles "circle") is that of "the Same within us, dominating by the power of the *Logos* the irrational mass of the four (material) elements" of the body of the Cosmos (*Timaeus* 42 C). Plato himself does not call the Fifth Element, which corresponds to the dodecahedron and which enforms (δια ξωγρα φῶν) the rest (*ib.* 55 C) by the name of "Ether," but rather "Soul" (the Goddess, Θεός, of *Laws* 897 B), and inasmuch as this Immortal Soul, that Zeus himself has "sown," is woven throughout the Universe and encircles it from without" (πάντη διαπλακεῖσα κύκλῳ τε αὐτὸν ἔξωθει περικαλύφασα) it is by "psychic bonds" that the astral bodies are bound together (*Timaeus* 41 D, 36 E, 38 E); and it is just because this "divine beginning (ἀρχη) of intelligent (ἔμρρων = *cetanavat*) life" (*ib.* 36 E) is thus ever omnipresent, and "has beheld all things both here in this world and there in Hades" that She, who is the self-moved Mover of all things everywhere, has it in her power to remember everything "throughout all time" (*Meno* 86 and *Laws* 896, 897). Cf. my "Recollection, Indian and Platonic," *JAOS. Supplement* 3, 1944, pp. 15, 16.

On Plato's "Soul" as the Fifth Element, cf. Plutarch's discussion (*Mor.* 423 A) of the five worlds of earth, water, air, fire and Soul, the latter "surrounding" or "embracing" (περιέχων) the four others, and represented by the dodecahedron with its pentagonal sides, with which the elemental triangles are incommensurable.

surcharged all its parts" (ἐγκεκόλπισται δὲ τὰ ὅλα καὶ διὰ τῶν τοῦ παντὸς μερῶν διελήλυθε. *Confessions* 136-137).[1] We remark, accordingly, a consistent use of the verb σφίγγε = δέω as a technical term in theology throughout a period of some five hundred years, extending from Empedocles to Philo;[2] and to the extent that the meaning of a noun can be deduced from the corresponding verb, this is as much as to say that σφίγξ implies the etherial Bond and omnipresent Power that keeps the world in being. At the same time and by the same token the Sphinx as subject of the verb ἁρπάξω is a harpy, and as such the Fate that refers the immortal principles of all things back to their source and centre when their time comes. This is to equate the Sphinx at once with Love and Death. It is, in fact, explicit that the Theban Sphinx "ravages the city and bears away (refers, translates) the Cadmean folk to the light of the untrodden Ether" (ἁρπαγαῖσι πόλιω . . . φέρεν αἰθέρος εἰς ἄβατον φῶς γένναν, Euripedes, *Phoen.* 48, 809).[3]

We are now in a position to take up the main problem of the present article [/chapter], that of the real meaning of the Sphinx in Greek literature and art. For this we must resort to the actual iconography, the literary sources, and the studies of modern scholars.[4] In the Greek Geometric and Orientalising

Figure 89: Griffin and male sphinx with "lily crown"; each in pairs as guardians of a tree. Bronze from Eleutherae, 5th century B.C. After H. Payne, *Necrocorinthia*, Fig. 1.

[1] Ἵνα μή ποτε λυθείη, cf. *Migr.* 190, echoed in Dante's *tal vime, che giammai non si divime, Paradiso* XXIX.36; διελήλυθε, an echo of Plato, *Timaeus* 58 A, B where it is "Fire" (i.e. the "ever-living fire" of Heracleitus, Philo's "fire unquenchable") that "most of all surcharges all things."

[2] When Plutarch (*Mor.* 394 A) says that Apollo συνδεῖ the οὐσιά of the world by his presence in it, he might just as well have said Ἐγκεκόλπισται like περικαλύφασα in *Timaeus* 36 E; similarly in 423 A περιέχοντα is tantamount to σφίγγων περ ι κύκλον ἅπαντα.

[3] With φῶς here cf. Aeschylus, *Pr.* 1092 αἰθηρ κολνὸν φάος εἱλίσσων; Plutarch, *Mor.* 390 A ὠπάνον . . . φῶς . . . αἰθέρα . . . πέμπτην οὐσίαν. The Ether is always thought of as "bright" (as in Indian *ākāśa*, root *kāś*, "shine"), while the Air is "naturally black" (Philo, *Opif.* 29, *Moses* II.86) or "blue" (Arist., *De col.* 794 A).

One "escapes" to the Ether (Euripedes, *Orestes* 1375-7, *Phoen.* 1216), but the living fear for one beloved μὴ πρὸς αἰθέπα ἀμπτάμεωος φύγη, *Iph. in T.* 844-5. In Euripedes' *Orestes* 275, Orestes seeks to drive away the Erinyes, *Kēres* and Eumenides to Ether ἐξακρίξετ αἰθέραπτεροῖς), as if to their natural habitat. Cf. Aeschylus, *Septerion* 543.

[4] Most of the references will be found in Roscher, Pauly-Wissowa, and Daremberg *et* Saglio. J. Ilberg, *Die Sphinx in der griechischen Kunst und Sage*, Leipzig, 1896, is a valuable source book.

Figure 90: Bellerophon and Chimaera, [with] paired [female] sphinxes guarding tree, seventh century B.C. MFA 95.10.

art, and on the archaic vases of the eighth and seventh centuries B.C. and later, there are numerous representations of paired affronted or addorsed sphinxes, occasionally male (Fig. 89) but usually female (Fig. 90), having between them a vegetative motive, palmette or rosette, of which they are evidently the guardians, like their Oriental prototypes, and like the Hebraic Cherubim who keep the way of the Tree of Life, or, in the place of the sphinxes, the Tree of Life or Light may be guarded by equivalent griffins (Fig. 91).[1] Paired sphinxes occur also with Hermes standing between them, holding his herald's staff;[2] the composition corresponds to Philo's Trinity of the *Logos* with attendant Powers, and Hermes himself to the Sumerian Nabū or Mummu, creative *Logos*, recording angel and messenger of the gods,[3] and probably also to the Indian Piṅgala, one of the Sun-god's two male attendants.[4] Representations of sphinxes forming parts of thrones, usually

Figure 91: Griffins and Minoan column. From C.W. Blegen, *Prosyma*, 1937, Number 576, pp. 266-7.

1 Literary evidence for the equation of the sphinxes with griffins will be cited below. For the close resemblance in form and function cf. Figs. 89, 90 and 91.

2 Lenormant *et* de Witte, *Élite céramogr.* p. 247 and pl. LXXVII; Ilberg, *l.c.* p. 29, citing also a representation of Hermes with *Kēres*.

3 For Nabū see S. Langdon, *Semitic Mythology*, 1931, pp. 104, 158, 277, 290; and A. Jeremias, *Old Testament in the Light of the Ancient East*, p. 9. For the Indian Breath (*prāṅah*) as recording angel see *Jaiminīya Brāhmaṇa* I.18.1.

4 Piṅgala and Daṇḍa are discussed by J. Hackin, *Mém. arch. de la Délégation Française en Afganistan*, VII, Paris, 1936, reviewed by L. Bachhofer in *JAOS.* 57 [1937], pp. 326-329. Piṅgala carries writing utensils (like Nabū), and Daṇḍa is armed with a shield and a spear, and it is quite obvious that these two represent the sacerdotal and royal powers, creative and punitive, that are united in the Sun himself; the *daṇḍa* (rod) is one of the most familiar symbols of Yama (Death, as Judge) and of the King, in his punitive capacity.

Figure 92: Achilles and Memnon fighting, with affronted sphinxes. Attic black-figured, sixth century B.C. After Gerhard, *Auserlesene griechischer Vasenbilder*, CCXX.

those of gods or goddesses (Zeus, Hera, Athene, Aphrodite) are not uncommon:[1] Pausanias records of the throne of Zeus at Olympia, made by Phidias, that its front legs bore the images of sphinxes holding the Theban youths whom they have carried off (ἡρπασμένοι).[2] The conception obviously parallels that of the Hebraic God for whom the Cherubim are a seat, and it may not be out of place to repeat here that these Cherubim are, in Palestinian art, actually represented by sphinxes. There are also representations of paired sphinxes or equivalent sirens associated with battle scenes, of which they are the spectators (Figs. 92 and 93) and that their function there is similar to that of the Valkyries, who in the Norse mythology conduct the slain warrior to Valhalla, is suggested not only by this association with the battlefield, but also by the fact that the sphinxes associated with a hunting scene on an archaic vase in Munich[3] are accompanied by inscriptions consisting [of] "*deren Name* (Σ+ΙΦΣ *oder* ΣΦΙ+Σ) *zugleich mit besondrer Betonung* (ΗΕΔΕ) *und mit gewöhnter palästrischen Gruss* (+ΑΙΡΕ)." This salutation, χαῖρε (or equivalent χαῖρων) is a word (like [the] Sanskrit *svagā*)[4] of welcome or farewell, and in the latter sense often uttered by or to those who are about to die (e.g. Euripedes, *Herakleidai* 600); here, I think, addressed to the slain warriors whom the Sphinxes will carry off, and in the sense of the Homeric words, σὺ δέ μοι χαῖρων ἀφίκόιο *Odyssey* XV.128, "Fare thee well and mayst thou arrive," addressed to Telemachus, setting out to return to his "home and fatherland" (ἐς πατρίδα γαῖαν), and that would be no less appropriate if addressed to the Spirit of the deceased, departing, as Philo says, "to find a father in Ether" (*Heres* 283).

---

1 *"In Griechenland . . . vor allem wurden die Throne der Götter mit solcher Verzierung versehen. Sphinxe schmücken die Rücklehne, wie am Throne des amykläischen Apollon* (Pausanias III.18.4); *sie sind neben oder unter dem Sessel, auch an der Fussbank angebracht und dienen oft statt der Füsse"* (Ilberg, *loc. cit.* p. 46, with references).

2 Pausanias V.11.12.

3 Meleagros and Theseus hunting the Caledonian boar (*Iliad* IX.543 f., Apollodorus I.8.2 f.); E. Gerhard, *Auserlesene griechische Vasenbilder*, 1858, III.156 and pls. CXXXV, CXXXVI.

4 *Taittirīya Saṁhitā* III.5.5.3, *Śatapatha Brāhmaṇa* I.8.3.11, literally "self-going," i.e. to a desired destination; in *Śatapatha Brāhmaṇa* specifically with reference to ritual death and prefigured *Himmelfahrt*. *Svagā*, only in the sense of "farewell," and to be distinguished from *svāgatam* (*sva* + *āgatam*, "self-come," or *su* + *āgatam*, "well come"), "welcome." Cf. Parmedides in Sextus Empiricus.

Figure 93: Achilles and Memnon fighting, with affronted sirens or harpies. Italo-Corinthian. MFA, Boston 95.14.

Figure 94: Sphinx in Sundoor, between griffins. Geometric-Orientalising; Arkadia, Crete; eighth or seventh century B.C. After Doro Levi, "Early Hellenic Pottery of Crete," *Hesperia* XIV, 1945. Cf. Valentin Muller, "*Minoisches Nachleben oder Orientalischer Einfluss in der fruhkretische Kunst*?" *Ath. Mith.* L [1925], pp. 51-58, and Abb. 1.

The single Sphinx appears in early Orientalising vase painting from Crete. The remarkable example illustrated in Fig. 94 [page 111] is important from several points of view. In the first place, she is seated between the two jambs of the *Janua Coeli*, in the position occupied by the Sun [here as a pillar of light] in Fig. 91 [page 109], of which Sundoor the paired griffins, right and left, must be regarded as guardian *genii*; and secondly, the details of the iconography are amongst those that point most clearly to the Hittite sources of this type, as to which see further below. Single sphinxes on vase paintings are also found in the central medallions of Attic black figured craters, a position in which a great variety of other solar motives are met. The single Sphinx appears also as a shield device;[1] Aeschylus, for example, describes Parthenopaeus' shield as having upon it the figure of a "raw-devouring" sphinx, holding her Cadmean prey beneath her (φέρεί δ'ὑφ' αὑτὴ),[2] a figure in relief (ἔκκρουστον) and "cunningly constructed with pivots" (προσμεμηχανημένην γόμφοις, *Septerion* 541-544), on which it must, I think, have moved when the shield was swung.[3]

Figure 95: Two sphinxes, one with living prey. Attic black-figured sherd, [sixth century B.C.] After Furtwangler, *Münchner Jahrbuch* I, Abb. 9. [Liebieghaus, Frankfort, LI 549, from a *loutrophore*. — Ed.]

---

1 For some references to representations in vase painting see G.H. Chase, "The Shield Devices of the Greeks," *Harvard Studies in Classical Philology*, XIII, p. 122.

2 With φέρεί is to be understood, however, ἄεθέπος εὶς ἄβατοω φῶς, Euripedes, *Phoen.* 809!

3 I digress to remark that Euripedes describes another apparently moveable shield device, which consisted of madly racing mares, "whirled from within by pivots ingeniously" (ἔν πως στρόριοφιγξιω ἐνδοθεν κυκλοῦμενα ι, *Phoen.* 1124-27). The words στρόφιγξ and γόμμφος, rendered by "pivot," are used elsewhere to denote the joints of living bodies (Plato, *Timaeus* 43 A; Aristotle, *Part. an.* II.5.9), γόμμφος also for the hinges of doors. Aristotle, moreover, witnesses that artists actually constructed wonderful machines in which a visible circle was made to revolve by means of a primary circle hidden from sight, "so that the marvel of the machine (τοῦ μηχανήματος . . . θαυμαστόν) is alone apparent, while its cause is invisible" (*Mech.* 848 a 35). It can hardly be doubted that such "machines," prototypes of clockwork, were actually models of the universe, of which the *prima rota* is unseen. The actual device of the mares racing in a circle belongs to the well known solar *Tierwirbeln* with from three to seven equine or other *protomas*, of which a very striking example is illustrated by Graef and Langlotz, *Die antike Vasen von der Akropolis* I, pl. 32 (no. 606) and 59 (no. 933 a). On the type more generally see A. Roes, "*Tierwirbel*" in IPEK XI [1936-7]; for some of the oldest forms [see] L. Legrain, *Culture of the Babylonians*, 1925, pl. LV; and for its persistence [see] J. Baltrusaitis, "*Quelques survivances de symboles solaires dans l'art du Moyen Age*," *Gaz. des Beaux-Arts*, [1937], pp. 75-82.

Figure 96: [Sphinx from a tomb in Xanthos, ca. 480 B.C. (A photograph of this motif on the monument is shown on page 96, Fig. 82 a.) British Museum. A.K. Coomaraswamy captioned his illustration with a reference to Euripedes, *Rhesus* 890 f. — Ed.]

There are many such representations of the Theban Sphinx with her prey, with which she is sometimes flying away; sometimes or even usually the victim is manifestly clinging to its bearer (Fig. 95).[1] Like the later Greek poets, one thinks of them as always "Theban" sphinxes, because of the prominence of the Oedipus saga in our minds.[2] But it is even more likely that some of these are simply representations of the Sphinx in her general capacity of soul-bearer, for the whole development is identical with that of the other winged messengers of death: *Erinyes*, *Kēres*, harpies and sirens. The forms of the latter, carrying off the souls of the dead, exhibit all transitions from the terrible Gorgon-like forms to others manifestly expressive of a truly maternal love and tenderness, of which the well-known Harpy Monument from Xanthos ([fifth] century [B.C.]), in the British Museum, is a striking example (Fig. 96).[3]

Of the sculptured single sphinxes the most important are that of Aegina and that of Naxian origin dedicated at Delphi (Fig. 97 [page 114]), where there are remains of many others. The Naxian Sphinx is colossal (2.5 meters) and was set up on an Ionic column 10 meters in height near the rock of the Sibyl, a significant association,[4] for like the Sphynx the Pythian oracle always speaks

---

1 A. Furtwangler, "*Die Sphinx von Aegina*," *Münchner Jahrb.* I [1906], Fig. 9 (our Fig. 95), an Attic black figured (6th century B.C.) sherd: One arm of the living burden around the Sphinx's neck, cf. the siren of Weicker's Fig. 5 (*Der Seelenvogel*, p. 7). Furtwangler cites other examples, published in *Gaz. Arch.* 1876, p. 77 and *Wiener Vorlegebl.* 1889, pls. 8 and 9. For similar representations on the throne of Zeus at Olympus see Pausanias V.2.2.

2 The Oedipus saga, as many scholars have recognized, is certainly not the origin or kernel of the Sphinx concept, but only a particular application of it.

3 G. Weicker, *Der Seenelvogel*, Leipzig, 1902, pp. 6, 7 ("*aus dem Todesdämon wird der Todesengel*"), pp. 125 and 127-130 (on the mixed types of Sphinx and Siren). Bearded as well as feminine sirens are known (*ib.* p. 32). The corresponding Indian *kinnaras* are of both sexes, and like sirens [are] both musical and amorous, but never associated with death. In the case of Rhesus [in Euripedes,] the Muse who carries him off is really his mother.

4 Poulsen, *Delphi*, p. 99, discounts the significance of the association, and remarks that "the Sphinx was so decorative a creature of legend that the Greeks could employ it anywhere and everywhere". But this is to refer a quite modern conception of "decoration" to an age where ornament had not yet been divorced from meaning.

[There are other] "significant associations" in this area of the sacred precinct at Delphi over which the Naxian Sphinx hovered. It was called *Halos* (a threshing floor). "There, every eight

(Continued on following page.)

Figure 97: Colossal Sphinx from Naxos at Delphi; early Archaic [sixth century B.C.]

Figure 98: Aphrodite with sphinxes, Corinthian mirror handle; ca. 510 B.C. After H. Payne, *Necrocorinthia*, p. 246 and pl. 46, 4.

(Continued from preceding page.)
years, a religious drama, the *Septerion*, was acted out [reenacting] the killing of Python by Apollo. A child whose parents must both be alive acted the part of Apollo. The priests led the child up the staircase called *Doloneia* to a hut in the *Halos* to shoot the dragon who was hiding there. Then the child made believe he was going to [the] Temple to atone for the murder as the god had done." Basil. Chr. Petracos, *Delphi*, Athens, 1871, p. 17.

Vincent Scully has described the ascent of the pilgrim to the Temple of Apollo in his *The Earth, the Temple, and the Gods*, p. 113, "The flank of the Athenian treasury directed the eye up the rising path where the Bouleuterion thrust its corner toward the roadway. Above the Bouleuterion the high Ionic column which supported the winged Sphinx of the Naxians would have been seen: Rising, appropriately treelike, near the cleft rocks which marked the sanctuary of Gaia, [Goddess of] the Earth, out of which the Pythoness was supposed originally to have prophesied . . . Above the rocks was the temple, and above the whole opened the V of the cliff's smaller pair of horns. The man-made forms were now seen and judged against the cliff, and the contrast was both intense and subtle." In this way, the Sphinx on its columnar tree, significantly Ionic, interposed itself for a *moment* between the rocks of the Phraedriades, the Shining Rocks, potentially clashing like Symplegades in this earthquake-prone area.
(Continued on following page.)

in riddles and somewhat harshly.[1] [Many of the] sphinx[es at] Aegina appear to have been *acroterion*[*s*] on the temple of [Aphaia[2]], ca. 460 B.C. Furtwanger remarks that "*dieser Würgerin ist klein hässliche Daemon, sie ist schön, berückend durch Leibreix, bezaubernd durch Anmut . . . Der Todt, den sie bringt, ist hinter Schönheit versteckt*," and he describes his first sight of her face, as it was uncovered, in remarkable words: " . . . *das war ein Moment, den ich nie vergessen werde; denn ich war gänzlich gefangen, berauscht von den bestichenden Zauber dieser dämonischen Schönheit; und ich empfand: Von ihr Klausen zerfleischt zu werden, müsste Wolluste sein.*"[3] This use of sphinxes as *acroteria* [. . .] reminds us [of] the handle of an archaic mirror [. . .] formed as an image of Aphrodite with a pair of sphinxes seated on her shoulder[4] (Fig. 98) [like the *acroteria* of a temple]. We have seen already that her throne, like that of Zeus, may be furnished with sphinxes, and we must not overlook that she, like other divinities, is one who chooses and carries off (ἀναρεφαμένη) her elect, making of Phäeton, for example, a "divine *genius*" (Hesiod, *Theog.* 990). These winged

(Continued from preceding page.)

What defined this early theatrical area on the north was the great polygonal retaining wall built to support the Temple of Apollo in 548 B.C. This wall was the dedicatory offering of slaves in thanks for the obtaining of freedom. In this way an association of "binding" was emphasized, and in this case a "loosening of bonds." It was before this wall that the Athenians built an Ionic *stoa* in 478 B.C. inscribed with the phrase in archaic letters: "The Athenians offered the portico and the arms and the *acroteria* captured from the enemy." "According to the findings of modern archaeological research, the *arms* referred to in the inscription were the ropes used to fasten the bridges over the Hellespont which had enabled Xerxes and his army to cross the water and invade Greece while the *acroteria* were figure-heads of Persian ships." Petracos, *l.c.* p. 17. Again, we find in this dedication significant reference to the symbolism of "binding" and also here the ineluctable workings of fate and destiny, which both led to the binding together of Asia and Europe and to the severing of that bond. Moreover, the Ionic order of the column was deliberately echoed in the *stoa*, so that as one turned the corner of the polygonal wall and began the final ascent to the God, in looking briefly back one would have seen the "marching line" of the *stoa*'s Ionic order leading the eye to the high Ionic column and over all the brooding Sphinx of Naxos.

[This page of the manuscript has been revised by Ananda Kentish Coomaraswamy. The early version possessed a brief discussion of the iconography of the Theban Sphinx, most of which was later used. However, one line was excised and it is appropriate to include it here:] In the unriddling of the enigma by Oedipus, the Theban Sphinx is seated on the capital of an Ionic column (Fig. 99 [page 116]), or perched on a crag.

1 Cf. Plutarch, *Mor.* 397, 404 E. The Sphinx is sometimes called an oracle (παρθένος χρησμῳδός), Sophocles, *Oedipus Tyr.* 1199; χρησμολόγος and speaking δύσγυωστα, *scolia* on Euripedes, *Phoen.* 45 and 1760.

[2 Ananda Kentish Coomaraswamy quotes Furtwangler as giving this now famous and well-preserved temple to Aphrodite; however, it has since been recognized as belonging to the local Aeginetan deity called Aphaia. It is pertinent to note that this goddess was the subject of divine betrothal and "rapture." — Ed.]

3 A. Furtwangler, "*Die Sphinx von Aegina*," *Münchner Jahrb.* I, 1906. Cf. Dante, *Paradiso* 26; *Hinduism and Buddhism*, p. 23.

4 Cf. *Arch. Zeitung.*, 1876, p. 181; Payne, *Necrocorinthia*, 1931, p. 246 and pl. 46,4 (Our Fig. 98). It can hardly be doubted that the specific meaning of the Sphinx as an attribute depends on that of the deity with which the form is combined; with Aphrodite the sense is erotic, with Athene that of wisdom, with Ares fear-inspiring, and in connection with thrones and with the Tree, protective.

On Aphrodite's and Christian doves, cf. G. Weicker, *Der Seelenvogel*, 1902, p. 26.

Figure 99: Cup, Oedipus Painter; ca. 470 B.C. Vatican 16.541.

powers are surely her messengers, and in the last analysis not to be distinguished from her doves, or, indeed, from the doves of Christian iconography where they represent both "soul-birds" [Fig. 100] and also the Spirit of the Lord, of which it is said that it "caught away" (ἥρπασε) Philip (*Acts* VIII.39), as Christ also "caught away" (ήρπασε) Nonna, to be reborn with her husband in heaven (*Anth. Pal.* VIII.103), playing the part of Charon (*Anth. Pal.* XVI.385, 603); all these are in some sense harpies, "*raffender Todesdämonen*," *His* messengers "who slaying doth from death to life translate."

Like the Indian Gandharvas, the Sphinx in her different aspects can be thought of as either good or evil, according to our point of view. Undoubtedly, the specific meaning of the Sphinx as an attribute depends upon that of the specific deity with which the form is connected. This association of the sphinxes with Aphrodite is to be interpreted, I think, in connection with their erotic character, which is also the *raison d'être* of their beauty, which, as Ilberg has very rightly pointed out, is much rather the expression of the sensual consequence of the flowering of Greek art;[1] and if Aphrodite's "hounds" (as

[1] Perhaps an echo of Ilberg who (*l.c.* p. 32) speaks of the "*Schönheit . . . bezauberner Anmut . . . berückende Liebreitz*" of the Sphinx. Plutarch (*Stob. Floril.* 64.31) remarks upon the "inviting variegation" (ἐπαγωγὸν τὸ ποικίλμα) of the Sphinx's wings and compares her allure to that of Eros. Anaxilas says "men call the Theban Sphinx a light of live"; and this amorousness reminds us both of Eros and [of] the the Vedic Uṣas.

sphinxes are often called) are in effect *Erotes*, and "cherubs" in this sense, this in no way reduces their deadly power; for she and Eros, mother and son, are hardly distinguishable in their operation, as terrible as it is irresistible.[1] The unity of Love and Death has been recognized in all traditions; it was as true for the Greeks as for Meister Eckhart that "the kingdom of heaven is for none but the thoroughly *dead*"; and we find the prayer expressed, "Never may the Eros of the mightier gods cast upon me (προσδράκοι) the glance from which there is no escape."[2] It has been remarked that the special connection of Eros with Psyche is relatively late in Greece, but if this is true for the developed story of "Cupid and Psyche," the *Kēres* and Harpies and the stories of the high gods who carry off souls are not late, and the interesting facts are that Love had been originally a more generalized spirit and in fact a *Kēr* "of double nature, good and bad . . . fructifying or death-bringing,"[3] like the Indian Death (Mṛtyu) who is also the God of Love (Kāmadeva) and an archer in both capacities, and "devours his children as well as generates them,"[4] and that even in such late versions as Apuleius' the conception of Amor is by no means altogether sentimentalized.

[*Figure 100:* From a mosaic in the Baptistry at Albenga, 5th century A.D. In G. de Jerphanion, *La voie des monuments*, 1930, p. 150.]

---

1 Euripedes, *Hipp.* 522 f. and *passim*; cf. *Medea* 632-4. In Lycophron, *Al.* 605, her "love" is compared to the snare of the Erinyes.

2 Aeschylus, *Prom.* 903, cf. *Hipp.* 525 ("Not me, not me!") and *Medea* 632 ("Not at me!"). οσδράκοι recalls the whole class of other-world guardians whose glance is unendurable. In Apuleius, *Met.*, Amor is described as a fiery *draco*, i.e. what in Biblical language would be a seraph. The *Erinyes* that haunt Orestes are winged, but also ophidian (δρακοντώδεις, Euripedes, *Orestes* 256). The full sense of these implications pertains to the history of Sagittarius.

3 J. Harrison, *Prolegomena to Greek Religion*, pp. 175, 631.

4 *Pañcaviṁśa Brāhmaṇa* XXI.2.1.

In connection with the erotic aspect of the Sphinx and Siren, in which they are the lovers of those whom they carry off, it must not be overlooked that with only a slightly different colouring the concept is of worldwide distribution in the form of the "folklore" motive of the "fairy bride," in that of the theft of mortals by fairies, and in the legends of "Swan-maidens." The derivation is valid even etymologically, inasmuch as "fairy" is a form of *fata*,[1] Latin equivalent of Greek μοῖρα; (as "edict"); and it has long been recognized that "fairyland" is that other-world from which there is normally "no return," at least for those who have partaken of its food — an other-world that, like Hades, can be regarded as either a Land of Delight and Lasting Life, or as [the] more dreadful Realm of the Dead. The connection is most apparent in the case of the Celtic daughters of the Land-Under-Wave or Overseas who literally seduce their chosen mates, of whom it will suffice to cite the examples of [the Lorelei and the Mermaid of Celtic legend.[2]]

Men shrink from death, as a matter of course; but the death of all component things is inevitable, and for the dead to be translated to the untrodden, shining Ether, the substance of God and homeland of the Immortals, is the antithesis of an undesirable fate: "No evil Fate (μοῖρα) was that, that led thee hither, far from the pathways of men"![3] It is to reach our destination: For "all that from Ether sprouts seeds back again to the celestial orbit,"[4] "all things are etherized, being dissolved again into the Etherial Fire according to the great cycles";[5] and what applies to a *maha-pralaya* applies as well to the individual *pralaya* (ἀνάλυτις),[6] so that when we give up the Ghost (πνεῦμα ἀφιέναι or ἀωιέναι = *prāṇa-tyāga*, *-utsarga*)

---

1 One would like to cite also "fey" in the sense of "doomed," and also "fetch" in the sense of one's "double" seen as an omen of death; but the etymology of both these words is uncertain.

[2 These last references were not found in the original manuscript. — Ed.]

3 Parmenides, cited in Sextus Empiricus, *Adv. Dogm.* 111; the whole context is one of the most magnificent descriptions of a *Himmelfahrt* extant. "Led thee hither," that is by "the far-famed road of the Daimon," the *Logos Prompompos*, to the Etherial Gates of which the keys are held by "Much Retributive" or "Punitive Justice" (Δίκη πολόποινος), the safekeeper of the records of things-done [Bury's version, "of things," misses the point, which is that Punitive Justice is the "bookkeeper"]. Parmenides' "chariot" corresponds to the *devaratha* of *Aitareya Āraṇyaka* II.3.8, the "road" to the *devayana*, and and the *Prompompos* to Agni *adhvapati* and *puraētṛ*.

Euripedes, *Hipp.* 541 makes Aphrodite the Chatelaine; and these two keepers of the *Janua Coeli* correspond, I think, to the "beneficent" and "punitive" powers of Philo's Cherubim (*Heres* 166, *Abraham* 145, etc.), and in general to the "Mercy and Majesty" of the Islamic and other traditions, e.g. in Christianity the "Love and Wrath" of God, in the Priesthood and Kingship (Judgment) of Christ, in India represented by Mitra and Varuṇa.

4 Euripedes, fr. 836 (in Marcus Aurelius VII.50), i.e. to Zeus (Euripedes fr. 386 τὸνδ' ἄπειπον αἰθέρα . . . τοῦτον νόμιξε Ζῆνα). The most undesirable of fates is to be unfated (αμοιρα), [i.e., having] nowhere to go.

5 Eusebius, *Praep. evang.* XV.18.1 (κατὰ περιόδους τιοὰς τας μεγίστας) i.e. in Indian terms, when a *Kalpa* is completed).

6 As in *II Timothy* IV.6 where St. Paul speaks of his imminent ἀνάλυσις, which he is very surely *not* thinking of as an annihilation. Philo (*Somn.* II.67, cf. *Fug.* 59) says of Nadab and his brother Abihu that they "were not carried off (ἁρπασθέυτες) by a savage and evil beast" [I see in this wording an allusion to the Theban Sphinx,] but "resolved (ἀναλυθέυτες) into etherial rays of light."

our "spirit dies away into the Ether" (πνεῦμ' ἀφ εἰς αἰθέρα),[1] just as in India *ākāśam ātmā apyeti* or, in other words, "goes home" (*astaṁ gacchati*). And that is a desired consummation, for, as the Platonizing *Axiochus* tells us (366), the Immortal Soul, imprisoned in the earthly tabernacle that Nature has tacked onto us, "is ever longing for its heavenly native Ether" (τὸν οὐράνιον ποθεῖ καὶ τόμφυλον αἰθερά). In a remarkable passage, Philo says that at death, when the four elements of our physical constitution are returned to their sources, "the (immortal) Soul, whose nature is intellectual and celestial, will depart to find a father in Ether, the purest of the substances," as is only natural, seeing that the soul herself is a participation (μοῖρα) of that Fifth Substance that dominates the other four,[2] a participation (μοῖρα) of the Etherial Nature, and herself etherial,[3] a spark (απόσπασμα) of the divine and blessed Nature from which it can never be disconnected.[4] In all these contexts, of course, the "Soul" is not the carnal "soul" but the "Soul of the soul"[5] or Spirit (πνεῦμα); as in *Spec.* IV.123 where the essences of man's two souls or selves are distinguished, the substance of "that other Soul" being the "Divine Spirit" (πνεῦμα θεῖον) or "Etherial Spirit" (αἰθερίον πνεῦμα) which God inbreathed into the face of man as the breath of life (πνοὴ ξωῆς), and in *Somn.* I.138 f., where earthly souls return to earthly

---

1 Euripedes, fr. 971 cited in Plutarch, *Mor.* 416 D, and recalling the "measures of fire" that are kindled (ἅπτεται) from the "ever-living (ἀει ξωον = ἀσβεστος) Fire" at our birth and quenched (ἀποσβέννυται) therein at our death (Heracleitus, frs. XX, LXVII). Σβέννυμι and ἀπόσβεννυμι have all the values of Sanskrit *udvā* and *nirvā* (for which values cf. on *nibbāyati* in *HJAS.* IV [1939] 158f.). Σβέσις and *nirvāṇa*, indeed, imply a dying, but not necessarily an annihilation, although σβέσις often seems to have this meaning for Philo and Marcus Aurelius; Philo, for example, explains that death is "not an extinction of the soul" (μὴ σβέσις ψυῆς) but her separation from the body and return to her source, which is God (*Abraham* 258). The use of such terms is perfectly correct, however, because, as has been recognized in every traditional philosophy, "all change is a dying," and, in this sense, in the words of St. Thomas Aquinas, "no creature can attain a higher grade of nature without ceasing to exist" (*Sum. Theol.* I.63.3). Eusebius, discussing the Stoic [but doubtless much older] doctrine of *Ekpyrosis*, i.e. the "etherization" of all things, their "analysis" into the etherial Fire, points out that the words ἀνάλυσις and φθορά (death) were never understood literally but meant a translation, transformation, migration or change (μεταβολή, *Praep. evang.* XVIII.1-3) — and might as well have been discussing the meaning of *nirvāṇa*. Ἀνάλυσις and μεταβολή correspond to λύσις (ἀπὸ τῶν δεσμῶν) and μεταστποφή ἐπὶ τὰ εἰδωλα καῖ τὀφὼς in *Republic* 522 B. The Soul, considered apart from its earthly integuments, is ἄσβεστος καὶ ἀθάνατος (*Heres* 276), like the Ether, "that holy Fire, a flame unquenchable" (φλόξ . . . ἄσβεστος, *Confessions* 156-7) and so returns as like to like.

On *Ekpyrosis* see also Philo, *Aet.* 102, *Heres* 228, *Spec.* 208 with Colson's note, p. 621. The doctrine of cycles and final conflagration is also Indian.

2 *Heres* 282-3.

3 *LA.* III.161.

4 *Det.* 89, 90. ἀφ' αὖ ἀπέσπασται) is immortal." It is said that this argument for the immortality of the Soul appears for the first time in Pindar, *Dirge* 131 (96), "while the body of all men is subject to death, the image of life remaineth alive," but it may be taken for granted that it was one of much older invention. This image (εἴδωλον) is thought of as asleep when we are active, but awakening when our activity is stilled. Ἀπόσπασμα, *scintilla*, Sanskrit *sphur*, cf. *Maitri Upaniṣad* 24 and 26.

5 *Heres* 55; ψυχή ψυχῆς, like *ātmano' tmā*, *Maitri Upaniṣad* VI.7, *antaḥ puruśa*, *ib.* III.3, ὁ ἐντος ἄνθρωπος.

bodies, others "ascend on light wings to the Ether"[1] — "the pathway of 'birds'."[2] All of which is virtually a commentary on *Ecclesiastes* XII.7, "Then shall the dust return to the dust as it was: And the spirit return unto God who gave it" and *Psalms* CIV.29, 30, "Thou takest away their breath, they die, and return to their dust. Thou sendest forth thy spirit, they are created."[3] The Hebrews, like all other peoples, clearly distinguished the mortal "soul" (*nefeṣ*) from the immortal spirit (*ruaḥ*).

The Indian doctrines are identical, both as regards the fundamental principle, *duo sunt in homine*,[4] and as regards the identification of Ether with God, as the origin, life and end of all things.[5] The Ether (*ākāśa*) is not merely the Fifth Element,[6] but the very substance and abode of the supreme Deity,

---

1 On this *lev*itation and *elev*ation cf. Phaedrus 247-8; *Pañcaviṁśa Brāhmaṇa* XIV.1.12-13 (the gnostic is winged, and flies away; the agnostic are wingless and fall); Dante, *Paradiso* X.74, 75 (*chi no s'impenna che lassù voli, dal muto aspetti quindi le novelle*), XV.54 (*ch' all' alto volo ti vest'i le piume*); my *Hinduism and Buddhism*, note 269.

Plutarch, referring to Plato (*Timaeus* 55 C), and like Philo, thinks of the Ether as the summit of the soul's perfection; for he says that she "comes to rest in the Fifth when she has attained the power of reason and has perfected (τελεώσασα) her nature" (*Mor.* 390 F), i.e. that Fifth Essence which he calls "Sky" and says that others call it "Light" (φῶς) and others "Ether" and that it corresponds to the dodecahedron which "embraces" (περιέχων) the four and is the form appropriate to the cycles and motions of the soul (*ib.* 390 A, 423 A); in Plutarch, of the five senses, it is that of sight that corresponds to Ether and Light, but in India it is sound that is associated with the Ether, as being the principle of extension and, in particular, the source of every prophetic and heavenly "voice" (*vāg ākāśāt*), cf. *Abraham* 176 ἀπ ἀέπος φωνῆ.

2 Aeschylus, *Pr. V.* 282. Cf. Sanskrit *ākāśa-ga*, *khe-cara*, "bird."

3 *Chāndogya Upaniṣad* VI.11.3.

4 *Nirvahana upasaniharam*, see *Brahmaṇa Upaniṣad* IV.4.3.

5 St. Thomas Aquinas, *Sum. Theol.* I-II.26.4. These are the inner and outer man of St. Paul's Epistles (*II Corinthians* IV.16), and Plato's two parts of the soul, respectively mortal and immortal, of which one corresponds to Hebrew, "soul" (*nefeṣ*) and the other to the "spirit" (*ruaḥ*), one to the ψυχή and the other to the πνεῦμα, which the Word of God divides (*Hebrews* IV.12). In India, the distinction of the two souls or selves, mortal and immortal, that dwell together in us, is fundamental (e.g. *Aitareya Āraṇyaka* II.1.8, II.3.7, *Jaiminīya Brahmaṇa* I.17, *Chāndogya Upaniṣad* VIII.12.1, *Maitri Upaniṣad* II.3); a distinction in terms of "blood" and "seed" is made in *Aitareya Āraṇyaka* II.3.7, *Jaiminīya Upaniśad Brahmaṇa* III.37.6 and *Jaiminīya Brāhmaṇa* I.17, cf. *John* III.6-8 and *Galatians* VI.8. For Philo's distinction of the blood-soul (ἡ ἕναιμεος χυχή) from the Spirit (πνεῦμα) see *Heres* 55, 61, *Det.* 83, *Spec.* IV.123, *LA.* II.56 — highly significant for the criticism of the modern doctrines of "blood" and "race." [Cf.] Διπλοῦς . . . (Hermes Trismegistos, *Lib.* I.15).

That there are "two in us" must have been evident to man from the time that he first envisaged an afterlife; since it is only too obvious that the visible one of these two is corruptible and mortal. It is astonishing that Rohde (*Psyche*, p. 6) should have thought of this belief in an "other self" as a thing that "may well seem strange to us" (moderns), since that there are two in us is taken for granted in countless phrases still in daily use (e.g., "my better self," "self-mastery," "con-science," etc.), and no one supposes that a "selfless" man is not a self! It is equally surprising that so many scholars, meeting with some universal doctrine in a given context, so often think of it as a local peculiarity: Waley, for example, with reference to the *Tao Tē Ching*, 10, remarks that "there are two souls in a man, according to Chinese thinking . . . the spirit soul (*hun*) and the physical soul (*po*)" — as if this had been a peculiarly Chinese belief, and not actually of worldwide distribution and still current apart from the limited sects of the "nothing morists."

6 *Aitareya Āraṇyaka* II.6, and *Upaniṣads, passim.* There is an allusion to this as an Indian doctrine, curious because it seems to imply a Greek ignorance of the Fifth Element, in Philostatus, *Life of Apollonius* III.34.

whose nature is etherial (*ākāśatman*), and who "from that very Ether awakens this conceptual world, which comes into being by his act of contemplation (*anena . . . dhyāyate*), and then again in him goes home" (*praty astam yāti*).[1] So, when all the factors of our component personality are returned to their principles at death, "the Spirit enters into (or dies away in) the Ether (*ākāśam ātmā apyeti*),[2] becoming a god enters into the company of gods" (*devo bhūtvā devān apyeti*),[3] "being Brahma, dies into him" (*brahmaiva san brahmāpyeti*).[4] He being also the Spirit (*ātman*), it is to him that our spirit enters when the body is cut off — if, indeed we have known "in whom" we are departing then.[5] He is also the Gale (*vāyu, vāta*) of the Spirit, "the one entire deity," homeless himself but into whom all other gods and men "go home," and hence the funeral benediction, "Thy spirit to the Gale!" (*gacchatu vātem ātmā*) and the prayer of the dying man, "My gale to the immortal Wind!" (*vāyur anilam amṛtam*),[6] i.e. "Into thy hands, O Lord, I commend my spirit"[7] — "To Prajāpati let me entrust myself."[8]

[Illustration from a medieval Christian bestiary.]

1 Cf. *Śatapatha Brāhmaṇa* X.6.16.
2 *Maitri Upaniṣad* VI.17.
3 *Brāhmaṇa Upaniṣad* III.2.13.
4 *Brāhmaṇa Upaniṣad* IV.1.2.
5 *Brāhmaṇa Upaniṣad* IV.6.6.
6 *Ṛgveda* X.16.5.
7 *Brahmaṇa Upaniṣad* V.15.1.
8 Cf. *Chāndogya Upaniṣad* II.22.5.

[Eagle with Ganymeda or Psyche;] 5th century B.C. [From] C. Trever, *Nouveax Peats Sasanides de l'Ermitage*, Moscow-Leningrad, 1937.

Chapter VII

The Immortal Soul as Psychopomp

WE HAVE SPOKEN SO FAR OF THE SOUL AS CARRIED OFF BY WINGED powers other than itself. But the soul herself is a "bird," alike from the Greek point of view and that of the Indian and other traditions; and when her wings are grown, it is on these wings of her own that she flies away.[1] But such souls as are "afraid of the unseen and of Hades,"[2] and are attached to earthly things, linger below, "and flit about the monuments and tombs where their dim phantasms (σκιοειδη φαντάσματα) have been seen" — for such souls as have died unpurified, and still participate in the perceptible, have this sort of image (εἴδωλα).[3] It is only after much delay and resistance that such a soul is "led away with violence, and hardly even so, by her appointed daimon"; whereas "the orderly and intelligent soul follows its guide (ἡγεμών) and understands what is taking place."[4] We know who this guide is, for it has just been said[5] that "after death, each one's daimon, (ὁ ἑκάστου δαίμων), to whom he has been allotted in life, leads him to the place where the dead must be assembled and judged" after which they are taken charge of by two other guides, of whom one leads them to their place in Hades and the other brings them back to birth "after long periods of time."[6] Furthermore, we know who it is that is called "each one's daimon" — or, as we should say in India, *Yakṣa*, "*Genius*," and *ārakkha devatā*, "guardian

---

1 *Phaedrus* 247, 248. *Anth. Pal.* VII.62.

2 There is a play on the words ἀειδής, "formless" (cf. Philo, *Gig.* 54) and Ἅιδης, "Hades," both implying "invisible" or "unknown"; but elsewhere Plato thinks that Hades is not so called from his invisibility (ἀειδές) but "from knowing (εἰδέναι) all things fair" and that he is the perfect sophist and philosopher, a benefactor both here and in the other world, where he only associates with those who are pure of all the evils and desires of the body; and no one ever desires, "not the Sirens themselves," to leave that other world of his, where he holds his guests "in bonds (δήσας) by their desire of virtue" (*Cratylus* 403 E-404 A, B). This explanation is probably "hermeneutic" (*nirutka, nirvacana*) rather than "etymological"; the root in any case is the Sanskrit *vid*, English *wit*, etc.

Hades (or Pluto), originally the son of Chronos and brother of Zeus — or identified with him (Euripedes, Nauck fr. 912; Justin, *Cohort.* C.15) or with the Sun (cf. G.H. Macurdy, *Troy and Paeonia*, 1925, chapter iii), or with Dionysos (Heracleitus, fr. CXXVII) — and corresponding to the Indian Yama, God of Death and associated with Varuṇa in Paradise, is for Plato more often the place than the person; and as a place, one of happiness and greater than that of this world, and where alone true wisdom is to be found (*Apology* 41, *Phaedo* 63, etc.). Only those who have done evil have cause to fear (Plato, *Laws* 959 B).

3 The contrast between such murky forms as these, and such radiant εἴδωλα as that of Helen that Zeus reveals to Menelaus, "in folds of Ether," i.e. Light. In general, although by no means necessarily, εἴδωλον stand for the realities of things, and φαντάσμα for our mere apprehensions or impressions of things (cf. *Republic* 520 C, 532 B, with σαιοειδῆ, cf. *Republic* 532 B μεταστροθή ἀπὸ τῶν σκιῶν).

4 *Phaedo* 108 A, B.

5 *Phaedo* 107 D.

6 *Phaedo* 107 D, cf. 113 D and *Laws* 732 C. In *Republic* 617 E, cf. 620 E, however, each one chooses his own daimon and vocation.

(Continued on following page.)

angel"[1] — for "God has given to each one of us his daimon (δαίμουα θεὸς ἑκαστῳ δέδωκε), that form[2] (εἶδος) of the soul that is housed in the top (ἐπ ἄκρῳ)[3] of the body, and which lifts us . . . up from the Earth towards our kinship in Heaven" and one "who ever tends this godhood (θεῖον) and well entertains (εὖ . . . κεκοσμημένων) the inhabitant daimon, will be a man felicitous" (εὐδαμονός).[4]

Now let us follow up the implications of the words ἐπ' ἀκρῳτῷ σώματι and ἀκροπόλις in the preceding contexts. The "top" of the body, which is the seat of the daimon, the most lordly part of the soul (*ut supra*), "the immortal principle of the soul" (ἀρχὴ φυχῆς ἀθάνατον,[5] *Timaeus* 69 C), "the immortal part of us that is to be obeyed as Law" (*Laws* 714) and "real self of each of us" (τὸι δὲ ὄντα ἑκαστον ὄντως *Laws* 959 B)[6] is, of course, the "head" (κεφαλή), which is "a spherical body in imitation of the spherical figure of the Universe,

---

(Continued from preceding page.)

For the two "other guides" cf. *Republic* 617 D. ff; and the Hermetic fragment XXVI.3, Scott, *Hermetica* I.616, "for there are two guardsmen of the Universal Providence, one the Cure of Souls (ψυχοταμίας) and the other the Conductor of Souls (ψυχοπομπός) . . . both of whom act according to the mind of God."

The allotted space in "Hades" (the "other world") is according to the soul's deserts, those who have done wrong being sent below, while those who have done well are conducted to the surface of "the pure earth that is in Heaven, which those who speak of such matters call the Ether" *(Phaedo* 109 C f).

For the "long periods," cf. *Bhagavad Gītā* VI.41 and Eusebius, *Praep. evang.* XV.1. These periods are of a "thousand" years (*Phaedrus* 249 A, B; *Republic* 615 A) — the duration of a *Kalpa* or "Day of Brahma" *Bhagavad Gītā* VIII.17) or *Jahve* (*Psalms* XC.4; *II Peter* III.8), and an Aeon of the Gods and of Prajāpati (*Śatapatha Brāhmaṇa* XI.1.6.6, 14), the (Great) Year; while man's life is alike for Plato and the Brahmans one of a hundred human years, this "not dying" (prematurely) here corresponding to an "immortality" there.

For "assembled," cf. Sanskrit Yama as *samganana*.

1 Sanskrit *yakṣa* and Greek δαίμον are almost identical in range of meaning, from "god" to "spirit" of any quality; see my "Yakṣa of the Vedas and Upanisads" in *Quarterly Journal of the Mythic Society* XXVIII [1938], especially page numbers 231-240 and note 21 (add *Samyutta Nikāya* I.32 "Who is that Yakṣa who does not hanker for food?" and *Majjhima Nikāya* I.386, the Buddha as the *āhavanīya* Yakṣa to whom the obligation is due). For the Yakṣa as guardian angel (as in Hesiod, *Works and Days* 121 f., Plato, *Phaedo* 620 E δαίμων . . . φύλαξ and Menander, frs. 550, 551, δαίμωω ἀνδρὶ . . . μυσταγωγός) see my *Yakṣas I*, Washington [D.C.], 1928, pp. 13-16, 31.

[2 There are two "forms" of the soul: Carnal and spiritual, mortal and immortal (*Timaeus* 90 D, *Republic* 439 E, *Phaedo* 79 A, B). When Plato also speaks of three kinds or castes (γένος) in the soul, there is a division of the mortal soul into a better and a worse part, θυμος and επιθυμια.]

3 "Housed at the Top," i.e. in the head; when man is thought of as a "city" (πολις = *pura*), then it is for the better part of the mortal soul to hear and obey and serve "the word from the Acropolis" (*Timaeus* 70 A). i.e. the voice of the conscience (συνεσις with which Apuleius rightly identified "the God of Socrates" (see *Laws* 969 C and *Timaeus* 90 C).

4 "Felicitous" [is] the normal rendering of εὐδαιμουος (see *Cratylus* 398 B, C).

5 Philo's ἡγεμονικὸν, ψυχήψυχῆς, *Q. rerum div., Heres* 55; *ātmano'tmā netā amṛtākhyaḥ, Maitri Upaniṣad* VI.7 ("Self of the self, immortal leader).

6 The doctrine of "man's two selves," regarding which the question is often asked, "By which self does one attain the *summum bonum*?" or "In whom, when I depart hence, shall I be going forth?" (*Bṛhadāraṇyaka Upaniṣad* IV.3.7, *Praśna Upaniṣad* VI.3; in Buddhism, *Sutta Nipāta*, 508). The two selves, born respectively of the human and divine wombs in *Jaiminīya Brāhmaṇa* I.17 (see *JAOS*. XIX.115) are the same as those born of the flesh and born of the spirit in *John* III.6.

and now we call it 'head' for that it is the most divine part and the ruler of the universe within us" (*Timaeus* 44 D, E).[1]

Observe that the expression "head" does not here mean merely the cranium, but also metaphorically the "head of the community"; and that in fact the immortal and divine and lordly principle, which is also the smaller part and to be contrasted with the multitude of the rest (*Republic* 431 C), is "housed" (προσῳκο δομέω), *Timaeus* 69 C) and "dwells together with" (σύνοικον ἐω αὐτῶ, *Timaeus* 90 A, C, etc.) the mortal soul in the microcosmic house of the body.[2] Bearing this in mind, we cannot fail to see that in ἐπ' ἀκρῳ τῷ σώματι . . . κεφαλή . . . θειότατον . . . κυριωτάτον . . . ούναικον taken together are, to say the least, suggestive of the κεφαλὴ γωνίας . . . ὄντος ἀκρογωνιαίου αὐτοῦ χριστοῦ ἴησοῦ, ἐν ῷ πᾶσα οἰκοδομὴ συναρμολογουμ ένη ἀυξει εἰσναὸω ἅγιου ἐν κυρυῷ, ἐν ῷ καὶ ὑμεῖς συνοικοδομεῖσθε εἰς κατοικητήριον τοῦ θεοῦ ἐν πνεύματι, *Luke* XX.17 and *Ephesians* II.20. Alike for Plato and [the] New Testament the immanent deity is the "top" or "head" of the microcosmic composite, as is the intelligible Sun the top and head and focus of all that it enlightens in the macrocosm.

[Prof. E. Panofsky,[3] René Guénon[4] and myself, having referred to the *lapis in caput anguli* as a "keystone" and regarding it as such, have found it of great interest that] Pausanias (IX.38.3) refers to "the very topmost of the stones" of a round building with a rather blunt top as "the harmony (ἁρμονία) of the whole building." The word ἁρμονία means both "fastening" or "bond" and "harmony"; the point at which they are "harmonized." Miss Jane Harrison, quite properly, renders the word by "keystone" (*Themis*, p. 401). In this sense the word is the precise equivalent of the Indian *kaṇṇikā*, or roof-plate of a domed building, by which the rafters of the dome are supported and in which they are met together and are thus unified. We have shown that such a roof-plate was the symbol of the Sun, that it was perforated and that it could be used as an exit by such as possessed the requisite powers of flight.[5] In this architectural sense the Sun is described as a harmony by Dionysius, *De div. nom.*, Ch. IV: "The Sun is so-called (ἥλιος) because he summeth up (αολλψποιεῖ) all things and unites the scattered elements of the soul and so conjoineth together all spiritual and rational beings, uniting them in one."[6] The Sun is, indeed, "the Spirit of all

---

1 Cf. *Maitri Upaniṣad* VI.7 "The light-world is the head of Prajāpati's cosmic body," and *Bṛhadāraṇyaka Upaniṣad* II.1.2. "The Person who is yonder in the Sun . . . I worship him as the outstanding head and king of all beings." In the sacrificial ritual, because this body has been decapitated by the separation of Sky and Earth in the beginning, an important part is played by the rites of "heading" (*Webster* 2) the Sacrifice in which the bodies of the Sacrificer and the Deity are simultaneously reconstituted.

[2 Just as in the Indian texts Earth and Sky, *Sacerdotum* and *Regnum*, when the *daivam mithunam* = ἱερος γάμος has been celebrated, are said to be "cohabitant" (*samokasā*) here in the realm or in the individual body.]

3 *Art Bulletin* XVII, p. 450.

4 "*La Pierre angulaire*," *Études Traditionelles*, 45, 1940 *Avril et Mai*.

5 In "The Symbolism of the Dome," etc.

6 Based on *Cratylus* 409 A where ἥλεος, Doric ἅλιος "might be derived from collecting (ἁλιςειν) men when he rises." Similarly in our Sanskrit sources, where the Sun is identified with *prāṇa*, the "breath of life" and *prāṇa* is derived from *prāṇī*, to "lead forth," cf. *Praśna Upaniṣad* I.8 "Yonder Sun arises as the life (*prāṇa*) of beings" and *Aitareya Brāhmaṇa* V.31 "The Sun as he rises leads forward (*prāṇyati*) all creatures, therefore they call him the 'Breath'" (*prāṇa*).

that is in motion or at rest" (*Ṛgveda* I.115.1), and the "fastening" (*āsañjanum*) to which all things are linked by his rays or threads of pneumatic light[1] of which he is himself the "seventh and best" (*Śatapatha Brāhmaṇa* I.9.3.10, VI.7.1.17, VIII.7.3.10, X.2.6.8 etc.).[2] The Sun as a "harmony" in these senses is manifestly the unique principle "in whom ye are all builded together."[3]

Now we have seen that the roof-plate of a domed structure — whether that of an actual building or that of the cosmos — is typically perforated; the "eye" of the dome being either actually or vestigially the foramen or luffer by which the smoke from the hearth below it escapes, and at the same time the "light" by which the interior is illuminated. We find accordingly διὰ τῆς ὀπαίας κεραμίδος = "through the eyed tile" = διὰ τῆς καπνίας, "through the luffer"; and ὀπή, "hole or eye in the roof, serving as a chimney" = κάπνη, καπνο ςόχη (Sanskrit *dhūma nirgamana*).[4] The Sun is "golden-eyed" (χρυσωπός).[5]

From Hermes Trismegistus, *Lib.* I.12-20, we can cite a splendid passage in which the cosmic ἁρμονία is indeed the "eye" through which the Son of God

---

[1] In accordance with the well known "thread spirit" (*sūtrātman*) doctrine (*loc. cit.*, and *Atharva Veda* X.8.38, *Jaiminīya Upaniṣad Brāhmaṇa* III.4.1, *Bhagavad Gītā* VII.7 ("All this is threaded upon me . . . "), *Tripura Rahasya* IV.119; Plato, *Laws* 644 D, E, *Theatetus* 153 C, D; *John* XII.32; Shams-i-Tabriz (Nicholson, *Ode* 28) "He gave me the end of a golden thread . . . ," *Hafiz* I.368.2; Blake, "I give you the end of a golden string . . . "

[2] The six rays are the six directions (East, South, West, North, Zenith and Nadir) of the cosmic cross (of which the two-armed cross is a plane diagram), the seventh the solar point of their intersection; this point corresponding also to the "nail of the cross" in the *Acts of Peter* XXXVIII. It is upon this cosmic basis that the importance of the number seven in all the other connections depends. These formulations are of the greatest importance to the theologian and iconologist: For example, the mediaeval representations of the "Seven Gifts of the Spirit" (Mâle, *Religious Art in France of the Thirteenth Century*, Figs. 91, 93) are essentially six-spoked Sun-wheels. The number seven recurs in solar symbolism everywhere from the Neolithic onwards.

[3] In *Ephesians* II.20, 21 Christ is the keystone (ἀκρογωγιαίος) "in whom all the structure is harmonized (σὺναρμολογομὲνη) . . . in whom ye are all builded together"; in other words, the "harmony" of all the parts. Another sense in which Christ might have been spoken of as a "harmony" is that of the "Bridegroom" (ἁρμοστῆς), implied in *II Corinthians* XI.12 "I have espoused (ἡρμοσαμην) you to one husband . . . Christ" — the Vedic Aryaman and Gandharva from whom all human wives are, so to say, borrowed.

[4] For ὀπαίος and ὀπή see Liddell and Scott. Cf. Ernest Diez in *Ars Islamica* V.39, 45, speaking of buildings "in which space was the primary problem and was placed in relation to, and dependent on, infinite space by means of a widely open *opaion* in the zenith of the cupola. The relation to open space was always emphasized by the skylight lantern in Western architecture . . . Islamic art appears as individuation of its metaphysical basis" (*unendliche Grund*). Later, becomes a designation of any window; cf. Sanskrit *gavākṣa*, "bullseye," probably originally the round sky-light overhead, but in the extant literature any round window. The faces that, in the actual architecture, are often represented as looking out of such windows are rightly termed *gandharva-mukha*, that is "face of the solar Eros" (the Sun as Vena, etc.), and this designation is good evidence for the equation "bullseye" = sun's eye; the same applies to the "bullseye" of a target.

In the archetypal *domus*, smoke rises from a central hearth to escape through the luffer, and in the same way if the *domus* is a temple. When Euripedes (*Ion* 89, 90) says that the fragrant smoke from the altar of the temple of Apollo at Delphi "flies like a bird (πεταται) = Sanskrit *patati*) to the roof" it is certain that there must have been an "eye" through which it escaped; and in the same way in the case of outdoor altars where the Sky is the roof. In all these cosmic constructions the altar is "the navel of the Earth," and the eye above it the nave of the Sun-wheel; the column of smoke is one of the many types of the *Axis Mundi*.

[5] Euripedes, *Electra* 740.

surveys all that is "under the sun."[1] Here the Man of Eternal Substance who is "the Son and Image of God, the (first) Mind, the Father of all, he who is Life and Light," while still "in the sphere of the Demiurge (God, as aforesaid),[2] himself too willed to create (δημιουρνεῖν);[3] and the Father gave him leave. . . (Accordingly) he willed to break through the orbits of the Governors (τῶ

---

1 Scott in the text and notes of the *Hermetica* is mistaken in supposing that it is through the moon that the Man looks out. All the heavenly bodies had been thought of as wheels having a single aperture described as a breathing-hole (see citations from Hippolytus and Aetios in Burnet, *Early Greek Philosophy*, 1930, pp. 66, 67). In just the same way the "Three Lights" (Agni, Vāyu and Āditya — Fire, Air and Sun) in the Indian cosmology are represented in the construction of the fire-altar by the three ringstones called the "Self-perforates" (*svayamātṛṇṇa*), the openings being explicitly both "for the passage of the breaths" and "for looking through"; furthermore, the way up and down these worlds leads through these holes, the lights themselves being spoken of accordingly as the stepping stones or rungs of a ladder by which one ascends or descends. Similar formulae are met with in the accounts of the *Himmelfahrten* of the Siberian Shamans. All this and much more material is collected in my "*Svayamātṛṇṇā: Janua Coeli*," which was in type and due to appear in *Zalmoxis II*, in Bucharest, nearly two years ago.

It is, accordingly, true that the Son of God looks through the Moon and sees the sublunary world, his eye is really far away, the Sun is the eye piece of his cosmic telescope, and the Moon only its most distant lens. To say, as Scott says (*Hermetica* I.121, Note 5) that it must have been the lunar sphere that the Man broke through cannot be reconciled with his evidently right pronouncement in another place (*Hermetica* II.63) that it was the eighth and outermost sphere, that of the fixed stars (from above all the planets, that is) that the Man looked out.

Another reference to the *Aussichtspunkt* will be found in Plato's *Statesman*, 272 E. Here, at the end of the cycle (i.e. Sanskrit *yuga* or *kalpa* preceding ours) God (χπονος, θεος, ὀμεγίστος δαίμιον) "let go the handle of the rudders and withdrew to his place of outlook" (εἰς τὴν αὑτοῦ περιωπήν), i.e. to the "crow's nest" of the cosmic vessel, the Ship of Life, of which the mast is the same as the *Axis Mundi*. It is in the same way that in the *Śatapatha Brāhmaṇa* XI.2.3.3 Brahma "withdrew to the farther half" (*parārdham agacchat*). The point of greatest interest here is that the "place of outlook, or circumspection" is precisely an "eye" (ὤψ in περι-ωπή), an eye that can only be the sun. It is not without interest that the analogous *pari-caks*, is to "overlook" in [the] secondary sense of "neglect." It is in just this sense that the *Deus absconditus* "over-looks" the world, but from the same place that his Son again "surveys" the world "with a view to" entering it at the beginning of another round.

[Coomaraswamy appended the note:]

. . . how best to navigate the "ship of life through this voyage of existence" *Laws* 803 B.]

2 "I the Creator and Father of works" (ἐγω δημιουργὸς πατὴρ τε ἔργων); the Father's works being "that which is beautifully framed" (τόρὴν καλῶς ἁρμόσθεν) and may not be dissolved (ἄλυτα) save by his will (*Timaeus* 41 A, B), i.e. until the end of time, at the Great Dissolution (*mahāpralaya*). This is really the answer to the question, asked by Stryzgowski, "Whence arises the idea of building a cupola with rafters?" (*Early Church Art in Northern Europe*, p. 63).

Mark the word ἁρμόσθεν; it implies that the Father of works is a carpenter (ἁρμόστης); the frame of the universe and the analogous human body is quite literally a "harmony," a piece of joinery. And since the "material" of which the world is made is "wood" (ὕλη, primary matter) we begin to see exactly why the Son of God is called "the carpenter's son" and "the carpenter" (*Matthew* XIII.55 ὁ τοῦ τέκτονος υἱός, *Mark* VI.3 ὁ τέκτων; cf. *Iliad* V.59, 60 τέκτονος υἱὸν Ἁρμονίδεω): By what other craftsman could the world have been fitly framed? In the same way [the] Sanskrit Tvaṣṭr is "the Carpenter" and the solar Indra, his son, Visvakarma, "the All-maker" (later, in a more restricted sense, the patron deity of the craftsmen's guilds); and that of which the world is made is likewise a "wood" (*vana*, *Ṛgveda* X.31.7 and X.81.4).

The root ἁρμονία, etc., is root *ar*, Sanskrit *ṛ* ("set in motion," "infix"), present also in such notable words as αρετή, αριντος, ἀριθμός, ἅρμα; Latin *ars* (art); Sanskrit *aram* ("sufficient," "adequate"), *arya* ("noble"), *arc* ("project," "shine," "sing"), *ṛta* ("order," "rite") and *ṛtu* ("season").

3 "Through him all things were made" (*John* I.3). The Sun is the "All-maker," Visvakarma. When this Eye is opened, then his image-bearing light implants all forms according to the power of the recipients to receive them.

διοικητόρων);[1] and having all power over the mortal and irrational living beings in the cosmos, he leaned-and-looked-out through the Harmony (διὰ τῆς ἁπμονίασ),[2] broke through the cupola (τὸ κύτος),[3] and showed to downward tending Nature the beautiful form of God. And Nature, seeing the beauty of the form of God, smiled with insatiable love of the Man, showing the reflection of that most beautiful form in the water[4] and its shadow on the Earth." Because of the union of the man with Nature, man is mortal as regards his body, and immortal as regards the Man, who is "born a slave of Fate,[5] but

---

1 The seven planets, governing as Fate, *ib.* I.10. The "Seven Seers" of *Ṛgveda Samhitā* X.82.2, and microcosmically the "Seven Breaths" (powers of the soul) in *Bṛhadāraṇyaka Upaniṣad* II.2.3.

2 For the Sun as God's all-seeing eye innumerable texts could be cited from Indian and other sources.

3 With special reference to the spherical form of the head, which is "a copy of the spherical form of the universe" (Plato, *Timaeus* 44 D). Cf. *Timaeus* 45 A to τὸ πῆς κεφαλῆς κύτος, and Hermes Trismegistus *Lib.* X.11 ὁ κόσμος σραιρά ἐστι, τουτέστι κεφαλή. So also in the *Bṛhadāraṇyaka Upaniṣad* II.2.3, with reference to [the] vault of heaven and the human cranium, "There is a bowl with mouth below and base above [. . .] it is the head, for this is a bowl with mouth below and base above"; and in *Maitri Upaniṣad* VI.6 the Sky is the "head of Prajāpati's world-form . . . its eye(s) the Sun . . . He (Prajāpati) is the Spirit of the All, the Eye of the All . . . This is his all-supporting form; this whole world is therein contained"; and *Jaiminīya Upaniṣad Brāhmaṇa*, "The summit (*agram*), that is His head; thence he expressed the Sky; that (head) of his the Sky accompanies." So for "broke through the cupola" we might have said "through the skull-cap of the world"; cf *Mark* I.10 "He saw the heavens opened and the Spirit . . . descending."

Now what is above the sun is transcendental to the world "under the Sun," just as what is above the crown of the head is transcendental to the man below. The Sky or skull-cap, in other words, is the boundary (*sīman*) between the finite and infinite, measured and immeasurable space, the mortal and the immortal. "Boundary," then, becomes the designation of the cranial suture in the middle of the head" (*Aitareya Brāhmaṇa* IV.22), or cranial foramen (*Brahmarandhra*, *Hamsa Upaniṣad* I.3). It is by the way of this boundary that Brahma, Ātman, the Spirit, enters the world and is born therein in all beings. And accordingly, just as in Hermes the Man of Eternal Substance reveals the image of the Father, so Vena, the "yearning Sun" "hath made manifest the Brahma, first born of old from the shining boundary" (*sīmatas*, *Atharva Veda Saṁhitā* IV.1.1 and *passim*); or as stated more fully in the *Aitareya Upaniṣad* III.11.12, "He (Ātman) considered (*īkṣata*, 'saw'), 'How now can this world exist without me?' So cleaving apart this very boundary (*sīman*), by that door he entered . . . That is the 'delighting'." This "delighting" *nandana*) suggests *Hermes* I.14 where the Man and Nature are "in love with one another" (ἐρώμενοι), and actually implies a participation of that divine beatitude (*ānanda*) "without some share in which none might live or breathe" (*Bṛhadāraṇyaka Upaniṣad* IV.3.32, *Taittirīya Upaniṣad* II.7).

Now Jupiter Terminus is the "boundary God," and we see why his worship must be hypaethral. He corresponds to the Agni "standing as a pillar of life in the nest of the Supernal, at the parting of the (seven) ways" (*Ṛgveda Samhitā* X.5.6) and the Sun as *Axis Mundi* and goal-post (*Jaiminīya Upaniṣad Brāhmaṇa* I.10.9, *Pañcaviṁśa Brāhmaṇa* IX.1.35, etc.). And hence "Even today, lest he (Jupiter Terminus) see aught above him but the stars, have temple roofs their *exiguum foramen*" Ovid, *Fast.* II.667); "*Quam angusta porta et arta via quae ducit ad vitam: Et pauci sunt qui inveniunt eam*" (*Math.* VI.14).

4 Closely paralleled in the *Pañcaviṁśa Brāhmaṇa* VII.8.1 "Unto the Waters came their season. The Gale (of the Spirit) moved over the surface. Thence came into being a something beautiful. Therein Mitra-varunau saw themselves reflected: They said, 'A something beautiful, indeed, has here been born amongst the Gods'." Similarly *Ṛgveda* I.164.25 "He (God) beheld the Sun reflected in the vehicle."

5 εἱρμαρμίνη, (sc. μοῖρα) is literally "allotted destiny": The essential meaning of the root (present also in Latin *mors*) is "to receive one's portion, with collateral notion of being one's due" (Liddell and Scott); μοῖρα is sometimes simply "inheritance," and to be ἄμοιρος is to be deprived of one's due share, usually of something good; κατὰ μοὶραν is tantamount to κατὰ φύσιν, "naturally,"

(Continued on following page.)

also exalted above the Harmony." When the first bisexual beings had been separated as man and woman, then "God's Foreknowing (ἡ πρόγοια, Providence),[1] working by means of Fate and of the Harmony (διὰ τῆς

(Continued from preceding page.)

"duly," "rightly." The notion of Fate is very often misunderstood to mean something arbitrarily imposed upon us from without; what it really implies is that which we must and ought to expect; one who is born is "fated" to die, one who puts his hand in the fire is "fated" to be burnt; all the mortal part of us is "fey." Nothing in Plato contradicts the orthodox view, implied in the word μοῖρα itself, that "Fate lies in the created causes themselves" (St. Thomas Aquinas, *Sum. Theol.* I.116.2); "There are no special doors for calamity and happiness; they come as men themselves summon them" (*Thai-Shang*, *SBE.* XL.235); "It is destined (εἵμαρται) that he who does evil things shall suffer evil, and to this end he does it, in that he may suffer the penalty for having done it . . . the punishment is self-inflicted" (Hermes Trismegistus *Lib.* XIII.1.5 and X.19 A); in the vernacular, "what is coming to us" is just "what we ask for." The First Cause is directly the cause of our *being* (and this is also a participation), but only indirectly, through the mediate causes, the powers that we called forces and of which the ancients spoke as "gods," the cause of our being *what* we are. What we are at any given moment is the resultant of all "things that have been done" (Sanskrit *karma*), of which we are precisely the heirs. Had it been otherwise, as St. Thomas Aquinas expresses it, "The world would have been deprived of the perfection of causality"; actually, "Nothing happens by chance."

So, as Plato says, all that is done by the "Draughts-player" (the "Aeon" of Heracleitus fr. lxxix) is "to shift the character that grows better to a superior place, and the worse to a worse, according to what belongs to each of them, thus apportioning an appropriate Fate . . . It was to this end that He designed the rule . . . For according to the trend of our desires and the natures of our souls each of us usually becomes of a like character [paralleled almost word for word in *Bṛhadāraṇyaka Upaniṣad* IV.4.5 and *Maitri Upaniṣad* VI.34.3 c] . . . the divinely virtuous "being transported by a holy road [= Sanskrit *devayana*, *brahmayana*] to another and better place and *vice-versa*; and, addressing those who think they have been left uncared for by the gods, he says "*This* is the 'Judgment' of the gods who dwell on Olympus" (*Laws* 903 D [to] 904 D). The judgments of human law are just as if they are of the same kind (*Laws* 728).

We cannot here enter into the problem of "liberation" from Fate and being "no longer under the law" except to say that since it is the mortal part of us that is fatally determined, "freedom" can only mean to have our consciousness of being only in the immortal part of us, that is "knowing ourselves" and becoming what we really are, rather than what we seem to be. This could be by an extended citation of parallel passages from Plato, the *Upaniṣads* and other sources, notably Boethius, *De consol.* IV.6: "Everything is by so much the freer from Fate, by how much it draweth nigh to the Pivot (*cardo*). And if it sticketh to the stability of the Supernal Mind, free from motion, it surpasses also the necessity of Fate." This derives from Plato's *Laws* 893. Meanings of *cardo* are "hinge" (of a door), "fitting together of beams," "point" (of the Pole), "that on which everything turns"; Greek ἀκή, ἀκμή, ἄκρον; Sanskrit *agra*. Boethius himself has just previously spoken of the circles that turn about the same centre, "of which the inmost approaches the simplicity of the midst, which is as it were the pivot (*cardo*) of the rest." That the etymological equivalent κράδη has for its primary meaning the "tip of a branch, especially of fig-trees" (cf. Hesiod, *Works* 679) presents at least a curious coincidence, since they say of the Tree of Life, at the top of which the solar eagle nests, that "At its top the fig is sweet; none gaineth it who knoweth not the Father" (*Ṛgveda* I.164.22). In any case it is clear that Boethius' *cardo* is the top of the *Axis Mundi* and the point at which this Axis penetrates the Sky that it "supports," in other words that he is referring to the Sun, as the "Cardinal" of the world, i.e. above the whole "structure" of the universe and above its solar construction.

1 Sanskrit *prajñā*, etymologically and semantically "prognosis," and *prajñātman*, the "Foreknowing Spirit"; the "incorporeal foreknowing solar Self" that "mounts" the corporeal (mortal) self as its vehicle (*Aitareya Āraṇyaka* III.2.3 with *Bṛhadāraṇyaka Upaniṣad* IV.3.21), just as in *Timaeus* 44 D [to] 45 B ἡ τῆς ψυχῆς πρόνοια, "the most divine and ruling part of us" has the body "for its chariot and vehicle."

This is "He who dwelling in the Sun, yet is other than the Sun . . . whose body the Sun is . . . He who dwelling in the semen is yet other than the semen . . . is your Self, the Inner

(Continued on following page.)

εἱμαρμένης καὶ ἁρμονίας),[1] brought about the unions of male and female, and set the births agoing."[2]

When this much has been said, Hermes asks to be told about "the upward road of the Birth,[3] how I may participate in Life." Poimander answers, "At the dissolution of your hylic body . . . the bodily senses return to their own sources, becoming parts of the Cosmos, and entering into fresh combinations to do other work; the brave and desirous parts[4] return to irrational nature; and it remains, then,

---

(Continued from preceding page.)

Controller, Immortal" (*Bṛhadāraṇyaka Upaniṣad* III.7.9, 23), who then enters into the corporeal self as its Life (*prāna*) "grasps and upraises the body," where these two, the Spirit and the Life, "dwell together" and from which they depart together (*Kauṣītaki Upaniṣad* II.3, IV.20, cf. *Aitareya Āraṇyaka* II.6).

Hence it is said that creatures "are born providentially" (*yathā prajñām hi sambhavaḥ, Aitareya Āraṇyaka* II.3.2); and that when the Spirit departs with the Life and is about to enter a new body, then "awareness, works and ancient Providence take hold of it" (*tam vidyakarmahī samanvārabhete pūrva-prajñā ca, Bṛhadāraṇyaka Upaniṣad* IV.4.2). In all such contexts it must be remembered that it is not "this man" but God that is born again: As Sankara says, "It is the Lord alone that wanders about (from one body to another)" (*satyam, nesvarad anyah samsari, Brahmasūtra-bhāṣya* I.1.5 — a doctrine amply supported by the texts (e.g. *Muṇḍaka Upaniṣad* II.2.6, *Maitri Upaniṣad* II.7). The Lord is the First Cause, and as such the "fifth and Divine (*daivyam*) cause" in *Bhagavad Gītā* XVIII.14-15, where the word is rightly rendered by Barnett as "Providence." "Works" are the "mediate causes" of our being "what we are" (*etāvat*). The Spirit makes a temporary home in successive bodies; it is the source of our being, but the manner of our being is predetermined by the mediate causes, *karma*, or as we should express it, by heredity.

1 "Fate," as explained in the preceding note; the resultant of the aforesaid "mediate causes" working *in* us, rather than *upon* us. The "Harmony" is the disc or body of the Sun, whose rays are the vivifying radii of the Spirit that become the Life in each of us (*Śatapatha Brāhmaṇa* II.33.3.7); these, in Plato's language, are the "golden cords" by which the best in us is suspended like a puppet" from that region whence first our soul was gotten" and to which we should hold fast (*Timaeus* 90 D, *Laws* 644 D, E, 803); that Plato knew the "thread-spirit" (*sūtrātmam*) doctrine is clear from his interpretation of *Iliad* VIII.18 f. in *Theatetus* 153 C. Cf. *Hermes* XVI.

2 The whole doctrine of the Sun's progenitive power is best known from Aristotle's "Man and Sun generate man" *Phys.* ii.2), but is quite universal, cf. references and citations in my "Primitive Mentality" in Quarterly Journal of the Mythic Society XXXI, October 1940 and "Sunkiss" in *JAOS.* 60, 1940. In the last mentioned article, page 57, on "taking by the hand," I should have added a reference to *Aitareya Brāhmaṇa* V.31 where man at sunrise stretches out his hand with an offering and the Sun is said to "take him by the hand and draw him upwards into the realm of heavenly light" and the Sun is called "Life" (*prāna*) "because he leads forth (*praṇayati*) all beings"; the "handfasting" and the "leading" also implying that the Sun is the Bridegroom and the man the Bride (as in *Bṛhadāraṇyaka Upaniṣad* IV.3.21 where he is "embraced by the fore-knowing Spirit" and *Chāndogya Upaniṣad* VII.25.2 where "he whose Bridegroom is the Spirit (*ātma-mithunaḥ*) . . . becomes a Mover-at-will and autonomous." In an Egyptian representation of Amenhotep IV and his family all of the Sun's rays end in hands — and of those rays, those which are extended to the eyes of the Pharoah and of his wife hold the symbol of life (see Kurt Lange, *Ägyptische Kunst*, 1939, Pl. 79).

We need hardly add that the doctrine that God is our *real* Father survives in Christianity: For example, "The power of the soul, which is in the semen, through the spirit contained therein, fashions the body" (St. Thomas Aquinas, *Sum. Theol.* III.32.1 as in *Kausītaki Upaniṣad* cited above), and "The *Spirit* is the Fountain of Life, which flows forth from God, to Feed, and Maintain the Breath of Life in the Body. When the time of Death comes, this Spirit draws back to their Head again those streams of Life, by which it went forth into the Body" (*Peter Sterry, Puritan and Platonist*, by V. de S. Pinto, page 156, like *Bṛhadāraṇyaka Upaniṣad* IV.4.2, 3 and other texts cited above).

3 Ἄνοδος τὴς γίνομενής = *Republic* 517 B εἰς τὸν νοητὸν τοπον τῆς ψυχῆς ἄνοδος, the way up [and] out of the Cave (body, cosmos, tomb) into the Light.

4 Ὁ θυμὸς κὰι ἡ ἐπιθυμία; the two parts of the "mortal soul" (*Republic* 440, etc.), distinguished from the "immortal soul that is our real self" (*Laws* 959 A, B). In the *Upaniṣads*, the "corporal self" (*sarira atman*) consisting of the sense powers (*prāṇāḥ*) and unclean mind (*aśuddha manas*) as distinguished from the "incorporeal Self" (*aśarıra ātman*), the pure mind (*śuddha manas*).

for the Man to ascend by way of the Harmony.[1] Passing through the spheres of the seven planets, he "is stripped of all that has been wrought upon him by the Harmony,"[2] and thus "attains to the eighth nature, possest of his own Power . . . and he sings with those who are there . . . And being made like those with whom he is, he hears the Powers that are above the substance of the eighth nature. And from time to time, in due order, these mount upward to the Father; they deliver up themselves (ἑαυτοὺς παραδιδόασι) to the Powers,[3] and becoming Powers themselves, are born in God (ἐν θεῷγίνονται). That is the Good, that the Perfection (τέλος) of those who have gotten Gnosis" (γλωσις = Sanskrit *jñāna*).

In Book XI Hermes again describes the soul's excursion from the Cosmos, from which it wills to break forth (εἰ δεβουληθειης . . . διαρρ — ή ξασθαι) just as the Man had willed at first to break in (ηροολήθη αναρρήξαι, *Lib.* I.13 b). "Bid your soul to travel to any land you choose" he says, "and sooner than you bid it go, it will be there[4] . . . Bid it fly up to the Sky, and it will have no need of

---

1 The ascent reverses the descent (Heracleitus fr. lxix, and as always in the Indian texts). The "eighth nature" is the "sphere of the Demiurge from which the Man of eternal Substance first looked out through the Harmony." Hermes' "Harmony" seems to be, as Scott understands, the whole "structure of the heavens" rather than the keystone only as in Pausanias; this is nevertheless a logical rather than a real distinction; it is in the same way that the Sun in Indian texts is both the *Axis Mundi* as a shaft of light and the source of light at its summit. Each of the circles is all contained and constructed (*coedificatus*) at its nave through which the Axis passes; [at] each of these points [, through] which the Axis penetrates [as a felly does a] "wheel" (Sanskrit *cakra*, world) [,] is a straight gate or needle's eye that must be passed on the way up or down; though *facile decensus*!

The real problem is presented by the fact that the sun, "the greatest and the king and overlord of all the gods in [the] Sky" is not the last and highest of them, but "submits to have smaller stars circling above him" (*Lib.* V.3). The Sun is not the seventh, but the fourth of the seven planets (as also in Dante's cosmology). It will be seen that the fourth is the middle place in the series; it is from this point of view that the problem can be solved. See Appendix II, ["The Rotation of the Earth," page 146].

2 For this "stripping off" of evils as the soul ascends many parallels could be adduced from Sanskrit sources. A notable example is that of Apala (Psyche) reunited to the solar Indra (Eros) only when she [has] been drawn through the naves of the three world wheels, each of these strait passages removing a reptilian skin, until at last she is "sun-skinned" and can return to him as like to like (*Ṛgveda* VIII.91 and other texts for which see my "Darker Side of Dawn," *Smithsonian Miscellaneous Collection*).

3 In almost the same words Agni ("*Noster Deus ignis consumens*") is said to "know that he (the Sacrificer, who would be deified) has come to make an offering of himself to me" (*atmanam paridam me*) and "were he not to signify this, Agni would deprive him of himself" (*Śatapatha Brāhmaṇa* II.4.1.11 and IX.5.1.53, cf. *Chāndogya Upaniṣad* II.22.5). So "He that would save his life, let him lose it"! The Sacrificer is born again of the Fire and takes his name. The sacrifice of selfhood (individuality, what can be defined and seen) is essential to any deification; for no one who still is anyone can enter into Him Who has never become anyone and is not any what. Cf. my "*Ākiṁcaññā*; Self-naughting" in *New Indian Antiquary* III, 1941. The "stripping" is the same as what is so often described in the Sanskrit texts as "shaking off one's bodies" or "striking off evil"; it represents that *ablatio omnis alteritatis et diversitatis* that, as the later Platonist, Nicolas of Cusa, repeats, are the *sine qua non* of a "*filiationem Dei quam Deificationem, quae et* θέωσις *graece dicitur*" (*De. fil. Dei.*, Ed. Bâle, 1565, pages 119, 123).

I cannot see the inconsistency discussed by Scott, *Hermetica,* Vol. II, page 60. If need be, the order of the sentences beginning καὶ ὁ θυμὸς . . . (which Scott omits from his translation) and καὶ οὕτως . . . could be reversed; but even without this it is easy to see that we have first a general statement about the purification, followed by a more detailed account of the stages by which it is effected.

4 "Nothing shall be impossible unto you" (*Matthew* XVII.20).

wings; nothing can bar its way,[1] neither the Sun's fire nor the vortex (δίνη) of the planets; cleaving its way through all, it will fly up until it reaches the outermost of all corporeal things.[2] And should you wish to break forth from the Cosmos itself, even that is permitted to you" (*Lib.* XI.ii.20 a).

Although — as we have so far seen — the solar "Harmony" is primarily architectural, it can be shown that an interpretation of the word in its secondary and more familiar sense of musical "Attunement," or perhaps "Keynote" would not be incorrect; and that the solar Harmony is in fact the "Music of the Spheres." In the Hymn of Praise to the Sun (*Lib.* XIII.17 f.), we find: "Let every bar of the universe be opened unto me.[3] I am about to sing His praise who is both the All and the One. Be ye opened, O ye Skies, and ye Winds, be still, let the Immortal Orb[4] receive my word (λόγος) . . . From you comes the praise-song and to you it proceeds . . . It is thy Word (λόγος) that through me sings thy praise; for by thee, O Mind, is my speech shepherded.[5] Through me accept from all the verbal sacrifice (λογικὴν ουσίαυ);[6] for the All is from thee, and to thee the All returns. O Light, illumine thou the mind[7] that is in us . . . I have seen . . . I am born again."

---

1 For the opening of doors to successive worlds at the Sacrificer's call, "Thrust back the bar," see *Chāndogya Upaniṣad* II.24.

2 Not as Scott implies in his footnote, "the outermost sphere of heaven" but "the top of the lower heaven," the "top of the wheel or vault beneath the Sky" as Plato expresses it in *Phaedrus* 247 B.

3 *Chāndogya Upaniṣad* II.24.15 *atihata parigham.*

4 ʽO κύκλος ὁἀθάνατος, i.e. ἥ λιοῦ κύκλος, as in Aeschylus, Pr. 91, the sun's wheel or disc; τῶν ἐντόρνων οὐσαν μίμημά τι κύκλον, *Laws* 898 A. For wheels in Greek ritual see Guthrie, *Orpheus*, page 208. Into the connected symbolism of ladders we cannot enter here, except to say that it plays an important part equally in Indian, Egyptian, Christian, American Indian and Siberian Shamanistic mysteries and might be expected in Greece. In a notable Vedic ritual (*Taittirīya Saṁhitā* .7.8), the priest on behalf of the sacrifice takes his seat upon a wheel set up on a post and there mimes the driving of horses, making the wheel revolve.

5 Cf. *Republic* 440 D where the immanent λόγος checks the irascible power of the mortal soul "as a shepherd calls back his dog." I cannot but regard the "Shepherd" of Hermas, appointed to live in the same house with him, as this immanent λόγος, his mentor, the Socratic δαίμων that "always holds me back from what I want to do" (*Phaedrus* 242 B, C), and Hermes' "Poimander" as of the same sort. This immanent δαίμων and guardian angel becomes the Synteresis of the Schoolmen.

6 Like the smoke of the burnt-offering, the echo of the music of the liturgy is returned to the Sun in which it originated; discarding its verbal embodiments as it rises until it returns as pure "tone" (*svara*) to the archetypal Cantor who "goeth forth with song unto all this universe," "who goes on his way intoning" (*Aitareya Āraṇyaka* II.2.2 with *Jaiminīya Upaniṣad Brāhmaṇa* I.15-21); of the divine and human Cantors, the songs are the same and the name (*udgātr*) is the same. "Those who sing here on the harp sing Him" (*Chāndogya Upaniṣad* I.7.5, 6). The Sacrificer himself ascends with the chant "on wings of sound" (*svara-pakṣa, Jaiminīya Upaniṣad Brāhmaṇa* III.13.10) or light (*jyotiṣ-pakṣa, Pañcavimśa Brāhmaṇa* X.4.5), the metrical wings" (*chando-pakṣa*) of *Atharva Veda* VIII.9.12.

[7 Throughout the tradition we meet with the distinction of the two minds, human and divine. These minds are respectively "unclean" by connection with desire, and "clean" when divorced from desiring, and beyond these is the still higher condition of "mindlessness" (*Maitri Upaniṣad* VI.34). The "Divine Mind" is the Sun's; the superhuman "Mindless" cf. *Ion* 534 and *Timaeus* 71 D-72 B) will not be confused with its antitype, the "mindlessness" of irrational beings, the distinction between the same as that between the two orders of "madness" (*Phaedrus* 244 A, etc.).]

We have seen that the soul is an "apportionment" of the etherial nature,[1] i.e. of divinity; and the etymological connection of this μοῖρα with the εἱμαρμένη, of which it is the bearer, will be obvious. The whole conception is Platonic; for him it is the fact that "man participates in a divine inheritance (μοῖρα) that makes him a kinsman (σθγγενής, cognate) of God and the only one of living beings that acknowledges the gods"[2] — makes him, that is to say, a re*lig*ious animal, one bound up and attached to the life in which he originates.[3] It is in the virtue of the presence of this "Same and Uniform within him" that man can rule by Reason (λόγῳ κρατήσας) the composite irrational mass of the four elements that adheres to him.[4] In other words, the immanent *Logos*, Reason so governs the Necessity (ἀνάγκη, "*karma*") by which our births are determined, as to conduct the greater parts of born beings to the best end.[5] For He who generated all things, having said that "in my Will (βουγῆσις) ye have a bond (δεσμός) mightier and more sovereign than those wherewith ye were bound up at birth . . . declared unto the (created) souls the Laws of Destiny (νόμους τετοὺς εἱμαρμένοας) . . . how that each was bound (δέοι), when each had been sown into his own organ of time (i.e. appropriate body), to grow into the most God-revering (θεοσεβέστατον) of living things."[6]

Now, when "the immortal Soul which is our real Self, goes off (ἀπιέν αι = Sanskrit *praiti*) to other gods,[7] there to render its account"[8] it is thought of as

---

1 *LA.* III.16.

2 *Protagoras* 322 A, cf. *Timaeus* 41 E.

3 This, I hold, is the meaning of the word *religion*, implying our dependence on a higher than our own power; the irreligious being on the other hand [being] the neg*lig*ent man who renounces his al*leg*iance and denies his ob*lig*ations.

That chain that bound and made me, link by link,
Now it is snapped: I only eat and drink.
Bayard Simmons

The "emancipation" implied by the breaking of the links creates the specious "freedom of choice" (thinking, doing, making "what we like") which is actually nothing but a servile subjection to the contrary pulls of our own ruling passions, and in the case of the "economically determined" man (whose measure and criterion of value is "Will it pay?") a subjection to greed; the acceptance of the obligations that our Destiny lays upon us, and consequent doing the will of God, on the other hand, is an exercise of the real "freedom of spontaneity" of which we are the legitimate heirs because of the participation in the divine free-will.

4 *Timaeus* 42 C.

5 *Timaeus* 48 A.

6 *Timaeus* 41 B, E; cf. *Quran* LI.56. Note σέβομαι, cognate of Sanskrit *sev*, "attend upon," etc. The text goes on, "and since human nature is two-fold, the superior (κρεῖττον) kind is that which hereafter shall be called 'the Man'." This corresponds to Philo's equation of νοῦς (= *manas*) with "the Man" and of αισθησις (= *vāc*) with "the Woman." R.G. Bury makes out that it is the superior "sex" that shall be called the Man, as if Plato had been speaking, not of "the better and the worse" in every human being of whatever sex but of men and women as such. The question involved is that of self-mastery, of which both men and women are capable; not one of the domination of an inferior by a superior "sex"!

7 As in *Phaedo* 63 B, "to other wise and good gods, and moreover to perfected men (ἀνθρώπους τετελευεηκότα), better than are here." "Other" is also with reference to and in distinction from the chthonic deities of *Laws* 959 D. The return is to the soul's "celestial kinship" of *Timaeus* 90 A.

8 *Laws* 959 B. "To render its account" is Rev. R.G. Bury's version of δώσοντα λόγον. The immortal soul that dwells in and with us and is our "guardian angel" is often spoken of an the "accountant"

(Continued on following page.)

"ascending"; and since it is already at the top of the body we may assume that what is explicit in the Sanskrit texts, *viz.* that the departure of the real Self is by way of the scapular foramen, as if through the "eye" of the cranial dome, is implicit in our Greek sources. The departure from the bodily microcosm in which the immortal principle has been "housed" is analogous to the Indian "breaking through the roof-plate of a domed building,"[1] and "breaking through the Sundoor, the World-door"[2] by those of the departed who are "able."[3] Let us also not forget that Christ is the "Sun of men"[4] and says, "I am the door: By me if any man enter in, he shall be saved, and shall go in and out" (*John* X.9). In the symbolism of the Church this can be taken to refer both to the (usually Western) door by which one is admitted to the Church on the ground level (as in the *Shepherd of Hermas*, Sim. IX.12) and more eminently to the door that is represented by the eye of the dome above the altar. It is by the first door that we come *to* Him at the altar; and by the second to the Father to whom "no man cometh but *by* me" (*John* XIV.6), and as Eckhart says (*Evans* I.275) this "breaking through" and second death of the soul is "far more momentous than the first." There are two things that must be said regarding this, [first] that the Father's abiding place is in the *coelum empyrium*[5] and beyond the Sun, and [second] that as like can only be known as like, those who are able to pass through the Sun must be those who have fulfilled the

---

(Continued from preceding page.)

(λογιστικός), and at least in the present context it is presumably the "entire soul's" account that it presents here, as in the *Shepherd of Hermas*, where the "Shepherd," who is appointed to live with Hermas in his house and is called the "Angel of Repentance" (μετάνοια), says *Ego sum pastor, et validissime oportet de vobis reddere rationem* (*Sim.* IX.xxi.6).

There is, however, another important sense in which the "Accountant" is so called; he it is that can give a "true account" on such matters as the nature of the conflicting tensions by which the soul is pulled this way and that, but of which there is only one by which we should be guided (*Laws* 645 B). For this last "leading string" see Appendix [I, "On the Etymology of "Cherubim," page 145.]

1 A feat performed by the "able" (*arhat*), having the powers of levitation and of traveling through the air, see my "Symbolism of the Dome," *Indian Historical Quarterly* XIV, 1938, page 54. For the corresponding modern practice see Madame David-Neel, *Magic and Mystery in Tibet*, (New York, 1937 edition), page 208.

2 *Chāndogya Upaniṣad* VIII.6.5. "He ascends . . . comes to the Sun . . . the World-door, a way in for the wise, an arrest for the foolish"; cf. *Maitri Upaniṣad* VI.30, *Aitareya Brāhmaṇa* III.42, etc.

3 The question is asked in *Jaiminīya Upaniṣad Brāhmaṇa* I.6.1 "Who is able (*arhati*) to pass through the midst of the Sun?"

4 A familiar expression, prefigured in *Malachi* IV.2 and implied by many passages in [the] New Testament. Literally, "Sun of Men" (*sūrya nṝn*) in *Ṛgveda* I.146.4.

5 *Jaiminīya Upaniṣad Brāhmaṇa* I.6.4, *pareṇādityam* = *Aitareya Upaniṣad* I.2, *parena divan*, *Mahānārāyaṇa Upaniṣad* X.5 *pareṇa nakam* = *Ṛgveda* I.164.10 *pare ardhe*, *Kaṭha Upaniṣad* III.1 *pareme parārdhe*. There no Sun shines (*Kaṭha Upaniṣad* V.15, *Bhagavad Gītā* XV.6, *Udāna* 9, *Revelation* XXI.23); "only the Spirit is his light" (*Bṛhadāraṇyaka Upaniṣad* IV.3.6), "the Lamb is the light thereof" (*Revelation* XXI.23).

The Sun himself is "beyond the dust," "beyond the darkness" (*parorajas, tamsah parastāt*); at the top of the world, he is the door to what lies beyond them (the "what is left over," *ucchiṣta*, of *Atharva Veda* XI.7, "deposited in secret," *nihitaṁ guhāyam*, *Mahānārāyaṇa Upaniṣad* X.5. *Śatapatha Brāhmaṇa* X.82.2, *sapta ṛsm para disah paranam krautam.*

commandment, "Be ye perfect (τέλειοι), even as your Father in heaven is perfect" (τελει΄ως, *Matthew* V.48).[1]

We are now in a better position to consider Plato's account of the perfected soul's excursion from the universe, described in *Phaedrus* 246, 247: "The entire soul . . . traverses the whole sky, being sometimes in one form and sometimes in the other. But when she is perfect (τελέα) and has its wings it ascends and controls (διοικῖ)[2] the whole universe; but the soul which has lost its wings is borne along until it gets hold of something concrete, in which it makes its house, taking upon itself a body of earth,[3] which seems to be self-moving because of the power of the soul within it; and the whole, compounded of soul and body, is called a living being, and furthermore a mortal . . ."

---

[1] In *Phaedrus* 63 B the men who are dwelling with the celestial deities are referred to as "perfected." For ἀνθρώπους τετελευτηκότας we cannot accept either H.N. Fowler's "men who have died" or Jowett's "men departed"; for while it is true that the men referred to are "men who have died," the reference is not to the dead as a class, but to a particular class of the dead. In the same way in Plutarch, *Moralia* 382 F, where the bodies "of those who are believed τέλος ἔχειν" are said to be hidden away in the earth, it would be ridiculous to render "of those who are believed to be dead" since it is obvious that those who have been buried have died; what is intended is a contrast of the buried bodies with the deceased "themselves" who are regarded as "having attained perfection," as they must have if indeed they are "really themselves" in the sense of *Laws* 959 B and *Odyssey* XI.602, cf. Hermes Trismegistus, *Lib.* I.18.

It is true that the forms of τέλεω all imply a "finish," and death in some sense, for example the initiatory death of the *homo moriturus*. For to be "finished" or "perfected" is to have reached the end of a process of becoming and simply to "be"; cf. Sanskrit *parinirvá*, [first] to be despirated and [second] to be perfected. But simply to have died when the time comes is not necessarily to have died with what Eckhart calls the "real death": And if in many contexts τετελευτηκώς and τελευτησάς mean simply "dead" (τε θηκός), it is rather as we say "dead and gone to heaven," expressing a pious wish than stating a certain fact. There are other contexts, including the present, in which the forms of τέλεω are used more strictly to distinguish the perfected from the unperfected. In the present case it is the "perfected" that are associated with the gods; i.e. such of the dead as are "perfectly (παντελῶς) whole and hale," not such as are "imperfect (ἀ ελής) and mindless" and must return to Hades (*Timaeus* 44 C). The "perfected men" of our text are precisely such as "return to their star homes, and gain the blessed and associated life" (*Timaeus* 44 C). Τέλεω = Sanskrit *arhat* ("fit" or "able") and *sukṛtatman* ("perfected self").

[2] Rather "controls and inhabits," as it is explicit in *Laws* 896 E where it is agreed that "Since Soul controls and inhabits (διοικοῦσαν καὶ ὀνοικοῦσαν) all things everywhere that are moved, we must needs affirm that it controls (διοικεῖν) the Sky also." The "perfected" soul is universalized by a "transfusion of the one into the all" (Nicolas of Cusa, *De fil. dei*, see Vansteenberghe page 13, Note 2), "is bodiless, and yet has many bodies, or rather, is embodied in all bodies" Hermes Trismegistus, *Lib.* V.10 A); it becomes "the Spirit of all beings" (*Bṛhadāraṇyaka Upaniṣad* I.15.18), or "is fitted for embodiment in the emanated worlds" (*Kaṭha Upaniṣad* VI.4), "its pasture is unlimited," like the Buddha, *anantagocara* (*Dhammapada* 179); and, in other words is a "mover-at-will" "going up and down these worlds, eating what it will and assuming what likeness it will (*Taittirīya Upaniṣad* III.10.5 etc.). Cf. *Pistis Sophia*, 2nd document, 189^b-191^b.

[3] "Of those who ascend to the top (*agra*) of the great Tree, how do they fare thereafter? Those who have wings fly away, those without wings fall down. Those having wings are the wise, those without wings the foolish" (*Pañcaviṁśa Brāhmaṇa* XIV.1.12, 13). These "wise" and "foolish" are the same as those admitted or shut out by the Sundoor in *Chāndogya Upaniṣad* VIII.6.5; the same also as the "wise" and "foolish" virgins who are admitted to the banquet or excluded from it in *Matthew* XXV. So Beatrice reproaches Dante that he has not long since been "full-fledged" (*Purgatorio* XXI.51).

Plato (*Phaedrus* 246 D, E) explains that the natural power of the wing is to raise what is heavy to where the gods live; and that the wings of the soul are "nourished" (τρέφεται) and

(Continued on following page.)

Now the great leader of the sky, Zeus, driving in a winged chariot, goes first, ordering all things and caring for all things. He is followed by a host of gods and daimons, arrayed in eleven divisions . . . There are many blessed sights and many ways about and about within the Sky (ἐντὸς οὐρανοῦ), along which the beatific gods go to and fro, each one doing what it is his to do;[1] and whoever always has both the will and the power,[2] follows; for jealousy is excluded from the divine choir. But when they go to a feast or banquet, they climb the heights, until they reach the top of the vault below the Sky

---

(Continued from preceding page.)

grow by "beauty, wisdom, goodness and the like." These are, manifestly, the "congenial food" (οἰκεῖα τροφή) with which we ought to tend the divine part of us, *viz.* the immanent δαίμων, so as to participate in immortality (*Timaeus* 90 C, D).

"Where is the soul's abode? Upon the pinions of the wind. The pinions are the powers of the divine nature" (Eckhart, Pfeiffer, page 513). The symbolism of "birds" has to do not only with their flight, but also their "language," and plays a large part in all mythological iconography. Here the special point is that nothing without wings can pass through the Sun; even the chariot of Zeus is "winged."

1 In other words, the gods are "just"; for "to do what belongs to one to do" (τὸ ἑαυτοῦ πράττειν), i.e. to fulfil the vocation for which one is fitted by nature is Plato's type and definition of "justice" or "righteousness" (δικαιοσυνη, *Republic* 433) and sanity (σωφροσυνη, *Charmides* 161); cf. *Bhagavad Gītā* III.35 and XVIII.42-48.

A very close parallel to Plato's account of the divine excursion will be found in the *Maitri Upaniṣad* VII.176; here the gods are described as "rising in the East," South, West, North, Zenith and Nadir, "they shine, they rain, they praise (i.e. do what is theirs to do); they enter in again (*punar viśanty antar*) and look out through the opening" (*vivaren-eksanti*). It is most likely that the five different openings here correspond to the "five visible quarters" from which the Sun rises (in successive stages of our enlightenment) until it finally neither rises nor sets but "stands alone in the centre" (*Chāndogya Upaniṣad* III.6-11); the Sundoor (*saura-dvāra*), an open door (*dvāra-vivara*) of *Maitri Upaniṣad* VI.30, corresponds to this last orientation.

2 ʽΟἀεὶ ἐθέλων τε καὶ δυνάμενος. H.N. Fowler and Jowett both ignore the ʼαεί, "always," though in fact it marks the distinction drawn again below (248 C) where "if any soul be a follower of God and catch sight of any of the truths (i.e. any glimpse of the 'plain of truth' at the back of the Sky) it cannot suffer until the next cycle, and if it can do this *always*, then it is *always* safe; but when, through want of power to follow, its vision fails, and it happens to be overcome by forgetfulness and evil, and grows heavy and so loses its wings and falls to Earth, then it is the law that . . . (of such souls) the soul that has seen the most shall enter into the birth of a man who is to be a philosopher," etc.

The "always" of these passages recurs in Plotinus, *Enneads* IV.4.6 where, discussing "memory" in the gods, he concludes: "In other words, they have seen God and they do not remember? Ah, no: It is that they see God still and *always*, and that as long as they see, they cannot tell themselves that they have had the vision; such reminiscence is for souls that have lost it." It is a blessed thing, but not enough, to have had an intimation of the "eternal now," "some of the truths" that it encloses: But those alone are safe eternally who have seen not merely "some of the truths" but "the truth of truth," and see this whole *always*.

The words "cannot suffer until the next cycle" and the statement that "those who have seen the most" will be reborn, when the time comes, as "philosophers" are in the closest possible agreement with Indian formulae, e.g. *Bhagavad Gītā* VI.41-43, where the question has been asked, What becomes of one possest of faith, "who has failed to attain perfection in yoga" (defined as dispassion and mastery of oneself), and the answer given that "Having attained to the worlds of those whose works are pure (i.e. the lower heaven), and having dwelt therein for enduring years (i.e. until the end of the cycle), one who has fallen from yoga is born in an illustrious and fortunate household . . . or perhaps into a family of contemplative Yogis, though such a birth as this is very hard to win in this world; there he recovers that state of being harnessed to the pure intellect that had been that of the prior body, and thence once more strives for perfection."

(ἄκραν ὑπὸ τὴν ὑπουπάνιον ἁψῖδα),[1] where the chariots of the gods, whose well-matched horses obey the rein, advance easily, but the others with difficulty; for the horse of the evil nature weighs heavily, weighing down to Earth the charioteer whose horse is not well-trained;[2] there the utmost toil and trouble awaits the soul. But those whom we call immortal, when they are come to the top (πρὸς ἀκρῳ νένωνται)[3] pass outside and take their places

---

1 Ἀψεῖς is primarily a wheel; it is said to be primarily a "felly," but it must be remembered that early wheels were solid (except for the perforation of the nave), and that the expression ἄψιν τάμνειν . . . ἁμαξῃ (Hesiod, *Works* 426) can hardly mean anything but "hew a wagon wheel"; an axe is the tool to use, and it is certainly a farmer's ox-cart that is being made, for which nothing but solid wheels are at all likely at this period. So also τὴν ἡμερίαν ἁψῖδα (Euripedes, *Ion* 87, 88), like ὁ ἡμερήσιος κύκλος (Philo, *Leg. allegorica* III) is nothing but the Sun's disc. Secondarily, ἁψίς is any circle, vault or arch, and finally "apse" in the current architectural sense of the word. That the symbolism of the domes and wheels is essentially the same need hardly be argued here; both are circles with radii (ribs) of the dome or umbrella, spokes of the wheel, both are penetrated by a central eye, and both exemplify the first principles. The nave of the wheel corresponds to the keystone of the dome, the felly to its periphery, the spokes to the radiating beams; cf. *Bṛhadāraṇyaka Upaniṣad* II.5.15, "Verily, this Self (*ātman* = Brahma, solar Person, Spirit) is the Overlord and King of all things. Even as all the spokes are fastened-in-together (*samarpitāḥ*, as in ἁπμονία, συναρμόξω) between the hub and the felly of the wheel, so all things, all gods, all worlds, all breathing things, all these selves (*ātmanaḥ*, plural) are fastened-in-together in this Self" (*ātman*).

2 Alike in the Greek and Indian sources the immortal, incorporeal soul or spirit has for its vehicle the moveable "house" or "chariot" of the body (*Timaeus* 41 E, 44 E, 69 C, D, *Laws* 898 C f.; *Kaṭha Upaniṣad* III.3-9, *Jātaka* VI.252 and throughout the literature). The Indian words *ratha* and *vimāna* mean both house, palace, temple and vehicle; so that, for example, at Konarak we find a temple of the Sun provided with wheels and steeds. The physical vehicle in which we move is analogous to the chariot of light or fire in which the God or perfected soul is thought of as travelling at will. The steeds are the senses which like to feed upon their objects and must be curbed and guided if the goal is to be reached. The whole symbol can be reduced to that of a single steed or wheel.

For Plato more specifically one of the two horses is of noble blood, the other very different in breed and character (*Phaedrus* 246 B "The entire soul [. . .]" and *Bṛhadāraṇyaka Upaniṣad* IV, cf. *Laws* 903 E); and these two are evidently the two parts of the mortal soul, the Courageous (θυμοειδής) and the Desirous (τὸ ἐπιθυματικόν), of which the former listens to and naturally sides with the Reason and is rarely led astray by its mate, while the latter is most unruly (*Republic* 440 f. etc.). All this is taken for granted in our text. For the relation of the soul or person of the Sun to the chariot of the Sun in greater detail see *Laws* 898 f. In this context the "Soul of the Sun" ("He who dwelling in the Sun, yet is other than the Sun, whom the Sun does not know, whose body the Sun is, who controls the Sun from within, and is your own Self, Inner Controller, Immortal," *Bṛhadāraṇyaka Upaniṣad* III.7.9) seems to be thought of as in India as both one and many. *Laws* 903 D-904 D should be compared with *Bṛhadāraṇyaka Upaniṣad* IV.4.4, 5; 903 D "Soul, being coordinated now with one body, now with another" corresponds to Śaṅkarācārya's "There is none but the Lord that 'reincarnates'" (*Brahmasūtra-bhāṣya* I.1.5). It scarcely needs to be said that the whole subject of "reincarnation" in Greek and Indian texts demands a fresh investigation with a view to seeing what, if anything, remains of the supposed rebirth of individuals here on Earth, when all that pertains to daily, progenitive, initiatory and final rebirth and the Vedantic doctrine that it is the immanent deity that passes from body to body and the corresponding Buddhist doctrine that no concrete essence passes over from one body to another have been allowed for.

3 The "top of the Sky" is, of course, the same as the "top of the sky" that is the "stopping place" of the sun at midday (παύεται ἄκρου ἐκ ὀνρανοῦ *Homeric Hymns* XXXI.15), the turning point and limit of his daily course. It is by no means without pertinence that we find Sanskrit *kāṣṭha* both as "goal-post" (*Ṛgveda* VII.93.3 and IX.21.7); *Kaṭha Upaniṣad* III.11) and as the axle or pillar by which the two worlds, Sky and Earth, are propped apart, the sun in his daily course

(Continued on following page.)

on the back of the Sky . . . and they behold the things that are beyond the Sky. But the region above the Sky (τὸν δὲ ὑπερουράνιαν τολὸν) was never worthily sung by any earthly poet, nor ever will be . . . For the colorless, formless and intangible really-existent essence, with which all true science (ἐπιστήμη) is concerned, holds this region and is visible only to the Mind (νοῦς), the pilot of the soul.[1]

Now the intellection of a god, nurtured as it is on Mind and pure knowledge . . . not such knowledge as has a beginning and varies as it is associated with one or another of the things *we*[2] call realities, but that which is real and absolute; and in that same way it sees and feeds upon the other absolute realities, after which passing back again within the Sky, it goes home and there the Charioteer puts up the horses at the manger and "feeds them with ambrosia and gives them nectar to drink." Thus the perfected souls are forever "saved" and "go in and out, and find pasture" (*John* X.9).

The word ἁρμονία is used by Heracleitus always, I think, with direct or indirect reference to the Cosmos. In Fr. XLVII we are told that "The invisible

---

(Continued from preceding page.)

from East to West reaches (the top of) this pillar at noon; this position is what is called in Sanskrit *bradh ya viṣṭapa*, "the Ruddy-one's height," i.e. the uppermost of the "golden axle-points" (*viṣṭāntā hiraṇya-mayī = ānī*) of the Sun's chariot (*Ṛgveda* X.93.13), i.e. the poles of the *skambha* or *viṣtambha*, the *Axis Mundi*, the sense of "stepping place" is also present in *viṣṭapa*. This point is the sacrificer's "goal" because it is "the end of the road," not because there is no way on (through the Sun), but because this "way" is trackless, and cannot be called a "road."

Thus the top of the Sky, which is the top of the peaked roof of the world, is also the top of the *Axis Mundi*, which is itself the centre and principle of the whole house (δῶμα), Sanskrit *dama*, house and dome, from δέμω, "build," preserved in *tim*-ber): The *caput anguli* is the same as the capital of the king-post.

These relationships are very well displayed in a passage by Nonnos (*Dionysiaca* VI.66 f.), which is itself hardly more than a paraphrase of Plato, *Timaeus* 40 C, D, both contexts speaking of revolving models (εἰκών, μίμημα) of the universe. In Nonnos, Asterion's "spherical image of the Cosmos" revolves on a "pole": The demonstration is made by "turning the top of the axis," (ἄξονος ἄκρον ἑλισσῶν) and so "spinning the pole" (πόλον αμφελέλιξε) and "carrying the stars round the axle set in the middle" (ἄξονι μεσσατίῳ). This is a model of the Cosmos, not of the Earth only: It is evident that the Earth must revolve with the All of which it is a part, but not explicit that the Earth revolves on her own axis or, what comes to the same thing, that her axis is also the Axis of the Cosmos (though we think this is implied). In any case ἑλισσῶν means "causing to revolve"; just as in Sextus Empiricus, *Matthew* X.93 εἰλουμεναι σφαῖραι are certainly "revolving spheres." Both of these contexts have a bearing on the meaning of the words γῆν . . . εἰλλαμένην δὲ περὶ τὸν διὰ παντὸς πολον τεταμένον. [I]n *Timaeus* 40 B, we assert, they mean "Earth, rotating about the pole that strikes through the All," although not the sort of pole on which the modern "globe" (a model of the Earth) rotates. For what the rotation of the Earth implies, see Appendix II, "The Rotation of the Earth," page 146.

It is far from insignificant that the Axis is spoken of as striking or cutting through, or piercing (τέμνω) the All (cf. *Jaiminīya Upaniṣad Brāhmaṇa* I.10.3, where "these worlds are compenetrated — *samtṛṇṇāḥ* — by the *Oṁ*, as though by a needle"): For from the same root comes τάμιας, with the secondary senses of "dispenser" ([as in an epithet for] Zeus, *Iliad* IV.84), "controller" and "director," and also "store," for the *Axis Mundi* (the *skambhha* described in *Atharva Veda* X.7) is precisely all these things; and it is in the same sense that the "Thunderbolt" (κεραυνός, Sanskrit *vajra*) is said to "govern all things" (Heracleitus, fr. XXVIII). It is the sceptre of Zeus, Indra's bolt, that *works* all things.

[1 Cf. *Timaeus* 33 C and *Qalb* (Heart) doctrine.]

2 We, for whom "such knowledge as is not empirical is meaningless . . . and should not be described as knowledge" (Keith, *Aitareya Āraṇyaka*, 1909, page 42).

Harmony dominates (κρείσσων) the visible." It is obvious that if a harmony of sounds had been intended here we should have the "inaudible" and "audible" making equally good sense; but actually, by the *invisible* harmony"[1] we can only understand the intelligible form of the universe, the "one from which all things proceed" (Fr. LIX) and in which they are all built together, and by the "visible harmony" the world itself. One is the "world-picture painted by the Spirit on the canvas of the Spirit" (*Śaṅkarācārya*), "the picture not the colors" (*Laṅkāvatāra Sūtra*), the other its manifold image projected on the "wall."

Frs. XLIII, XLV, XLVI and LVI speak of the "harmony" of the pairs of opposites, which naturally tend to move in opposite directions, rather than to cooperate. The "pairs" instanced are "high and low" (tones), male and female, and opposite tensions of the bow and harp." Plato (*Symposium* 187 f.) and Plutarch (*Moralia* 396) understand that the reference is to the pairs of opposites of which the universe is built, and which if they are not composed must remain ineffectual and unprogenitive. It is by the Cosmic Eros, a "master craftsman" (ἀγα θὸς δημιουργός) that they are made to accept "harmony and mingling" (κρᾶσις = Sanskrit *sandhi*) and so to be productive. It is precisely with these "loves" (ἐρωτικά; Sanskrit *mithunāni*) that "all sacrifices (θυσία) and all that has to do with divination (μαντιαή, Sanskrit *mantraṇa*), that is to say all means of communion between gods and men" are occupied (*Symposium* 188 B, cf. 210 A), a statement in every way as applicable to Indian as to Greek rites.

In connection with Heracleitus' "opposite tensions" let us consider for a moment those of the bow. It has a string that approximates the two ends of the bow. We have no early authority for saying that these ends can be thought of as implying Sky and Earth, but will venture to say as much; on the other hand, a string or thread is one of the most universal symbols of the Spirit, with particular reference to the "pull" by which it draws and holds all things together, and to which "pull" in the present case is opposed the "push" of the bow itself (cf. *Republic* 439 B). That the like could be said about the lyre would be more obvious if we could suppose that this instrument was, as least in origin, a *Bogenharfe*, like the Sumerian and like the old Indian *viṇa*. In such an instrument the opposing tensions are those of the strings and the body of the instrument; this body, however, really consists of two parts, one the belly representing the lower parts of the body, and secondly the neck and head representing the upper part; as in the case of the bow, presumably the archetype of all stringed instruments, it is the "Spirit" that connects the extremes. The same will apply, only less obviously, to the lyre in its classical form, and in fact almost any stringed instrument in which the tension of a wooden body opposes that of a string or wire. It is, in any case, only when these tensions have been duly regulated by the "good artist," who must be "Love's disciple," that a result is obtained; which result is either the flight of

[1] The "divine harmony" of *Timaeus* 80 B.

the arrow (the regular symbol of the "winged word" directed to its mark), or the production of musical sounds. It is no wonder, indeed, that archery and music have been so often made the vehicles of the highest initiatory teaching.[1]

We have now considered "harmony" from several points of view. And since it is not least as a contribution to the history of architecture that the present article has been prepared, let us recall to mind that "harmony" is for Pausanias the name of the keystone of the actual building. For the history of art, as regards the origins of its forms, can never be understood by an analysis of its later, elaborated and relatively meaningless developments. As Andrae has so well said, "The sensible forms, in which there was at first a polar balance of physical and metaphysical, have been more and more voided of content on their way down to us."[2] If we want to understand the history of doors and pillars and roofs it will not be enough to consider only their physical functions, we must also consider the macrocosm to which they are analogous[3] and the microcosm for whose use they were built, not as we think of use but in accordance with the thinking of primitive man, all of whose utilities were designed to "satisfy the needs of the body and soul together." To understand his economy, we must first understand that "plan of creation" which the early Christian Fathers constantly spoke of as an "economy,"[4] knowing that the vaulted universe is the first house that was ever built, and the archetype of every other.

1 Cf. Joachim Heim, "*Bogenhandwerk und Bogensport bei den Osmanen*" in *Der Islam*, XIV and XV, 1925-26, and Nasu and Aker (Acker), *Tōyō kyūdō Kikan* (in English), privately printed, Tokyo 1937.

2 *Die ionische Saüle, Bauform oder Symbol*, 1933 (Schlusswort).

3 Cf. W.R. Lethaby, *Architecture, Mysticism and Myth*, London 1892. Lethaby quotes on his title page César Dalys's question "Are there symbols which may be called constant; proper to all races, all societies, and all countries?," and evidently thinks of his own work as an affirmative answer.

4 "Κατ' οἰκονομιαν, *selon le plan divine, est pour ainsi dire un terme technique de la langue chretienne*" (A. Siouville, "*Philosop-huema (de Hippolyte)*," *Les Textes du Christianisme* VI, Paris (no date), t. II, page 82, note 3.

Chapter VIII

[Conclusion]

There remains to be made a final synthesis. We have seen that in the mythological formulations, verbal and visual, winged pneumatic powers, whether we call them sirens, sphinxes, eagles or angels, convey the soul to the heavenly realms of etherial light; the soul itself not being winged, only clings to its bearer. On the other hand, Plato in the *Phaedrus*, speaks of the soul itself as growing her wings; Philo, similarly, speaks of souls that are purified from mundane attachments that "escaping as though from a prison or a grave, they are equipped for the Ether by light wings, and range the heights for ever" (*Somn.* I.139); and though we have concluded that it is primarily as psychopomp that the Sphinx, Siren or Eagle appears on tombs, we find in the *Palantine Anthology* VII.62 the question asked of the Eagle on a tomb, "Why standest thou there, and wherefore gazest thou upon the starry home of the gods?" and the answer given, "I am the image (εἴδωλον) of the Soul of Plato, that hath flown away to Olympus." In the same way Dante speaks of those who are, or are not "so winged that they may fly up there" (*Paradiso* X.74). In India, likewise, both formulations occur; on the one hand, it is the Eagle that conveys the Sacrificer, who holds on to him (*Taittirīya Samhitā* III.2.1), by means of the *Gayatri*, whose wings are of light, that one reaches the world of the Suns (*Pañcavimśa Brāhmaṇa* X.4.5 with XVI.14.4), on the other it is asked, what is their lot who reach to the top of the Tree (of Life), and answered that "the winged, those who are wise, fly away, but the wingless, the ignorant, fall down" (*Pañcavimśa Brāhmaṇa* XIV.1.12, 13); uplifted on wings of sound, the Sacrificer "both perches fearless in the world of heavenly light, and also moves" *Jaiminīya Upaniṣad Brāhmaṇa* III.13.9, 10), i.e. at will, "for wherever a winged one would go, all that it reaches" (*Pañcavimśa Brāhmaṇa* XXV.3.4). The two positions are combined in *Pañcavimśa Brāhmaṇa* XIX.11.8 whether the metre as discussed is described as winged, and the Comprehensor therefore one who "being winged and luminous, frequents the pure worlds."

Since writing all of the above, I have been delighted to find that I have been anticipated, as regards the Sphinx, by Clement of Alexandria. "The Sphinx," he says, "is a symbol of defense (ἀλκή) and of association (συνέσις)"[1] *Stromata* V.7.42. In another place, he speaks of the Egyptian "Sphinxes" (improperly called, here, perhaps for the first time) and explains them from his own, Greek, point of view, saying that the "Egyptians set up sphinxes before their temples, to show that the doctrine about the God-who-Is is enigmatic and obscure, and perhaps also to show that we ought both to love and fear the divinity . . . for the Sphinx displays at once the image of a wild beast and of a human being" (*ib.* V.5.31). In a longer passage he says that "whereas according to the poet Araton the Sphinx is not the common bond of the

1 See [next paragraph].

Whole and the circumference of the Universe (ἡ τῶν ὅλων σύν δεσις[1] καὶ ἡ τον κόσμου . . . περιφορά), nevertheless it may well be that it *is* the pneumatic chord (πνευματικος τόνος) that pervades and holds the Universe together (συνέχων), and that it is well to regard it as the Ether that holds all things together and constrains (πάντασυνέχοντα κας σφίγγουτα), even as says Empedocles:

> But come now, first I will speak of the Sun, the beginning,
> From whom sprang all things we now admire,
> Earth and the many billowed Sea, and moist Air,
> And Titan Ether that constrains all things in its circle [. . .]

(τιτὰν Ἀἰθὴρ σφίγγων περὶ κύκλον ἅπαντα, *ib.* V.8.48, quoting Empedocles Fr. [185]); and finally he quotes "μάρπτε σφίγξ, κλώψ ξβυχ θηδόν" which he says was a writing copy for children, explaining that μάρψαι is to "grasp" (καταλαβεῖν), and that "by the Sphinx is meant the Harmony of the World" (ἥτοῦ κόσμον ἁρμονία, *ib.* V.8.49). That is precisely the conclusion which I had reached independently, mainly by a collation of the uses of the verb σφίγγν[2] from which the noun "Sphinx" comes. We have been led to think of the Sphinx as a manifestation of the principle that joins all things together in a common nexus, and that of the luminous, pneumatic, etherial thread of the Spirit by which God "draws" all things unto Himself by an irresistible attraction.

My rendering of ἀλκή is determined in part by Clement's φοβεῖσθαι in V.5.31, cf. Plato, *Protagoras* 321 D αἱ Διὸς φυλακὰι φοβεραί, in part by correlation with ἀλκά qualifying the "fire-breathing Chimaera" in Euripedes, *Ion* 202-4, and partly by the etymological equivalence of ἀλκέω, *arceo* and Sanskrit *rakṣ* in *soma-rakṣas*, Gandharva "Soma-guardian." The literal rendering of συνέσις by "association" is determined mainly by Clement's φιλεῖν and ἁρμονία in V.5.31 and V.8.49, but is by no means intended to exclude the sense of "conscience" in its primary meaning of "con-sciousness," Sanskrit *saṁ-vitti*, or to exclude the "fullness of knowledge" (ἐπίγνωσις πολλή) that Clement says is the meaning of the word "Cherubim" (whom he also understands to be "glorifying spirits," cf. Philo, for whom the Cherubim represent ἐπίγνωσις καὶ ἐπιστήμη πολλή, as well as the beneficent and punitive, or creative and royal Powers of God that are emanations of the *Logos* (*Moses* II.97, *Fug.* 100, *Heres* 166, *Cherubim* 26-9). Συνέσις has near Sanskrit equivalents in *sa m-sthiti*, *sam-bhava*, *sam-astitā*, *sam-ādhi*, *saṁ-vitti* [and] *sam-jnāna*.

It seems to me that Clement's exegesis is both iconographically and philologically sound, and particularly so when he makes the Sphinx a symbol at once of love and terror, the human face expressing love and the leonine body terrifying power. For — bearing in mind that the Cherubim are actually represented in Western Asiatic art by pairs of sphinxes and that Philo does not distinguish seraphim from cherubim — Mercy and Majesty (the later

---

1 Manuscript synesis as emended by Sylbius.

[2 The remainder of this paragraph is an interpolated portion of the lecture "The Riddle of the Greek Sphinx." — Ed.]

Islamic *jamāl* and *jalāl*) are precisely the two aspects of the *Logos* which in his analysis are represented by the guardian Cherubim of the Old Testament. Again, when Clement substitutes "deference" and "association" for "terror" and "love," these are qualities equally well expressed by the two parts of the composite form. And it is finally the unifying *Logos* as the Spirit, Light or Word of God-who-Is, [who is] median in two ways, both inasmuch as he stands (like the apex of a triangle in relation to its other angles) above and between the creative-beneficent and royal-legislative Powers, representing by the Cherubim, dividing them and all other opposites from one another, and inasmuch as He stands on the border (μεθόπιος) "between the extremes of the created and the uncreated," acting as mediator — suppliant on man's behalf and ambassador on that of the Father, and like the Sun, whose place is that of the fourth in the middle of the seven planets. This centrality of the Solar *Logos* corresponds to that of the Indian Breath (*prāṇah*) or Universal Fire (Agni Vaisvanara) or[1] Supernal Sun — not the sun that all men see, but the Sun of the sun, the light of lights, as the *Vedas* and Plato express it. Furthermore, by a consideration of the verb σφίγγω from which the noun "Sphinx" comes, we have been led to think of the Sphinx as a manifestation of the principle that joins all things together in a common nexus, and of that luminous, pneumatic, etherial thread of the Spirit by which God "draws" all things unto Himself by an irresistible attraction.

Lastly [Clement] says, that "by the Sphinx is meant the Harmony of the Universe," "Harmony" here almost as if it were the name of the Goddess, and with reference to the root meaning of the word, "to join together," like the carpenter whom we — more literally — term a "joiner." I need not tell you that Christ was also a "carpenter" (ἁρμοστης) in just that sense, or that every form of the Artificer "through whom all things were made" must be a carpenter wherever we think of the stuff of which the world was made as a "wood" (ὕλη, or in Sanskrit *vana*). So the Sphinx, despite her femininity which corresponds to that of the divine "Nature," can be regarded as a type of Christ, or more precisely, like the Dove, as a figure of the Spirit in motion, for it is by it that he draws them to himself. The Sphinx, in other words, is Love; and though rather in the image of Aphrodite than in that of Eros, mother and son were originally hardly distinguishable in character or function. If you ask, "Is not the Sphinx also the symbol of Death?" need I but remind you [that] in all traditions Love and Death are one and the same Person, or that God has said of Himself in many scriptures that "I slay and make alive"?[2]

[1 We again interpolate a portion of the "Sphinx" lecture to complete this paragraph. — Ed.]

[2 Our last paragraph preserves *in toto* the last paragraph from the "Sphinx" lecture. — Ed.]

In all that change is a dying. "No creature can attain a higher grade of Nature without ceasing to exist" (St. Thomas Aquinas). The Ether is the soul's immortal covering — its subtle or glorious body.

When this Perfection has been realized, it will not be found to have been affected by our toil . . . our toiling was not essential to the *being* of its Perfection, our own Perfection, but only dispositive to our *realization* of it. As Eckhart expresses it, "When I enter there no one will ask me whence I came or whither I went." *The weary pilgrim is now become what he always was had he only known it.*

Appendix

I
On the Etymology of "Cherubim"

The derivation and significance of the Hebrew Cherubim have been discussed by Mm. Dhorme and Vincent.[1] The Akkadian origin of the word *kerūb* and the Babylonian origin of the plastic form in Hebrew literature and plastic art are indisputable. The Akkadian verb *karābu* (cf. Arabic *mubārak*) implies the act of blessing (in the case of a deity) or prayer (in the case of the worshipper), the latter sense tending to predominate. The *kāribu* (present participle of *karābu*) as subordinate deities "mediate between man and God."[2] In anthropomorphic forms, they present the devotee to the deity. Their typical form, however, is that of the šedu and *lamasu* — man-bulls and dragons — that are represented in pairs as the guardians of gateways or sacred emblems. They may be of either sex and many different composite forms: In general, intercessors and tutelary divinities, embodying the powers and functions of the deities they serve.

Mm. Dhorme and Vincent emphasize the intercessory character of the *karābu* and regard their anthropomorphic forms as prior to the theriomorphic (which seems to me unlikely). However, the characteristic gesture of the intercessors is that of an *orant*, with one or both hands raised, and this motive appears already in the prehistoric art, in which we find bird-headed men with raised hands as assistants beside a sacred symbol.

There is nothing whatever contradictory, of course, in the double function of guardianship and intercession, or rather exclusion and introduction; it is the proper business of any janitor or watchdog to keep out the unqualified and admit the qualified. So in the myth of Adapa, Tammuz and Giśzida are the guardians of the gates of Paradise, and after questioning Adapa introduce him to Anu;[3] and the terrible Scorpion-men, "who dwell at the ends of the Earth, as guardians of the Sun's rising and setting or supporters of his wings,"[4] examine Gilgamesh with hostile intent, but on being satisfied treat him kindly

---

1 P. Dhorme *et* L.H. Vincent, "*Les cherubims*," *Rev. Biblique* 35 [1926], pages 328-333 and 481-495. Cf. P. Dhorme. "*Le dieu et la deese intercesseurs*" in *La religion assyro-babylonienne*, pages 261 ff. It may be observed that the functions of guardianship and of presentation or introduction are both properly those of porters or janitors; and that in the Gilgamesh epic the guardian Scorpion-men (man and wife), whose representation as protectors of the Tree and supporters of the winged Sun survives all through Babylonian and Assyrian art, play both parts.

2 There can be no doubt that these "*Schutzgottheiten*" correspond on the one hand to the Greek *Daimons*, intermediate between man and the deity whose "powers" they embody, and on the other to the Indian Gandharva-*rakṣas*; and just as one of those, so it can be said of the *kāribu* — whether lions, bulls, dragons, dogs, rams, sphinxes, griffins, scorpions or "storms," in wholly theriopomorphic or partly anthropomorphic shapes, masculine or feminine — that "*wem die Götter gnädig gesinnt sein, den schützen gute Geister; wem die Götter zurnen, der ist in den Händen böser Dämonen*" (B. Meissner, *Babylonien und Assyrian* II, 1925, [page] 50).

3 S. Langdon, *Sumerian Epic of Paradise*, 1915, pages 42, 43.

4 H. Frankfort, *Seal Cylinders of Western Asia*, page 201, cf. 156, 201 [and] 215, and Plates XXXIII, b, e. Representations of the Scorpion-men as the Sun's assistants, supporters of his wings or defending his pillar, are common on seals of all periods, cf. Moortgart, *Vorderasiatitische Rollsiegel*, numbers 598, 599 [and] 709, and our Figures 17-21 [, pages 32-34].

and give him advice.[1] The type of the Scorpion-man, armed with bow and arrow, found on the Sumerian *kudurrus*, is one of the archetypes of Sagittarius, whose well known representations as a snake-tailed archer-centaur, or one with both equine and scorpion tails; these tails are the unmistakable vestige of these archetypal forms of the Defenders, whose basilisk glance, like that of the Gorgons and that of so many of the Indian forms of the Defenders of the *Janua Coeli*, is death.

II
THE ROTATION OF THE EARTH

FOR εἱλλομένην IN *TIMAEUS* 40 B JOWETT HAS "CLINGING ROUND," WITH a footnote, "or 'circling'"; Bury has "which is globed around"; and Cornford "as she winds round." All these versions reflect a doubt. We shall only deal with Professor Cornford's full discussion of the problem in *Plato's Cosmology*, pages 120 ff. We shall say in the first place that Hilda Richardson, cited on page 129, Note 1, is almost wholly right. In the second place, Plato could no more have thought of the Earth as a planet than of the Sky as a planet; the Earth is the floor, and the Sky the roof of the cosmic house. The orbits of the planets lie in the space between these limits. Thirdly, Earth "is the first and eldest of the gods that have come into being within the Sky," that is to say "under the Sky," ἐντός here in the sense of Liddell and Scott 2, Latin *'citra*, "on this side of"; "first and eldest" because in all traditions Sky and Earth were originally one, and must be separated in order to provide a space for the existence of other beings, whether gods or men. Fourth, Sky and Earth correspond to one another, like the roof and floor of a house; the one is an inverted bowl, the other a bowl of so large a radius as to be virtually flat; the horizon is their common periphery. Sky and Earth are at once held apart and connected by an (invisible) pillar, whether of fire or smoke or resonant or luminous or pneumatic, the trunk of the Tree of Life, and only pathway up and down these worlds; this pillar extending from Nadir to Zenith penetrates the naves of all the world-wheels (three or seven or three times seven) and is the Axis about which all these worlds revolve. At the foot of this axial pillar, with which the pillar of the sacrifice is also identified, at the "navel of the Earth," burns the "central Fire," and at its summit the solar Eagle nests, and from this eyrie he surveys all things in the worlds below him. The Sun is not merely, however, the capital of the pillar, but the sky-supporting pillar itself, and so the "single nave" on which all turn. These worlds are collectively his vehicle; and when we are thinking only of Sky and Earth, these are the "twin wheels" of his chariot, turning on a common axle-tree. The Earth on which the whole is supported floats like a flower on the primordial Waters, and is thought of as their consolidated foam. It is from these Waters that

---

1 British Museum, *Babylonian Story of the Deluge and the Epic of Gilgamesh*, 1920, pages 50, 51.

For the study of whose history the present article is, in part, preparatory. Here I shall only call attention to the notable representation of the scorpion-tailed Sagittarius centaur defending a sacred symbol against the griffin-hero Zū, on an Assyrian seal of ca. 800 B.C.

the Sun rises in the East, and to them that he returns from the West; it is because he passes behind the Earth from West to East at night that the Earth can be called the maker of day and night.

Like the Sun, the Earth is central because it is from the central Axis that the quarters radiate; just as the capital of a kingdom is traditionally its centre, surrounded by four provinces. The planets other than the Sun are only "excentric" in that they are bodies "wandering" on the peripheries of their orbits; and by analogy, whoever on Earth lives far away from its centre (and whether this be Benares, Jerusalem or Rome is a matter of ritual, not of geographical determination), whoever in any land does not sacrifice, whoever in his own person lives "superficially" and not at the centre of his being, is likewise "excentric."

A detailed documentation of the traditional cosmology outlined above would require a pamphlet by itself; we do not feel that such a documentation is necessary, because every serious student will already be familiar with these formulae. Taking for granted, then, the traditional cosmology, it will be seen that it not only "contains serious teachings concerning the relations of God to the universe and to man," as Professor Fowler[1] remarks on the Atreus myth in Plato's *Statesman*, but at the same time explains all conditions that Professor Cornford finds it so hard to reconcile: Those of a central Earth, a central fire, a central axis, a revolution about this axis, and the "making of day and night." The modern scholar's difficulties arise largely from the fact that he cannot forget his science and does not think in the technical terms of metaphysics, which terms are not those of an imperfect "science" but simply those of the appearances that are presented alike to primitive man and to our own eyes, to which the Sun still seems to rise in the East and set in the West. We as geologists who know that the Earth is spherical can only think of the "pole" that is represented in our own "globes." But I who have had a scientific training can *also* think in terms of a "flat" Earth; the Hindu trained and expert in modern astronomy can also take a sincere part in rites apotropaic of Rahu, the mythical cause of the eclipse.[2] Professor Cornford asks, "Why do we never see the Central Fire?" The answer is easy: Only because we do not want to, do not know what it means to "grasp with an incantation" (*Śatapatha Brāhmaṇa* III.1.1.4), or how to enchant some part of the Earth and make that part a central hearth. Our extroverted eyes are glued to the wall of the Cave and only see the flickering shadows, not the Fire that casts them. This may suit *us* well enough, but it will not help us to understand Plato; unless we can think in his terms, and not *only* scientifically, we cannot think his thoughts, and therefore cannot translate them.

Almost the same difficulties are met by W. Scott in his endeavor to explain (mainly by emendations and omissions) Hermes Trismegistus, *Lib.* XVI.5 f. Here the Sun is an expert charioteer, and has made fast and bound to himself the chariot of the Cosmos, lest it should away in disorder." [. . .] He "leads

[1 Ananda Kentish Coomaraswamy did not reference this essay of Murray Fowler. — Ed.]

2 The "conflict between religion and science" is something that I have only heard of, never experienced.

together (συνάγει, probably with marital implication) Sky and Earth, leading down (κατάγωω) being and leading up (ἀνάγων) matter . . . drawing to himself all things (εἰς αὐτὸν τὰ πάντα)[1] and giving forth all things from himself." [. . .] "With that part of his light that tends upwards, he maintains the immortal part of the Cosmos, and with what is shed downwards gives life to all that is below him, and sets birth (or 'becoming') in motion."[2] [. . .] "He is stationed in the midst and wears the Cosmos as a crown about him." [. . .] "And if there be an intelligible substance (i.e. if we can speak of νοῦς as a 'substance'), the light of the Sun must be the receptacle of that substance."[3] [. . .] "He is the preserver and maintainer of every kind of living being; and as the intelligible Cosmos, encompassing the sensible Cosmos,[4] he fills its space (ὄγκον)[5] with omniform images (παυτομόρ φοις ἰδέαις)."[6]

Scott's chief difficulties are as follows:[7]

(1.) How can the Sun be "in the middle," since it is very unlikely that Hermes could have thought of the Earth as traveling round the Sun — "Besides, the Sun is here compared to a charioteer, and that comparison would be unintelligible if he were thought of as stationary";

(2.) If the Moon and planet-stars are included amongst the immortal parts of the Cosmos, as "can hardly be doubted" (!), the Sun must be below the Moon, which is contrary to the usual Greek view;

---

1 "And I, if I be lifted up from the earth, will draw (ἑλκύσω) all unto me" *John* XII.32). Cf. *Iliad* VIII.18 f., as rightly understood by Plato to refer to a cord by which the Sun connects all things to himself (*Theatetus* 153 C, D). "The Sun is the fastening to whom these worlds are linked . . . He strings these worlds to himself by means of a thread; the thread is the gale of the Spirit" (*Śatapatha Brāhmaṇa* VI.7.1.17, VIII.7.3.10).

"All things are generated from the One, and are resolved into it" (ascribed to Orpheus' disciple Musaios, in Diogenes L., *Proem.* 3). Cf. *Bṛhadāraṇyaka Upaniṣad* V.1 (*Atharva Veda* X.8.29) and *Bhagavad Gītā* VII.6 "I am both the producer of the whole world and its dissolution."

2 In other words, the Sun is stationed at the boundary between the mortal and immortal, sensible and intelligible. [Ananda Kentish Coomaraswamy references a note on *sīman* here which appears to be missing from the manuscript. — Ed.] "All creatures below him are mortal, but those beyond him are the immortal gods . . . Everything under the Sun is in the power of Death" (*Śatapatha Brāhmaṇa* II.3.3.7 and X.5.1.4), "These things are said to be under the Sun" (St. Thomas Aquinas, *Summa Theologiae* I.103.5 ad 1 and III, *Supplement* 91.1 ad 1).

3 "He who dwelling in the light, yet is other than the light, whom the light does not know, whose body the light is, who controls the light from within — He is your Spirit (*atman*, Self), the Inner Controller, immortal" (*Bṛhadāraṇyaka Upaniṣad* III.7.14).

"With the Sun's rays dost Thou unite" (*Ṛgveda Saṁhitā* V.81.4).

4 "Verily, this Spirit (*ātman*) is the Overlord of all things, the King of all things. Just as all the spokes are fastened-in-together (*samar-pitaḥ* = συνερμοσμένοι) between the hub and felly of a wheel, so in this Spiritual-self (*ātman*) all things, all gods, all worlds, all breathing things, all these spiritual-selves (*ātmanaḥ*) are fastened-in-together" (*Bṛhadāraṇyaka Upaniṣad* II.5.15).

5 "The Sun, the Spirit (*ātman*) of all that is in motion or at rest, hath filled Sky, Earth and Air" (*Ṛgveda Saṁhitā* I.115.1). "Do I not fill heaven and earth?" (*Jeremiah* XXIII.24).

6 The Sun is "omniform" (*viśvarūpa* = παντόμορφος) and distributes these forms by means of his operation of mediate causes to receive, cf. my "Vedic Exemplarism" in *HJAS*. I. Every point on the circumference of a circle is "more eminently" represented at its centre.

7 See *Corpus Hermeticum* II.444 f.

(3.) The simile of the chariot-driver is inconsistent with the picturing of the Cosmos as a wreath or crown;

(4.) "The Earth is motionless";

(5.) "'The reins', i.e. the things by means of which the Sun controls the heavenly bodies . . . ought . . . to be the rays of light which the Sun emits";

(6.) "I can make nothing of ἕλικος τρόπον";

(7.) "The νοητὸς κοσμος is said to 'encompass' αἰσθητὸς κόσμος, because it is imagined to be situated in extra-cosmic space. But the Sun, being stationed 'in the middle', cannot be said to '*encompass* all things in the Kosmos'";

(8.) The Sun operates on all things by means of his light. But we are also told that he operates on all things through the agency of the troops of daemons commanded by the planets — "two distinct and inconsistent theories"; and

(9.) Διὰ τοῦ ἡλίου is to be eliminated because the ray of divine νοῦς is identified with God Himself, and cannot therefore be thought of as transmitted by the Sun.

I can only say that no one of these difficulties presents itself to one who approaches the subject from the standpoint of a traditional cosmology such as the Indian.

We cannot undertake to explain away all these difficulties here. But to consider them in order, in the first place it must be realized that being in the middle and being at the top are by no means irreconcilable conceptions. In the well known doctrine of the "seven rays" of the Sun, six of these rays correspond to the directions of space which form a three-dimensional cross, of which the arms extend to the limits of the spherical universe. The Sun's place is at the intersection of these arms. The seventh and best ray is that "ray of light from God by which the intellectual part of the soul is illumined" (*Hermes* XVI.16), and that "golden cord to which we should hold on and by no means let go of" (Plato, *Laws* 644); it is [by] one of his rays which "ascending and piercing through the solar orb, on to the Brahma-world extends; thereby men reach their highest goal" (*Maitri Upaniṣad* VI.30). It is this ray, of which the extension beyond the Sun cannot be represented in any model, because in passing through the Sun it passes out of the dimensioned Cosmos, which will enable us to understand in what sense the middle is also the top; we must not be misled by the fact that the physical nadir is above the physical zenith in our model, but must realize that the Brahma-world is above the Sun, who stands, as we have already seen, at the boundary between the finite Cosmos and the space that cannot be traversed outside it. The centre of our diagram is the nail that fastens the crossbar to the upright, the crossbar itself representing the Sky.

The Sun is not in every sense of the word motionless. The two wheels of his chariot are the Sky and [the] Earth, and the axle tree that connects them is the *Axis Mundi*; he inhabits this cosmic vehicle as we inhabit our bodily vehicles. Both the wheels of this chariot revolve upon the points of the axle;

but one of these poles is fixed (for we are thinking now of the Comprehensor for whom the Sun neither rises or sets, but is ever in the middle and for whom it is evermore day[1]); the other, in addition to its rotation has a forward and sunwise motion upon the ground of the Cosmos, represented by the the periphery of the cosmic sphere, on which periphery we stand. The complete revolution takes a "Year" (a period of time that can be understood in various senses). It will be seen that it is in view of this revolution correctly said that the pole of the solar chariot "faces all directions."[2] The Earth is far from motionless, but rather has two motions, about its own (solar) axis and about the Sun. As to the reins, they are indeed "rays," as is explicit in the Sanskrit sources, where the one word *raśmi* means both "ray" and "rein. We cannot discuss the spiral motion at length, but will point out only that the resultant of a centripetal motion by which we approach the Sun by "following" the golden chain and seventh ray, and the peripheral motion (one of these motions being independent of time and the other temporal) will be spiral; and that all tradition agrees in regarding both the descent and the ascent therefore as spiral motions.[3] The intelligible Cosmos "encompasses" the sensible Cosmos in the same sense that the Infinite encompasses the finite, the centre of the circle is the circle in principle, and in the same sense that the One is both the One and the Many.[4]

As for the eighth objection, I fail to see the "contradiction." The distinction between the Sun's direct operation and that of the daimons who are subject to the Sun is that of the first from mediate causes.[5] There is nothing in Hermes' text contrary to the orthodox (universal) doctrine that the Sun (spirit) is directly the author of our being, but only indirectly (providentially) the cause of the manner of our being.[6] This already disposes of the "inconsistency." But it will be useful to observe the working of Heres' daimons more closely. They are energies or forces or tendencies rather than persons (δαίμονς νὰρ οὐσία ἐωέρνεια); they are seated in our "nerves" (νεῦρα) and "veins";[7] some are

1 *Chāndogya Upaniṣad* III.11.1-3.

2 *Ṛgveda* X.135.3.

3 See also René Guénon, *Le Symbolisme de la Croix*, Paris, 1931.

4 As, for example, in *Śatapatha Brāhmaṇa* X, where "He is one as he is in himself, but many in his children." "The Sun's rays are his children" (*Jaiminīya Upaniśad Brāhmaṇa*).

5 On the distinction of first from mediate causes, cf. Plato, *Laws* 904, *Republic* 617 E, *Theatetus* 155 E, *Timaeus* 42 D.

6 "The (primary) forces (ἐνέρνειαι) are, as it were, God's rayings; the natural forces are the rayings of the Cosmos; the arts and sciences are man's rayings" (*Lib.* X.22 b). Hermes' Daimons (the natural forces by which our "destiny" is shaped) are to be contrasted with the one "Good Daimon," Intellect (νοῦς, *Lib.* X.23 and XIII b). It must be remembered in this connection that neither Hermes nor Plato speak of Intellect or Reason (νοῦς, λόγος) in the narrow sense of the words, but rather as the Scholastics speak of *intellectus vel spiritu*.

7 These "nerves" are "attached to the heart" (*Lib.* V.6); they are the same as the reins that extend from the heart to the objects of the senses (*Maitri Upaniśad* II.6, etc.), while the "veins" correspond to the Indian "channels" (*naḍi, hite*) of sense perception. These "nerves" or "rays" must not be thought of as parts of the physical body, but are extensions of the soul, connecting it with the objects to which it is at-*tracted*; these objects themselves exert their attraction by which the soul may be entangled. The "nerves" are intangible lines of force, directions of aesthetic reaction and instinctive response; not the "nerves" of physiology, but the "tendencies" of psychology.

good and others bad in their tendency; they "pull" our souls towards them in opposite ways (ἀνθέλκουσι τὰς ψυχὰς ἡμῶς εἰς ἑαυτούς);[1] they take charge of us at birth.[2] They are the passions or affections (πάθη) that Hermes elsewhere (*Lib.* XII.i.10 f.) speaks of as "chains" or "wires" (ὁρμαί), telling us that "since in irrational animals [the] mind works together with these wires, which wires are the affections, it seems that [the] mind is always passible (παθητός), being colored (συγχρωματίξων) by them." Thus Hermes is simply repeating the Platonic doctrine of the passions or affections (πάθη) in us "which like nerves (νεῦρα) or cords (μήινθοί) pull upon us, and being opposed to one another pull in opposite directions (ἀλλήλαις ἀνθέλκουσιν εναντίαι ὄυσαι) towards contrary actions, and therein lies the dividing line between virtue and vice. But, as our story tells, there is one of these tractors (ἕλξις) that every man should always follow and nowise leave go of . . . and whereas the other cords are hard and steely and of every shape and likeness, this one is flexible and single, being of gold. With that most excellent leading string of Law we ought always to cooperate . . . so that the golden kind within us may vanquish the other kinds" (*Laws* 644-645). Hermes differs from Plato only in this respect, that instead of speaking of the golden "cord" by holding onto which the other pulls are overcome, he says that "the man who is illuminated by a 'ray' of light from God, passing through the Sun, for him the workings of the daimons are brought to naught; for no Daimon of God (star) has power against a single ray from God." Hermes and Plato are at one in the essential, in distinguishing the single guidance of the "thread spirit" — "cord" or "ray" — by which the Sun "operates" directly, from the many and contrary of the demons of sensation. As in the *Chāndogya Upaniṣad* VIII.6.6 and *Maitri Upaniṣad* VI.30, "Endless are his (the Sun's) rays, who like a lamp dwells in the heart; one of these, ascending, passes through the head and penetrating the Sun's disk leads on to immortality in the world of Brahma; but by its (the heart's) downward tending rays one wanders there helplessly." These rays or reins extend from the heart to the objects of the senses, and the mortal soul, losing control of them, is overcome by the pairs of opposites" (*Maitri Upaniṣad* III.02) — "opposites" that correspond to the contrary strains referred to by Plato's ἀνθέ λκοθσινιεπ' ἐντίασπραξεις. And just as Hermes calls these powers of the soul (Sanskrit *indriyāṇī*, *prāṇah*, etc.) "Daimons," so in the Indian texts they are very commonly spoken of as *Devas*, "Gods"; they are, in fact, "Demons" (*Asuras*) insofar as they are used as means to the sensation, but gods (*Devas*) insofar as they are used as means to the understanding of realities (Śaṅkara on *Bṛhadāraṇyaka Upaniṣad* I.3.1). But whether as *Asuras* or *Devas*, they are equally the children of the Progenitor (*Bṛhadāraṇyaka Upaniṣad* V.2 etc.). And this brings us back again to the distinction of mediate from first causes, that of the many from the one, that of the sons of God from God Himself (see Plato, *Laws* 904, *Timaeus* 42 D, *Republic* 617 E, *Theatetus* 155 E).

---

1 Scott renders ἀνθίλκουσι only by "pull away," missing the notion of pull in opposite directions, επὲναντίας in the Platonic context from which Hermes' [is derived].

2 Karmic character [is] destiny, [i.e.] inborn tendencies.

III
On "Stephanos"

On certain well known Orphic tablets, discussed amongst others by Guthrie (*Orpheus*, page 171 f., and 208, 209, citing the references), are found the words, "I have flown out of the sorrowful, weary circle, I have passed with swift feet to the diadem (crown, or garland) desired. Happy and blessed one, thou shalt be god instead of mortal. A kid, I have fallen into milk." It need not concern us whether this forms part of an initiatory ritual or is a recitation of what is understood to have befallen the deceased; for such rituals always prefigure what is to take place after death, and in effect ensure that the initiate shall have "died before he dies." The first line cited is, from an Indian point of view, sufficiently clear: The perfected soul has escaped on wings from "the storm of the world's flow," the causally determined world of becoming, *bhava-cakra* or *saṃsāra*; it has willed and been able to pass through the Sundoor. The "milk" may very well refer to the initiate's or deceased's acceptance as a legitimate son of God; to receive the milk that springs, sometimes like a river, from the breasts of the Queen of Heaven is a token of divine filiation well attested from Egyptian, Etruscan and Christian sources.[1]

Our main purpose, however, is to discuss the word στέφανος, rendered above by "diadem" (crown or garland). It has often been thought that a crown or garland of victory is intended, such a "crown of glory" or "of life" (*Revelation* II.10) as is won by Christian saints and is often represented in the iconography only by a solar "halo" or "nimbus."

We are told in *Republic*, 363 C, D, that the "justified" (ὅσιοι) are "crowned" (εστεφανωμένοι) and that they feast with the gods, "who deem that the fairest mead of virtue is to be forever drunk with mead."[2] In supposing that the Orphic στέφανος was really a "crown of glory," and in fact a nimbus, there is nothing new; it is the obvious interpretation, which many scholars have endorsed. It is rather with the fact that *stephanos* also means "a wall" that we wish to deal. It has been suggested on this basis that it was some kind of heavenly city or enclosure that the initiate ran. Guthrie (page 181) thinks that Pindar's (VIII.42) "minded to make a s*tephanos* for Ilion" does not mean a "wall encircling Ilion" but "a crowning glory for Ilion," and that one would not gather from the words "Cortona lifts to heaven the diadem of her towers" that the word *diadem* had come to mean in English *a thing that encloses*. We shall first begin to realize that Pindar's *stephanos* means both "a wall" *and* a

---

1 For some of the references see my "The Virgin suckling St. Bernard" and "*La Voie Lactée*" in *Études Traditionnelles* 42 [1937] and 43 [1938]; and Moret, *Du caractere religieuse de la royauté pharaonique*, Paris (Museé Guimet), 1902.

[Cf.] Philo, *LA*. III.74 [and] Hermes XVI.7.

2 There is no need whatever to suppose that Plato is sarcastic here. What the gods drink there is not *our* "*eau de vie*," but veritably "living water," ambrosia, *amṛta*, *rasa*, *Soma*. The notion of a divine convivium is universal (cf. *Ṛgveda* X.135.1; *Phaedrus* 247 A; *Matthew* XXII.2 f. and *John* II.1-10). See also Emile Dermenghem, *L'Eloge du Vin*, Paris, 1931.

"crowning glory," and that a "diadem of towers" is precisely "a thing that encloses," if we recall that the most distinctive feature of the iconography of a Greek "city goddess" — the *Fortuna* (τυχή) of the city — is precisely a "*mural* crown," a turreted or battlemented circlet. When Homer says that "children are a man's 'crown', the towers of the city" (*Epigrams*, XIII)[1] one can hardly tell whether his στέφανος is not rather a defensive wall than a crown. In any case a city wall is in the most literal sense of the words her *crowning* glory. The Byzantine crown is still unmistakably mural.

Perhaps it may be said that all crowns are in this sense walls; for the crown that can be worn by "this man" who is himself "a city" (Plato, πόλις, and Sanskrit, *pura*, *brakmapura*) must be analogous to the nimbus (root as in Sanskrit *nabha*, sky) that encircles the heavenly city (*brahmapura*) of the Sun himself; and as Sky is actually the "wall" that separates the Cosmos from the Empyrean, and the "veil" or "curtain" that divides the "green room" from the cosmic stage. The Sun's headgear is in fact his "defense" (*varūtham*, *Ṛgveda Saṁhita* X.27.13) and it is in the same way that a crown can be also a helmet.

It is, moreover, a striking parallel to what has been said above on the semantics of *stephanos* that the Indian turban[2] (*uṣṇīṣa*), originally a sacerdotal and royal prerogative is in every respect an equivalent of a crown; for in the architectural terminology of the *stūpa* the coping of the encircling *prakāra* is precisely a "coronet" (*uṣṇīṣa*). Now a crown, like a turban, is originally and essentially a headband, fillet or wreath; the top of the head is not concealed, but seen above it. And the dome of a *stūpa* is iconographically a cranium. It will be realized accordingly that the relation of *stephanos* as "wall" to the political city, that of *stephanos* as crown to the individual "city," and that of an *uṣṇīṣa* as coronet to a *stūpa* are identical; in each case the Acropolis is encircled by and seen above a mural crown, a crown that is a wall, or wall that is a crown.

Whether we render *stephanos* by "crown" or "wall" will depend upon the context; the fact that *stephanos* can mean either "crown" or "mural crown" or "wall" — and is in any case something that encloses — offers no ground for supposing that in the Orphic context it means anything but a victor's crown, and as such, archetype of the crowns or glories of the Christian saints.[3]

1 It is pertinent to this to recall that "The Sun's rays are his children" (*Jaiminīya Upaniśad Brāhmaṇa* II.9.10) and also that it is by these rays that the way in through the Sun is defended (*ibid.* I.3.6, I.7.2; *Isa Upaniśad* 15, 16, etc.).

[2 For the detailed symbolism of the turban and umbrella see my "*Usnisa* and *Chatra*, Turban and Umbrella" in the *Poona Orientalist*, Volume III, 1938, and René Guénon, "*Le Dome et la Roue*" in *Études Traditionnelles*, Volume 43 (1938).]

[3 Cf. Hermes Trismegistus XVI.7, where the Sun "is stationed in the midst and wears the Cosmos as a crown."]

"The problem vanishes, in fact, in the light of self-knowledge, if we have been able to recognize ourselves not in the mortal outer man, but in the immanent divinity, Our Self, the self's immortal Leader, alike in life and at death; for if we have known Who we are, it is our Self that flies away with us, and in our Self that we fly away."

— *Clement of Alexandria*

"So 'He that would save his life, let him lose it'! . . . The sacrifice of selfhood (individuality, what can be defined and seen) is essential to any deification; for no one who still is anyone can enter into Him Who has never become anyone and is not any what."

—*Ananda K. Coomaraswamy, "Self-Naughting"*

Patron's Dedication

To my twin sons, Beldon and Seton.

All existence comes from the One
And takes form in the Duality.
Just as you were created from the single
And were manifest as the two,
So shall you one day return home
To the formless within the Unitive.

— *Peter Schroeder*

BIBLIOGRAPHY

List of available works of Ananda K. Coomaraswamy, where many of the references cited in this volume can be found:

1. Selected Papers, Bollingen Series LXXXIX (Volume I contains especially the article on Sympleglades).
2. *The Essential Ananda K. Coomaraswamy*, World Wisdom Books.
3. *Spiritual Authority and Temporal Power in the Indian Theory of Government*, Indira Gandhi National Center for the Arts, Janpath, New Delhi, India.
4. *What is Civilisation? And Other Essays*, Golgonooza Press, Ipswich, England.
5. *The Living Thoughts of Gotama the Buddha*, Fons Vitae, Louisville, Ky.
6. A Complete Bibliography, entitled *A Bibliography of Ananda Kentish Coomaraswamy* by James Crouch, also published by the Indira Gandhi National Center for the Arts, Janpath, New Delhi.

OTHER RELATED FONS VITAE AND QUINTA ESSENTIA TITLES

Sacred Art in East and West • Titus Burckhardt

Alchemy — Science of the Cosmos, Science of the Soul • Titus Burckhardt

Fundamental Symbols — The Universal Language of Sacred Science • René Guénon

Symbol and Archetype — A Study of the Meaning of Existence • Martin Lings

A Return to the Spirit: Questions and Answers •
Martin Lings (Forthcoming, 2004)

The Art of Living — Essays on Christian Art •
Ananda K. Coomaraswamy (Forthcoming, 2005)